"Attic" and Baroque Prose Style

ESSAYS BY MORRIS W. CROLL

"Attic"
and
Baroque Prose Style

THE ANTI-CICERONIAN MOVEMENT

Essays by Morris W. Croll

EDITED BY J. MAX PATRICK
AND ROBERT O. EVANS,
WITH JOHN M. WALLACE

PRINCETON, NEW JERSEY
PRINCETON UNIVERSITY PRESS

First Princeton Paperback Printing, 1969

Publication of this book has been aided by
the Annan Fund of Princeton University

Printed in the United States of America
by Princeton University Press, Princeton, New Jersey

Preface

When the essays contained in this volume were prepared for reprinting in *Style, Rhetoric, and Rhythm*, the editors took the opportunity to rectify typographical errors silently and to correct a few errors in dating and the like, which are duly noted. More liberty was taken with the footnotes, for, although Morris W. Croll sustained a high level of scholarship and accuracy in his main texts, he was rather cavalier about notes. Accordingly, they have frequently been reworded and standardized for clarity; references have been filled in; and citations have sometimes been changed to texts more accessible than those he used. As a result, the footnotes may not be in his words, but they are true to his intention. Added material has been put in brackets. These modifications are retained here; and we have taken the occasion to rectify a few minor errors which eluded us previously.

Parts II and III of *Style, Rhetoric, and Rhythm*, not reprinted here, contain "The Sources of Euphuistic Rhetoric," originally an introduction to *Euphues: The Anatomy of Wit*; *Euphues and his England* (1916); "The Cadence of English Oratorical Prose" (1919); "The Rhythm of English Verse" (mimeographed, 1929); and "Music and Metrics: a Reconsideration" (1923). Croll's other works were "Tom Jones," in *Papers Read before the Novel Club of Cleveland* (Cleveland, 1899); his University of Pennsylvania dissertation, *The Works of Fulke Greville* (Philadelphia, 1903); a textbook anthology, *English Lyrics from Dryden to Burns* (New York, 1912); a brief entry, "John Florio," in *Modern Language Notes*, XXXIV (1919), 376; and reviews of Williamson, *The Donne Tradition*, White, *English Devotional Literature*, and Nethercot, *Abraham Cowley*, in *Modern Philology* (1930-1931).

Professor Croll's papers and lecture notes are preserved in Princeton University Library. They contain little, if anything, which he polished to publishable form, but it is to be hoped that this collec-

PREFACE

tion will inspire some qualified scholar to select and edit the best
portions of these unperfected works, particularly the essay on the
sermons and sermon style of Thomas Adams.

J. Max Patrick

Biographical Note

MORRIS WILLIAM CROLL was born at Gettysburg, Pennsylvania, April 16, 1872, the son of Luther Henry and Jane Crawford Smyth Croll. His father was Professor of Mathematics at Pennsylvania (Gettysburg) College, which Morris attended in due course, receiving the A.B. degree in 1889 and the A.M. in 1892. In 1931 his old college was to award him an honorary Litt.D. He continued his studies at Harvard, from which he received an A.B. in 1894 and an A.M. in 1895. From 1895 to 1899 he taught in the University School, Cleveland, Ohio. Completing graduate study at the University of Pennsylvania, he wrote his dissertation on the works of Fulke Greville under the direction of Professor Felix Schelling, receiving his Ph.D. in 1901. From 1901 to 1905 he was an Associate Editor of the *Lippincott-Worcester Dictionary*. Returning to teaching, he was brought to Princeton in 1905 by President Woodrow Wilson as one of the fifty "preceptor guys" in the new plan of undergraduate instruction. He was promoted from Instructor in English Literature to Assistant Professor in 1906, to Associate Professor in 1918, to Professor in 1921. He retired in February 1932. Early in World War I he served on Herbert Hoover's Commission for the Relief of Belgium, for which in September 1919 he was awarded the Cross of King Albert. Professor Croll never married. For the last years of his life he resided with his sister, Miss Elsie L. Croll, at 40 Bayard Lane, Princeton. Never robust in health, after his retirement he became less and less active, with long periods of confinement to his rooms. He died at Saranac Lake, New York, where he was spending the summer, on August 17, 1947.

In the fall of 1916 Mr. Croll met his preceptorial in English Romanticism in a cubbyhole at the top of the old School of Science. His tall, somewhat stooping figure suggested Sargent's portrait of R. L. S. at Bournemouth. A general impression of physical frailty grew on acquaintance, but this was not the effect of any slackness in his manner. One was first struck by his soft and precise enunciation, with an occasional sibilant emphasis just rising above a whisper. This furnished a striking contrast to the vigorous and sometimes explosive delivery of J. Duncan Spaeth, the lecturer in the course. There was nothing of the pundit in his comments, but the quiet note of authority that marked matters of special interest to him commanded respect. Because he was gentle in criticism of the callow responses of his students, his rare displays of irritation were more effective in consequence. Perhaps most notable in his presentation of literature was the pervasive evidence of a sensitive appreciation.

In the autumn after the United States entered the war, many senior classes contained only a handful of students. Professor Croll's course in Poetics and a group permitted to enroll for Advanced Composition, five in all, met in his rooms, 6 North Reunion. His graduate courses in the immediate postwar years, English Prose Style 1500-1680 and the English Lyric, not much larger, foregathered in his study at 7½ Greenholm. He was probably at his best with these small, intimate groups. In both undergraduate and graduate courses might be noted his impatience with lecture notes or reading from a prepared manuscript. On more than one occasion, beginning with a manuscript, he tossed it aside and continued the discussion without again consulting it. The only one of his courses in which the formal presentation of the subject permitted the writer to take highly organized class notes was Poetics. But even here what he remembers is rather Croll's reading of Bridges's "Whither, O splendid ship" and Yeats's "The Lake Isle of Innisfree," with an exposition of their metrical subtleties, than the historical and critical outline of lyric production. His method, of necessity, became more formalized when he met larger classes in the late twenties.

The writer particularly recalls the older man's sympathetic assistance when he was in great perplexity about his obligation to military service. Mr. Croll felt sadly that he was himself barred from active participation in the war effort. In the early summer of 1918 he worked on a Pennsylvania farm for six weeks, until the unwonted exertion wore him down, compelling him to complete rest for the remainder of the season. In September of that year he wrote from Bread Loaf Inn, Vermont: "It was a great pleasure to hear from you and know of your being at work on the great business. *Nothing* else is worth a young man's doing now, and I resent the *single* year (less!) which prevents me from being drafted in it. I'd rather be a private in the trenches than anything else in the world. And if I could only stand it—or have a shadow of a chance of standing it— I'd not balk at the morality of lying about my age."

Professor Croll must have enjoyed a period of comparative vigor in 1923, for in the latter half of the year he took sabbatical leave, traveling in England, and on his return after Christmas he appeared in good health and spirits.

He read widely, but his personal taste was conservative. One recalls a summer when he reported his reading as including *Lalla Rookh* and Trollope, and an afternoon when he was found deeply immersed in Scott's *Anne of Geierstein*. He was a founder of the Freneau Club, a student literary society which invited writers to the campus to read from their work and to discuss it informally. After a visit from Sinclair Lewis, Mr. Croll wrote: "His lecture was in good colyum style—to the delight of the U.G.'s. But *Main Street* is hard reading for all that. After all and all, the classics are still the classics—hey?" Nevertheless, his response to undergraduate creative efforts was un- forced and generous. *A Book of Princeton Verse II*, 1919, in whose publication he was the moving spirit, carried on the tradition of Princeton poetry that had been marked by two previous collections. For this volume Professor Croll was assisted in gathering contribu- tions by James Creese, '18, and with them were associated Henry Van Dyke and Maxwell Struthers Burt, the former writing the Preface. Of the thirty-four authors included, several were well known beyond the campus, but young aspirants were chiefly and liberally represented.

After the summer of 1927 the writer was seldom in Princeton, and on infrequent later visits Professor Croll was not often in the village. There was worsening news of his completely failing health. At Reunion 1943 the members of our Advanced Composition class in attendance telephoned Miss Elsie and begged to call on Saturday afternoon. She gave her permission, but stipulated that the visit be brief. Morris Croll was his gracious self, cordially welcoming his former students, but he was obviously very frail. The last note in the writer's possession was written a fortnight later from Saranac Lake, thanking us for a book we had brought him.

Professor Croll's most important book was the edition, with Harry Clemons, of Lyly's *Euphues*, which appeared in 1916. The work tentatively entitled *From Montaigne to Dryden*, a study of prose style in the seventeenth century, achieved only partial publication in journal and *Festschrift* articles. His interest in the musical basis of verse suggested an intellectual kinship with Sidney Lanier, and, like Lanier, Croll played the flute, though with something less than the mastery of the author of *The Science of English Verse*. *The Rhythm of English Verse* existed only in mimeographed form and has not hitherto been printed, perhaps because of the difficulty and expense of reproducing the metrical notation devised for it. Professor Croll's contributions, both to metrics and, especially, to "Attic" prose, have been extensively cited, but it has not been easy to lay one's hands on them. Their gathering in this volume is not only a fitting memorial to a fine scholar, but a sorely needed aid to contemporary scholarship.

Atlanta, Georgia   THOMAS H. ENGLISH
                                                      EMORY UNIVERSITY

Contents

Abbreviations

Abbreviations of titles of periodicals, etc. are standard ones as used in *PMLA*. In the notes, Croll's articles are referred to as follows:

APL: Essay IV, "Attic Prose: Lipsius, Montaigne, Bacon"

APS: Essay II, " 'Attic Prose' in the Seventeenth Century"

BS: Essay V, "The Baroque Style in Prose"

Lipse: Essay I, "Juste Lipse et le Mouvement Anticicéronien à la Fin du XVIe et au Début du XVIIe Siècle" (here summarized in English)

Muret: Essay III, "Muret and the History of 'Attic' Prose"

"Attic" and Baroque Prose Style:
The Anti-Ciceronian Movement

So that readers may follow the development of Croll's ideas, these
five essays are printed here in the order in which he prepared them
for publication. However, it should be borne in mind that Muret
initiated the Anti-Ciceronian movement, that Lipsius was his follower, and that Croll later acknowledged that Essay One needed
revision in part. Accordingly, those interested in grasping his developed ideas and in following the movement chronologically are
advised to begin with Essays Two and Three, and then to read the
English summary of Essay One in the light of the recapitulation in
the opening part of Essay Four.

Foreword to Essay One*

The precepts governing "Ciceronianism," the dominant academic prose style of sixteenth-century Europe, were prescriptive and proscriptive. Indeed, although this widely established mode of writing was based on exclusive imitation of Cicero, it lacked the flexibility and adaptability which that master of rhetoric himself exhibited in varied styles, particularly in his epistles. In the minds of its proponents and practitioners, this orthodox style and the rhetoric behind it were identified with law, order, propriety, decency, and, like themselves, with what today is called "the establishment." To depart from this style—for example, to lecture to students on Tacitus urging that imitation of his prose might be more rewarding and more relevant to the realities of the period after about 1575—was to threaten the social order, to undermine all virtue, and to corrupt the young, or so it seemed to the supporters of Ciceronianism. Nevertheless, opposition to this stylistic stranglehold developed into a movement which was anticipated by Montaigne, fomented by Muret, programmed by Lipsius,[1] advanced by Bacon, and carried to extremes by Gracián, to mention only a few of its practitioners. And it was associated with, and partly inspired by, an equally iconoclastic Neo-Stoic or libertine philosophy.

Morris W. Croll took the lead in perceiving this movement and in noting that it corresponded to a classical Anti-Ciceronian movement which began in Cicero's own lifetime and was largely inspired by that reaction. Other scholars followed, modifying and adding to

---

* In *Style, Rhetoric, and Rhythm: Essays by Morris W. Croll,* from which the essays in the present volume have been extracted, there was a Foreword to Essay One by John M. Wallace. Rather than distort it in summary here, I have composed a new Foreword which combines his main points with others of my own; but the debt to him is heavy. The footnotes follow his numbering and are largely owing to him, although they do incorporate some new material.

[1] For Lipsius' life and relevant scholarship since 1914, see Jason A. Saunders, *Justus Lipsius: The Philosophy of Renaissance Stoicism* (New York, 1955); also D. C. Cabeen, *A Critical Bibliography of French Literature,* Vol. II, *The Sixteenth Century,* ed. Alexander H. Schutz (Syracuse, 1956), under "Lipsius" in the index; for eds. of Lipsius' works, see F. van der Haeghen, *Biblioteca Belgica,* Vols. XV-XVII (Ghent, 1880-1890).

3

his perceptions: thus George Williamson maintains against Croll that the style of Lipsius was more Tacitean than Senecan; R. F. Jones contends that the new science, rather than imitation of ancient Anti-Ciceronianism, was the mainspring of the major stylistic shift; and, in a study published since the first appearance of the present collection, Robert Adolph, taking a cue from Croll's insistence that prose styles reflect their times, holds that the major influence on stylistic change was a utilitarian ethic and values associated with it.[2] Meanwhile, José Ruysschaert learned more about Lipsius' reading and rivalry with Muret;[3] E. Catherine Dunne discovered that Lipsius wanted to free the *ars dictaminis* from the classical oration and to renew the old connection between letter-writing and conversational dialogue;[4] and Wesley Trimpi indicated how Lipsius and others opened the familiar letter to subjects formerly restricted to other genres.[5] And long before them, in the year after Croll's essay on Lipsius appeared, G. P. Krapp made a contribution to the subject which is still valuable,[6] though what he failed to see throws into relief the originality and importance of what Croll perceived.

Croll notices in the character of Lipsius a fear of denying one truth while defending another. Something of the kind occurs in his own work. In most of his essay on Lipsius he treats the Anti-Ciceronian movement of the century following 1575 as a revolution corresponding to the stylistic reaction in ancient Rome, and in so doing he largely ignores the Middle Ages. But he also views the Lipsian

[2] Williamson, *The Senecan Amble: A Study in Prose Form from Bacon to Collier* (Chicago, 1951), pp. 121-149. See the Foreword to *BS* below. For Jones's writings, see the *Festschrift* honoring him, *The Seventeenth Century* (Palo Alto, 1961). Adolph, *The Rise of Modern Prose Style* (Cambridge, Mass., 1968): Adolph summarizes Croll's work, criticizes it brilliantly, adds references to relevant scholarship not mentioned here, and draws attention to Andrews Wanning's unpublished dissertation, "Some Changes in the Prose Style of the Seventeenth Century" (Cambridge University, 1936).

[3] *Bulletin de l'Institut Historique de Rome*, XXIV (1947-1948), 139-192; *Revue Belge de Philologie et d'Histoire*, XXIII (1944), 251-254.

[4] "Lipsius and the Art of Letter-Writing," *Studies in the Renaissance*, III (1956), 145-156.

[5] "Jonson and the Neo-Latin Authorities for the Plain Style," *PMLA*, LXXVII (1962), 21-26. His book, *Ben Jonson's Poems: A Study of the Plain Style* (Stanford, 1962), reflects Croll's influence and is henceforth referred to as "Trimpi."

[6] *The Rise of English Literary Prose* (New York, 1915).

movement as seeming sometimes to bridge the gulf between us and the Middle Ages and at other times as seeming to be more distantly medieval than the relatively simple, enthusiastic humanism of the early Renaissance. Indeed, two years after writing on Lipsius, he published his introduction to John Lyly's *Euphues: The Anatomy of Wit; Euphues and his England* (edited by himself and Harry Clemons), where he treated "The Sources of Euphuistic Rhetoric" largely in terms of medieval sermons. And he later linked all vernacular expression at about 1550 to medievalism. Nevertheless, in the essay on Lipsius he keeps trying to see Anti-Ciceronianism as a forecast of modernity, almost as the birth of the modern mind, as tending to a theory of modern style. In the words of John M. Wallace, "it is the growth of this theory in the subsequent history of Senecan prose which he outlined in the closing pages of this essay. The impulse toward personal freedom in thought and language seems to have remained the sole psychological explanation that Croll offered for the new style, and his belief in it grew with the years. It led him later to misunderstand the plain style in the Restoration, which he judged to be a mere revision of Senecanism, effected by the influences of Descartes, Baconian science, and *mondanité*. However, to take 'the heat and fever out of the imaginative naturalism of Montaigne, Bacon, and Browne,' is to create a rival style, not to introduce 'certain changes within the *cadres*' of Senecan prose,[7] and one concludes that Croll's theory is applicable chiefly to those early humanists from whom it was first derived. Here other scholars (notably Arnold Stein in his early essays on Donne, and Floyd Gray on Montaigne)[8] have not hesitated to follow him. His belief that the Anti-Ciceronians attempted to catch the movement of thought in all the ardor of its first conception in the mind remains truer of the geniuses than of the common run of their disciples."[9]

[7] Croll and R. S. Crane, review of R. F. Jones, "Science and Prose Style," *PQ*, x (1931), 185.

[8] Arnold Stein, "Donne and the Couplet," *PMLA* (1942), 676-696; "Donne's Obscurity and the Elizabethan Tradition," *ELH*, XIII (1946), 98-118. Floyd Gray, *Le Style de Montaigne* (Paris, 1958).

[9] *Style, Rhetoric, and Rhythm*, pp. 4-5. Wallace goes on to draw attention to

Essentially, Croll's idea here is that instead of subordinating ideas, spontaneity, and feelings to Ciceronian externals, forms, and dictates, men like Lipsius, Muret, and Bacon imitated Latin authors of the Silver Age, especially Seneca and Tacitus, who adjusted, manipulated, and subordinated form to make it answer the fire and feeling of a mind in the process of thinking. But it is probably more just to say that they strove for the *effect* of a mind developing ideas naturally, flexibly, and freely; that they *imitated the thinking mind*; and that they exploited the techniques and devices of both Ciceronians and Anti-Ciceronians to achieve such results. The reader has the impression that he develops ideas and feelings along with such authors and participates in the dynamics of their thought. On reflection and analysis, he recognizes, at least with the geniuses, that he is faced with products of incredible virtuosity in varied styles and is moved by the persuasive skill of master rhetoricians. But he will not be moved and influenced if he expects authors' styles to conform to the pedantic rigorism of grammarians and other prescribers.[10]

Croll's own writing reflects a mind changing, developing, modifying, sometimes near to reversing itself. What he means by terms such as *naturalism, positivism, modern, libertine, baroque,* and so on, shifts like the realities to which they approximate. Croll refuses to submit his concepts to the stranglehold of falsifying unchanging definition. Sometimes (for example in his use of *Augustan* to extend back to Ciceronian Latin), he is needlessly confusing; but the reader who, like Croll, rejects slavery to mere terminology, will find that he gradually acquires a sense of the rich complexity of what Croll conveys. It is for this reason, and because the footnotes to Essay One and its Foreword serve as a foundation for bibliography throughout this volume, that they have been retained almost in their entirety.

---

a development from Croll's thought made by Don Cameron Allen in "Style and Certitude," *ELH*, xv (1948), 167-175.

[10] This paragraph derives in part from my Introduction to *The Prose of John Milton*, ed. J. Max Patrick (New York, 1968), p. xxviii.

Justus Lipsius and the Anti-Ciceronian Movement at the End of the 16th and the Beginning of the 17th Century*

TRANSLATED AND SUMMARIZED
BY J. MAX PATRICK

✧ I ✧

The Man

IN THEIR period, Scaliger, Casaubon, and Lipsius (1547-1606) were equally esteemed.[1] Though their parity was again recognized in 1852, Lipsius came to be viewed as the weakest in this literary triumvirate.[2] ⟨8⟩ Because he left the Calvinists for the Jesuits

---

* *Revue du Seizième Siècle*, II (July 1914), 200-242; reprinted in *Style, Rhetoric, and Rhythm*, pp. 7-44 (in French), ed. John M. Wallace.
The following summary is based on the text as edited by Wallace and retains its footnote numbering. So that cross-references to his text and index entries to it may be readily followed up, its page numbers are indicated here in brackets. I have condensed the contents of the footnotes but have not deleted any of the bibliographical references in them. I am solely responsible for the bracketed material and the translations from French.—J.M.P.

[1] Charles Nisard, *Le Triumvirat Littéraire au XVIe Siècle: Juste Lipse, Joseph Scaliger, et Isaac Casaubon* (Paris, 1852), pp. 1-148. [On p. 3, Nisard cites Antoine Teissier on Lipsius in *Les Éloges des Hommes Savants Tirés de l'Histoire de M. de Thou* (Leiden, 1715), IV, 526.] Emile Amiel's *Un Publiciste du XVIe Siècle: Juste-Lipse* (Paris, 1884) is less valuable.

[2] See Mark Pattison on Lipsius in *The Encyclopaedia Britannica*, 9th ed. (Edinburgh, 1875). [J. Dana translated Lipsius' *De Bibliotecis Syntagma* as *A Brief Outline of the History of Libraries* (Chicago, 1907), and Albert Steur wrote an uncritical dissertation, *Die Philosophie des Justus Lipsius* (Münster, 1911). Partly due to Croll, interest in Lipsius has grown since 1914: *e.g.*, the works mentioned in the Foreword to this essay, and Léontine Zanta, *La Renaissance du Stoïcisme au XVIe Siecle* (Paris, 1914); Basil Anderton, "A Stoic of Louvain," *Sketches from a Library Window* (Cambridge, 1922), pp. 10-30; Guido Capitolo, *La Filosofia Stoica nel Secolo XVI in Francia* (Naples, 1931); V. Nordman, *Justus Lipsius als Geschichtsforscher und Geschichtslehrer* (Helsinki, 1932); and the eds. by Rudolf Kirk listed in n. 4 below. Related studies: F. L. Schoell, *Études sur l'Humanisme Continental en Angleterre* (Paris, 1926); C. B. Hilberry, *Ben Jonson's Ethics in Relation to Stoic and Humanistic Thought* (Chicago, 1933); Philip A. Smith, "Bishop Hall, 'Our English Seneca,'" *PMLA*, LXIII (1948), 1191-1204; H. W. Sams, "Anti-Stoicism in Seventeenth- and Early Eighteenth-Century

and justified repressing heretics with "fire and sword," ⟨9⟩ Protestant disciples (*e.g.*, Hall) prized his literary works but ridiculed his religious ones,[3] whereas the Jesuits Bouhours and Vavasseur suspected the inspiration of the former. Some readers after 1860 were led by such contrary opinions to find Lipsius unheroic. Never one to die for a viewpoint, he doubted his own views as readily as those of others. His submission to Jesuit authority was probably due to inability to fix on intellectual choices. ⟨10⟩ He similarly hesitated to commit himself to rigid literary opinions. Thus, having founded a school of prose, he became its first opponent!

Lipsius was unmanly in evading responsibilities, unhealthy in creating tableaux about massacres.[4] But the naive enthusiasms of Pico, Colet, and Melanchthon were no longer possible. In his own times Lipsius was modern, a precursor of a type of disillusioned contemplator, Stoic moralizer, and heroic egotist, which included Montaigne, Balzac, Burton, Browne, and even Pascal.

⟨11⟩ The nineteenth-century notion that Lipsius had only a rhetorician's interest in the ancients was false.[5] He did not Hellenize

England," *SP*, xli (1944), 65-78; Audrey Chew, "Joseph Hall and Neo-Stoicism," *PMLA*, lxv (1950), 1130-1145; Ralph G. Palmer, *Seneca's De Remediis Fortuitorum and the Elizabethans* (Chicago, 1953); Jonas A. Barish, *Ben Jonson and the Language of Prose Comedy* (Cambridge, Mass., 1960); George Williamson, *Seventeenth Century Contexts* (Chicago, 1961); Julien-Eymard d'Angers, "Le Stoïcisme dans l'Œuvre de J.-L. Guez de Balzac," *Revue des Sciences Humaines*, n.s. lxxxiii (July-Sept. 1956), 269-300. See also *APS*, n.36.]

[3] Joseph Hall in *Epistles*, i.5-6 (*Works*, Oxford, 1837, vi, 134-143) ridicules Lipsius' *Diva Virgo Hallensis Beneficia Ejus et Miracula* (1604) and *Diva Sichemiensis sive Aspricollis* (1605) and cites a passage on miraculous healing attributed to the Virgin. After Lipsius joined the Jesuits, Scaliger was embarrassed because he had praised his erudition; see Jacob Bernays, *Joseph Justus Scaliger* (Berlin, 1855), pp. 171-172. Scaliger was also a literary adversary (Nisard, pp. 128-130).

[4] Especially in *De Constantia, Libri Duo, qui Alloquium Praecipue Continent in Publicis Malis* (1584), which was put into English by Sir John Stradling in 1595 [also by R. G. in 1654 and Nathaniel Wanley in 1670]. It influenced Montaigne who, in turn, made use of it; cf. *Essais*, iii, ix-x, and Pierre Villey, *Les Sources et l'Évolution des Essais de Montaigne*, 2nd ed. (Paris, 1933), i, 178. It had an important role in the late sixteenth-century renaissance of Stoicism (*ibid.*, ii, 65-66), which aided the change in prose studied here. [See Rudolf Kirk, ed., *Tvvo Bookes of Constancie, by Justus Lipsius*, trans. Stradling (New Brunswick, N.J., 1939), *Heaven upon Earth* and *Characters of Vertues and Vices, by Joseph Hall* (1948), and *The Moral Philosophie of the Stoicks . . . by Guillaume Du Vair* (1951).]

[5] Pattison, "Lipsius," *Encyclopaedia Britannica*. [Croll was as yet unaware of John Edward Sandys, *A History of Classical Scholarship*, 3 vols. (Cambridge, 1900-1908), where Lipsius' merits as a classicist are recognized, especially as editor of Tacitus. According to Jason A. Saunders, p. 59, "there is scarcely a problem relating to Roman antiquities on which his criticism and judgment have not

or Romanize himself or venerate the classics uncritically: he judged
them and their relevance realistically and as a moralist interested in
inner life. ⟨12⟩ In an era of stress he found consolation in Stoic
detachment rather than Jesuit doctrine, and he even justified suicide.[6] Was he a Stoic? As Christian he submitted to the Church;
as philosopher he followed the ancients.[7] Tacitus and Seneca were
his models in style, but he was drawn to them as "the father of
prudence" and "the fountain of wisdom."[8] One of the first to react
⟨13⟩ against Renaissance enthusiasms, Lipsius revived the Stoic
doctrine of the mind's superiority over circumstances, which inspired Chapman, Greville, and Donne, and influenced Gracián's
somberness and Montaigne's maxims.

✧ II ✧

His Rhetoric

Bacon, Montaigne, and Lipsius represent a European prose
movement; but alone in his generation Lipsius formulated and
openly defended its rhetoric. When he began to publish, narrow
Ciceronianism flourished despite attacks by Erasmus and Ramus.[9]

---

thrown lasting light. . . . To Lipsius belongs the glory of having given to literary
and historical studies a fruitful and enduring stimulus."]

[6] See *Epistolarum Selectarum Centuria II, Miscellanea*, II.22,28 in *Opera Omnia*
(Antwerp, 1637), II, 79, 82. [Unless otherwise noted, this ed. is used for quota-
tions from Lipsius. He recurred to the subject of suicide in *Manuductionis ad
Stoicam Philosophiam Libri Tres* (1604), III.22-23; cf. Saunders, pp. 111-116.]

[7] C. Scribianus, *Justi Lipsi Defensio Posthuma* (Antwerp, 1608). [Ch. IX; in
Lipsius, *Opera*, II, 315.]

[8] *Ep. ad Italos et Hispanos*, 89, in *Opera*, II, 315.

[9] In the Renaissance controversy, Ciceronianism means not only admiration for,
and imitation of, Cicero but *exclusive* imitation of him; and Anti-Ciceronianism
covers *all* opposition to it. All the Anti-Ciceronians, Lipsius, Montaigne, and
Bacon, sincerely proclaimed that Cicero was the greatest master of Latin rhetoric
although they preferred other models. See John Edward Sandys, "The History of
Ciceronianism" in *Harvard Lectures on the Revival of Learning* (Cambridge,
1905), pp. 145-173; Izora Scott, *Controversies over the Imitation of Cicero as a
Model for Style and Some Phases of their Influence on the Schools of the Renais-
sance* (New York, 1910), pp. 106-111; Eduard Norden, *Die Antike Kunstprosa
vom VI. Jahrhundert von Chr. bis in die Zeit der Renaissance* (Leipzig, 1898 and
Darmstadt, 1958), II, 773-782. None of these books extends to the final Anti-
Ciceronian movement which we study here and which was crowned with success.
See also W. H. Woodward, *Vittorino da Feltre and Other Humanist Educators*
(Cambridge, 1897), pp. 10-13. [See Croll's essays below and their Forewords;
G. L. Hendrickson, "The Origin and Meaning of the Ancient Characters of Style,"
American Journal of Philology, XXVI (1905), 248-290; Trimpi, pp. 28-59 and
passim; J. W. Duff, "Augustan Prose and Livy" in *A Literary History of Rome
from the Origins to the Close of the Golden Age* (London, 1953); Wilbur Samuel

⟨14⟩ Men were then incapable of unbridled liberty and in danger of reverting to corrupt medieval Latin or succumbing to sophistical Greek rhetoric; ⟨15⟩ so it was untimely to urge imitation, particular or eclectic, of authors other than Cicero. In 1580 Muret opposed Ciceronianism, and he had wanted to lecture on Tacitus. But when he listed authors to imitate, he failed to discriminate harmful from beneficial models and gave no guidance to taste and choice.[10]

The revolt against Ciceronianism prepared for modern individualism and its advocacy of achieving a personal style ⟨16⟩ without leaning on guides or models. But Lipsius' generation could neither dispense with imitation nor trust an as yet unborn instinct for form.

Lipsius' program for liberation from Ciceronianism seemingly reconciled novelty with authority and conventions. In 1569 he was a master of Ciceronian periods; eight years later he avowed preference for Plautus' style and need for a style ⟨17⟩ more precise and mordant than the standard one.[11] Converted by studying Plautus' and Cicero's letters, conversations with Muret, and research for his edition of Tacitus (1575), he devoted himself to authors of the Roman Silver Age. His new style was so famous by 1585 that he had to oppose both its adversaries and imitators. He was already working on his edition of Seneca (1605).

⟨18⟩ Rivius[12] praises Lipsius for resuscitating the reputations of

---

Howell, *Logic and Rhetoric in England, 1500-1700* (Princeton, 1956); Sister Miriam Joseph, *Shakespeare's Use of the Arts of Language* (New York, 1947); Williamson, *Senecan Amble*, Ch. 1 and *passim*.]

[10] See Charles Dejob, *Marc Antoine Muret: un Professeur Français en Italie dans la Seconde Moitié du Seizième Siècle* (Paris, 1881) [and P. de Nolhac's corrective review of it in *Revue Critique d'Histoire et de Littérature*, XVI, N.S. XIII (June 19, 1882), 483-488. Cf. *APS*, n.38, and *Muret*, p. 108]. See Nisard for Muret's relations with Lipsius.

[11] [*Variae Lectiones* (1567), shortened to *Variarum Lectionum Libri Tres* (1577). *Epistolicae Quaestiones* (1577) made obvious Lipsius' preference for later Latin writers and a style not "extended and suave, such as you find in Cicero," but with "brevity, piquancy, and a sufficiency of ancient references" v.26, III.16; cf. Saunders, p. 17.] A letter to Janus Lernutus in June 1577 shows that Lipsius was much more advanced in his theory of style than he admitted publicly (*Ep. Misc.* I.13, in *Opera*, II, 16, describing Seneca and his imitators). [Cited in *APL*, p. 172. Cf. Williamson, *Senecan Amble*, p. 123; F. I. Merchant, "Seneca the Philosopher and his Theory of Style," *AJP*, XXVI (1905), 44-59; E. V. Arnold, *Roman Stoicism* (Cambridge, 1911); C. N. Smiley, "Seneca and the Stoic Theory of Literary Style," *Wisconsin Studies in Language and Literature*, III (1919), 50-61; J. F. D'Alton, *Roman Literary Theory and Criticism* (London, 1931).]

[12] Gaugericus Rivius, *Justi Lipsi Principatus Litterarius*, in Lipsius, *Opera*, I, lxxxii-lxxxiii.

Seneca,[13] Velleius Paterculus,[14] Pliny, and, especially, Lucius Annaeus Seneca ⟨19⟩ and Tacitus.[15] His eulogistic passage[16] shows how
Lipsius revived ⟨20⟩ unknown or scorned writers and helps us understand why Jonson and Gracián cite Paterculus, why Montaigne
and Burton knew Valerius Maximus, and why the younger Pliny's
panegyric on Trajan was widely imitated.[17] Lipsius helped create
the taste for Sallust, defended Silver Age Latinity, interpreted for
his era the Anti-Ciceronian movement which began in the days of
Cicero, and thus showed his contemporaries how to escape from
Ciceronianism.

He states his theories on style in letters. In 1586 he ⟨21⟩ admits
that he once imitated Cicero, but as a man he no longer finds
"Asiatic feasts" pleasing: "I prefer Attic banquets."[18] "Attic" may
seem inappropriate for the Anti-Ciceronian movement which Tacitus
and Seneca led, and for an artificial style which was far from
Cicero's elegance and Demosthenes' concision; but the ancients
used it, and it helps explain the corresponding movement in prose
between 1575 and 1675, especially its scorn for useless ornament
and hollow formalism, and its striving for terse precision.

According to Lipsius, allegations that his style corrupts youth
show that it lives—unlike the prevalent style which lacks energy

[13] Rivius jokingly indicates the tragic condition of Seneca's reputation by having
Lipsius find Seneca in a jail.

[14] Lipsius published annotations on Valerius Maximus in 1585 and remarks on
Paterculus in 1591.

[15] [Croll here cites the passage from Rivius in French translation, italicizing
two points or *acumina*, characteristic of the Anti-Ciceronian school. In the English rendering which he gives in *APL*, p. 174, these are: "they were bound who
had attached all humanity in bonds to themselves" and "they lay darkened in
filth who had cast a light beyond the limits of the world."] Croll notes that the
terseness and subtlety of Lipsius becomes obscurity and extravagance in his imitator: Anti-Ciceronianism turns into *concettismo*.

[16] In the translation the extravagance of the style is attenuated for compre-
hensibility. The work appeared in a volume edited by Joannis Moretus (1607)
containing various pieces by Lipsius, eulogies of him, and a fine portrait of him
adorned with symbolic figures. [It is described in *Justi Lipsi Sapientiae et Litterarum Antistitis Fama Posthuma* (Anvers, 1607); cf. F. van der Haeghen, *Bibli-
ographie Lipsienne* (Ghent, 1886-1888), III, 315-317.]

[17] Cf. Sir Henry Wotton, "A Panegyrick to King Charles," *Reliquiae Wot-
tonianae* (London, 1672), pp. 135-158, and the analysis of the "Panegyric on
Trajan" by Dom Jean Goulu (the adversary of Guez de Balzac) in the second
part of his *Lettres de Phyllarque à Ariste* (Paris, 1628); also, Lipsius, *Commen-
taribus in Opera*, IV, 283ff. Taste for this work and admiration for Tacitus were
in large measure results of the pervasive European study of the art of being a
courtier. The Anti-Ciceronian movement, Catholic reaction, and new monarchy
are interestingly intertwined. [See *APS*, n.58.]

[18] *Ep. Misc.*, II.10, *Opera*, II, 75. [*APS*, p. 71.]

and is apathetic in expression, sentiment, and rhythm; and it also shows that his opponents want him to support the despicably un-eloquent Melanchthon.[19] ⟨22⟩ Do they think themselves Ciceronians because they prize a tepid, listless mishmash? His own style aims for extraordinary piquancy and erudition, display of feeling, the fire of inspiration, not mere show.[20]

Thus late sixteenth-century Anti-Ciceronianism esteems expressive power over external beauty, attention to every detail over dispersal of interest for total effect, biting terseness over ceremonious elaboration; it tries to convey serious thought in the heat of its conception. It objects to a conventional, empty rhetorical method and at times seems to object to all traditional styles, forecasting the modern theory of personal expression which leaves little room for studying rhetoric. But its leaders envisaged no ⟨23⟩ such aim: they changed models but not method. In their view, imitation was necessary, and original, individualized expression was incompatible with it.

In *Epistolica Institutio*, Lipsius shows that imitation (harmonious conformity of style with that of the ancients) is the only means to perfection in rhetoric. He replaces exclusive imitation of Cicero with a three-stage plan. To acquire a uniform oratorical style based on a definite model, *boys* should study only Cicero, imitating him to learn periods, constructions, rhythms, and the art of organization. (If Calvus, Coelius, Brutus, etc. were extant, they might serve instead.) Otherwise ⟨24⟩ beginners, selecting from various authors, might develop stylistic instability.[21] *Youths* should gradually imitate other authors, beginning with those who depart least from Cicero rapidly perusing Fabius, Velleius Paterculus, and Caesar, and then studying Plautus and Terence for verbal aptness and Attic elegance, and Pliny despite his being sometimes unpleasing, prolix, and un-

---

[19] *Ep. ad Belgas*, III.28, in *Opera*, II, 486.

[20] *Ep. ad Germanos et Gallos*, 15, in *Opera*, II, 332. [*APL*, p. 177.]

[21] Lipsius' addition, that he is not ignorant of the causes of this error, suggests that he is thinking of Montaigne. In his style, as in Burton's and to some extent in Browne's, one sees the result of a wished-for individualism and scorn for turns, locutions, phrases, and conventional classical periods. Antiquity no longer serves to form their art but to enrich it with knowledge, to ornament it with noble details, and to embroider it with allusions. They are liberated from the laws of servile imitation, and that gives them a new and precious prerogative. They regard the classics as romantics, so to speak: they feel their charm, their remoteness as no conscientious humanist would have wanted to do.

manly; and also that modern who is greater than the moderns[22] in the art of letter-writing—the famous Politian.[23] Though ⟨25⟩ guilty of some straining and affectation, he seems to equal the ancients. Finally, to adorn eloquence's crown, *mature students* should gather all flowers freely in all gardens, preferring Sallust, Seneca, Tacitus, and others who cut through abundance with a sharp sword: imitation of them will develop a strong, precise, masculine style. But let Cicero be reread, especially before going to sleep.[24]

⟨26⟩ This distinctive plan of progressive study reflects Lipsius' own progress. It may seem weak today because it supposes that convention and imitation may be reconciled with originality and genial fire and because it assumes that rhetoric dominates over inspiration and vitality which, accordingly, may be taught like Ciceronian stylistic figures. Such a method could result in sterility of marshalled expression or in ⟨27⟩ temporarily triumphant emphasis and exaggeration. But the plan was suited to a generation which in the middle between medieval and modern was groping toward liberty of mind and originality and had not found a philosophy of independence although it had a glimpse of what was opening up for human reason. In sum, the era of the Anti-Ciceronian movement was the one which preceded Descartes and was the age of Bacon's philosophy; sometimes it seems to bridge the gulf between us and the Middle Ages; at other times it seems more remotely medieval than the simplicity of the early Renaissance.

[22] A typical point illustrating the *argutiae* which Lipsius condemns, without conviction, in Politian.

[23] Angelus Politian was one of the first Anti-Ciceronians. "Do you condemn Livy, Sallust, Quintilian, Seneca, and Pliny because they are barbarians?" he demanded in 1493 (*Epistolarum Libri XII*, v.1, in *Omnium Angeli Politiani Operum*, Paris, 1519, fol. 40v.).

[24] *Ep. Inst.*, Ch. xi, in *Opera*, ii, 538-539. [See *Muret*, n.66.] The advice to reread Cicero is typical of Lipsius' fear of denying one truth while defending another. He may be thinking of his imprudent students who mock Cicero out loud, or the passage may imitate Ciceronian enthusiasm: it recalls Erasmus' *Ciceronianus*. *Ep. Inst.* is condensed in two chapters of Jonson's *Discoveries*: parallel passages are noted in Maurice Castelain's ed. (Paris, 1906), pp. 110-116. [Jonson may have known the Lipsian original, but he derived his borrowings through John Hoskyns, *Direccons for Speech and Style*; see the ed. by H. H. Hudson (Princeton, 1935) and L. B. Osborn, *The Life, Letters, and Writings of John Hoskyns* (New Haven, 1937); also Dunn, "Lipsius and the Art of Letter-Writing," *SR*, iii; Trimpi, pp. 62-75; *Ben Jonson*, ed. C. H. Herford and P. and E. M. Simpson, 11 vols. (Oxford, 1925-1952), viii, 629-633 and xi, 275-278.] Some seventeenth-century English schools used Lipsius' letters as a rhetoric text: cf. Foster Watson, "Scholars and Scholarship, 1600-1660," *Cambridge History of English Literature* (New York, 1932), vi, 357; also his *The English Grammar Schools to 1660* (Cambridge, 1908), p. 415. [Cf. Trimpi, pp. 62-75; *APL*, p. 176.]

✧ III ✧

The Application of Lipsius' Theories

Lipsius led to many classical authors being imitated, especially Tacitus and Seneca. Their influence may be considered in relation to clarity. If one is going to be subtle and terse, one risks obscurity. Seneca tries to avoid that quality ⟨28⟩ and takes care to formulate his aphorisms so that an attentive intelligence apprehends them readily; but in his compact, expressive discourse, Tacitus deliberately adds obscurity, favoring paradoxes and ellipses. The seventeenth century attributed the obscurity of the Spanish *concettisti* to this "Prince of Darkness."[25]

Giving terseness primacy, Lipsius looks to four correctives—perspicuity, simplicity, graceful charm (*venustatem*), and appropriateness (*decentiam*)[26]—and makes "brevity and clarity" his formula, under Senecan influence.[27] His style is expressive, nervous, elliptical, precise; as in Seneca, sentences are neat, ellipses easily understood, points clarified by their expressed form: antithesis in thought accompanies antithesis in expression.

⟨29⟩ Lipsian style is characterized by (1) brevity—short phrases; brief locutions which make us fill out ellipses; avoidance of Ciceronian digressions, apologues, and exordiums;[28] (2) omission of conjunctions and transitions when possible; (3) avoidance of the matched phrasing, parallelisms, similitudes, etc., of Ciceronian concinnity: Lipsius likes to break rhythms, denying what the ear expects; (4) frequent parentheses and concise turns of phrase: Lipsius cuts the long Ciceronian period, stimulates mind while deceiving ear. Parentheses help identify his imitators;[29] (5) striv-

---

[25] [Croll attributes the phrase to Dominique Bouhours, *La Manière de Bien Penser dans les Ouvrages d'Esprit* (Amsterdam, 1688), which John Oldmixon translated as *The Arts of Logick and Rhetorick* (London, 1728). The fourth dialogue treats obscurity and Tacitus, but does not use this phrase.]

[26] *Ep. Inst.*, Ch. VIII, in *Opera*, II, 536. [Cf. Trimpi, pp. 248-249 and 258, n.13, where he observes that the Lipsian qualities of style approximate the virtues of Stoic style described by Diogenes Laertius in his "Life of Zeno," VII.59.]

[27] *Ep. Inst.*, Ch. VIII, in *Opera*, II, 537: "Write then, if you can, clearly and with concision, never forgetting that the latter quality is laudable, the first indispensable."

[28] Abrupt beginnings and endings for letters, prefaces, etc. are marks of an Anti-Ciceronian. Lipsius writes to Montaigne that neither of them would do otherwise, and Wotton's preface to his *Elements of Architecture* (1624) exemplifies this deliberate tightness.

[29] *E.g.*, Joseph Hall, of whom a friend wrote, "He was no talkative fellow: that to every short question returns answer able to fill a volume; with as many paren-

ing for points (*acumina*)—subtle thoughts usually brief and antithetical in form; ⟨30⟩ (6) fondness for metaphors: this distinguishes
seventeenth-century prose from sixteenth, which preferred clearer,
more expanded comparisons.[30]

Croll cites in Latin two passages by Lipsius which illustrate (a)
his choice of subtle, erudite figures in preference to the simple,
realistic, pretty images of the Ciceronians; *i.e.*, he chooses not Sidney's but Bacon's kind of image, ⟨31⟩ (b) his sententious humor,[31]
(c) style which approaches the biting pithiness of Bacon's essays,[32]
and (d) points couched antithetically in Senecan manner.

✧ IV ✧

His Place in Literary History

Lipsius' new ideas on rhetoric gained him many followers, notoriety for having inspired a sect ⟨32⟩ with his errors,[33] and such high
rank as a master rhetorician that he was a center of controversy
throughout the seventy-five years from the High Renaissance to
the prose of French Classicism. During his life and the next decade,
he was denounced as innovator and literary heretic by Henri

---

theses in one sentence as would serve Lipsius all his life" (*The Sermons of Thomas
Adams*, ed. John Brown, Cambridge, 1909, p. 197). [The Croll papers in Princeton Library include an unpublished article on Adams.]

[30] This quality is less notable in Lipsius than in other Anti-Ciceronians, no
doubt due to desire for clarity, but the new taste for concise figures is seen in
Ep. Inst., and the extreme terseness and piquancy of his style is seen in the epistle
to the reader (prefaced to his commentary on Pliny's panegyric, *Opera*, IV, 297)
in "quae didicisse oporteat magis quam discere."

[31] It recalls Polonius and Sir Henry Wotton's maxim for ambassadors, "The
thoughts close and the countenance loose" (*Life and Letters*, ed. Logan Pearsall
Smith, Oxford, 1907, I, 109).

[32] Croll cites passages in Latin from *Ep. Misc.*, I.22, in *Opera*, II, 21-22. The
letter was Englished as *A Direction for Travailers* by John Stradling (1594). An
extract from *Tvvo Bookes of Constancie* (London, 1595, p. 19), Stradling's translation of *De Constantia*, shows not only the penetrating concision of Lipsius' style
but also the cast of the rational and skeptical mind which links him to Montaigne:
"If fire should happen to be kindled in this cittie, we should have a generall out-
cry: the lame and almost the blind would hasten to help quench it. What think
you? For their countries sake? Aske them and you shall see, it was, because the
losse would have redounded to al, or at the least, the feare thereof. So falleth it
out in this case. Publike evils doe moove and disquiet many men, not for that the
harme toucheth a great number, but because themselves are of that number."

[33] *Lettres Diverses de Monsieur de Balzac* (Paris, 1663), sig. a5v. In *Socrate
Chrestien . . . et Autre Œuvres* (Paris, 1661), pp. 352, 355, Balzac claims that
Lipsius corrupted young people by preferring Seneca to Cicero; but he pardons
him, for in pleading Seneca's cause he pleaded his own also. [Cf. *APS*, p. 71.]

Estienne[34] ⟨33⟩ and by Joseph Scaliger: the latter, despite hostility, described Lipsius' style accurately.[35] Such attackers ⟨34⟩ repeated the phrases used by the ancient Ciceronians to express scorn for the two Senecas and their imitators.[36]

A new era in the history of prose began about 1625. French critics such as Descartes, Balzac, Caussin, and Vavasseur were prominent in it. Lipsius remained a center of disputes, but the nature of the attacks changed, for Ciceronianism was dead and a new style imitative of Tacitus and Seneca was in favor. Though its defects—obscurity and extravagance—were pointed out, those of Ciceronianism were as frankly recognized. Critics described the different kinds of classical prose and its imitations, indicated dangers, urged imitation of good features, and thus moved toward reason and taste.

Such was Nicholas Caussin's method. ⟨35⟩ He distinguished ten styles, one of which had biting terseness and penetrating subtlety. Without condemning the ancients who practiced it, he warns that it is not suited to all times and talents and that its adopters' styles may be disfigured by childish ineptitude.[37] But when he defends Ciceronianism he shows that the finest passages in Cicero had the

---

[34] In *De Lipsii Latinitate . . . nec Lipsiomini, nec Lipsiocolacis; multoque minus Lipsiomastigis. Libertas volo sit Latinitate, sed Licentia nolo detur illi* (Frankfort, 1595) (title abridged).

[35] *Silva Variorum Carminum*, No. 14, in *Poemata Omnia* (Leyden, 1615), p. 20, cited in Norden, II, 776, n.2. [Trimpi (p. 49) translates the epigram: "The uniform plainness, which Caesar and Cicero once cultivated, offends others, who are pleased by 'points' bound tight in the joints, which leap, rather than walk, through rough places (*Quae per salebras saltitant, non ambulant*) and, while the expectation of the reader hangs, need more to be understood than read."] In Joseph Justus Scaliger, *Scaligerana* (Cologne, 1667, p. 142), one finds the brief remark on Lipsius, *male scribit*. [Scaliger admired Lipsius' ed. of Tacitus (*Scaligerana*, Cologne, 1695, p. 243) but denounced the Lipsian books on miracles: *Lipsius crepitum edit, admirantur omnes* (p. 153). Cf. Muret, p. 157.]

[36] There is the same tone in a passage cited by Balzac (*Œuvres*, Paris, 1665, II, 608). [It derives from Daniel Heinsius' funeral oration on Joseph Scaliger: According to it, Lipsius urged students not to imitate him or his models, but they did so and, instead of his eloquence, achieved mannered roughness and awkward archaisms: "If anyone wished to write in Latin, dead words were fetched from as far back as Pacuvius and Ennius; sentences hopped along; a lean and jejune speech, juiceless and meagre, broken by some short phrases and plays on words, or by abrupt clauses and short questions, occasioned nausea and disgust." Such was the literary crisis faced by Scaliger when he succeeded Lipsius at the University of Leyden. (Trans. G. W. Robinson in his *Autobiography of Joseph Scaliger*, Cambridge, Mass., 1927, pp. 62-83.).]

[37] *Eloquentiae Sacrae et Humanae Parallela Libri XVI* (Louvain, 1609), II, xiv, p. 73. [Cf. *APS*, n.44.]

qualities prized by Seneca's partisans. Thus Caussin reveals how ideas on rhetoric had changed.

⟨36⟩ The reign of reason and of rules for taste which issued in French Classicism began in the first third of the seventeenth century, so that it is a link in the chain which connects Renaissance prose with that of the Classical period. The opinions of its greatest prosateur, Balzac, were usually like Caussin's, but they show the process of thought. Accepting the Anti-Ciceronian doctrines of Lipsius, Montaigne, and Bacon, Balzac as a youth immersed himself in the "modern" Attic style of Seneca and Tacitus. Though criticized for overyielding to points,[38] he remained Attic to the end;[39] however, he decided ⟨37⟩ that Lipsius, though right about style, erred in choosing mediocre models. Balzac himself sought the best Attic wherever he could find it, in Seneca and Tacitus, in the last, severest speeches of Cicero (the Phillipics), and, above all, in Demosthenes. Thus Balzac allotted the duty of choosing to reason. In general, his development corresponds to that of other writers in the transition between Anti-Ciceronianism and the eighteenth century's achievement of stable doctrine. The quest for a pure model which originated with the humanists began to take on a more liberal, more rational form: Caussin reasons like Balzac in advocating imitation of the best rather than the worst in authors; Vavasseur propounds almost the same program, but his Ciceronianism, like Caussin's, is extremely reactionary: both thought in terms of preaching and failed to understand how well the severest Attic style expressed the heroic morale which was integral to the seventeenth-century ideal.

Bacon seems to have reached a position like Balzac's. He con-

---

[38] Lipsius' earlier tastes are exposed by Frère André at the end of the first part of John Goulu, *Lettres de Phyllarque à Ariste* (Paris, 1628); also in François Ogier, *Apologie pour M. de Balzac.* [See Émile Roy, *De Joan. Lud. Guezio Balzacio contra Dom. Joan. Gulonium Disputante* (Paris, 1892).] To show that Balzac was a plagiarist, this work parallels one hundred ten passages of his with thirty-five by Seneca, fifteen by Tacitus, eleven by Plutarch, nine by Cicero, a score or so from various Latin authors, nine by Joseph Hall, and two from Bacon's *Essays.* Especially interesting in Ogier's apology is his praise of melancholy (pp. 234-240), which caused Balzac suffering but nourished his genius: "In the measure that they acquire experience and wisdom, all men acquire this melancholy disposition." This trait links Lipsius, Burton, Montaigne, and Browne. The study of seventeenth-century melancholy would greatly illuminate some obscure aspects of its literary history.

[39] The story that Lipsius met Balzac and praised him for mastering his stylistic principles is fictitious but shows that Balzac was regarded as a product of the Anti-Ciceronian movement.

tributed significantly to the Anti-Ciceronian movement with imitations of Tacitus and Seneca and with a famous passage in his *Advancement of Learning.* ⟨38⟩ Later, having observed the faults of the new style, he exposed its errors in 1622 with an insertion added to his Latin redaction of the *Advancement.*[40] It is probable that he arrived at the principle of reasoned choice of what to imitate, which his contemporaries formulated later.

The revised doctrine of imitation was a threat to itself; for tastes which are refined enough to distinguish merits and defects among classical models without any authority or guidance soon become independent and seek authority in simple realities and the natural laws of thought.

The first signs of this new phase are visible in Descartes, whose philosophy furnished a basis for independent judgment and human reasoning. In one of his letters ⟨39⟩ he lauds Balzac's style and describes the current fashions in prose: (1) the style like Cicero's: a lengthily exposed, tedious subject proves disappointing to an attentive mind; (2) the style like Seneca's: its sense-packed, rich sentences and noble reflections are pleasing, but their terseness is likely to become tiring and obscure. Then Descartes turns to (3) the dry, unornamented style; (4) the style of conceits and points; and (5) the style of Balzac, who avoids Ciceronian diffuseness without coarsening the grandeur and dignity of his sentences with verbal poverty;[41] and it is noteworthy that Descartes does not use

[40] [*The Advancement of Learning,* ed. William Aldis Wright, 5th ed. (Oxford, 1957), i.iv.2, pp. 28-30 (in *Works,* ed. Spedding, Ellis, and Heath, London, 1868, III, 282-284); *De Augmentis Scientiarum,* in *Works,* I, 452, paraphrased in III, 285, n.1. In Gilbert Wats's trans., *Of the Advancement and Proficiencie of Learning or the Partitions of Sciences* (Oxford, 1640), p. 29, the added passage reads:

Litle better is that kind of stile (yet neither is that altogether exempt from vanity) which neer about the same time succeeded this *Copy* and *superfluity of speech.* The labour here is altogether, *That words may be aculeate, sentences concise, and the whole contexture of the speech and discourse, rather rounding into it selfe, than spread and dilated*: So that it comes to passe by this Artifice, that every passage seemes more witty and waighty than indeed it is. Such a stile as this we finde more excessively in *Seneca*; more moderately in *Tacitus* and *Plinius Secundus*; and of late it hath bin very pleasing unto the eares of our time. And this kind of expression hath found such acceptance with meaner capacities, as to be a dignity and ornament to Learning; neverthelesse by the more exact judgements, it hath bin deservedly dispised, and may be set down *as distemper of Learning,* seeing it is nothing else but a hunting after words, and fine placing of them.

Cf. Williamson, *Senecan Amble,* p. 29 and Chs. III-IV, esp. pp. 112-120; *Muret,* n.54; and the significantly different translation (Croll's own?), in *APL,* p. 190.]
[41] *Lettres de Monsieur Descartes* (Paris, 1657), no. 100, pp. 572-573.

the ancient names for these new styles or uphold classic writers as models: Greeks and Romans are mentioned only as corrupters of pure eloquence in a heroic age. Moreover, he uses modern terms with modern meanings—"the language of the people corrected by usage," "elevated thoughts rendered in familiar terms," "a happy harmony between things and style," and "the natural elegance of speech." His theory seems to be that a good writer should try to delve out of men's ordinary language "corrigée par l'usage" the elements of beauty which are found there and should combine them in order to approximate, as closely as possible, the ideal beauty of natural style which (he thinks) existed at the beginning, in a Golden Age, before it was corrupted by the rhetoric of the sophists of antiquity.

But Descartes was ahead of his times, for the doctrine of imitation was not dead. Near the century's end, Bouhours ⟨40⟩ was defending Cicero, and Shaftesbury ridiculed servile imitation of Seneca.[42]

Thus the criticism of 1600-1640 almost universally reveals an Attic tendency inspired by ancient Anti-Ciceronianism, a tendency which opened a new era to the prose of different nations. Lipsius was regarded as the leader who made it triumph. But he was not alone: ⟨41⟩ there were Bacon, Hall, and Wotton in England; Montaigne, above all, in France; and Quevedo and Gracián who pushed the movement to extremes in Spain.

Lipsius' influence as philosopher and rhetorician was as strong in England as in France,[43] though his letters reveal no interest in Britain. He corresponded with Spaniards and ⟨42⟩ directly influenced Quevedo,[44] who tried to be the Spanish Christian Seneca of the Catholic reaction.[45] ⟨43⟩ Lipsius enjoyed a friendship of equals

[42] Saint-Évremond greatly influenced the admiration for imitating Seneca and the Anti-Ciceronians which continued in the last half of the seventeenth century, at least in England. See Auguste Bourgoin, *Les Maîtres de la Critique au XVIIe Siècle* (Paris, 1899), pp. 79-85, 112-116. Saint-Évremond's presence in England seems to have caused a revival of Montaigne's influence there. [Cf. Pierre Villey, "Montaigne en Angleterre," *Revue des Deux Mondes*, XVII (Sept. 1, 1913), 115-150.]

[43] In a letter Lipsius remarks that he converted William Paddy to his literary tastes (*Ep. Misc.*, II, 96, in *Opera*, II, 107-108).

[44] See *Muret*, pp. 126-127.

[45] Croll cites some of the correspondence, praising E. Mérimée, *Essai sur la Vie et les Œuvres de Francisco de Quevedo* (Paris, 1886). The letters are in *Sylloge Epistolarum a Viris Illustribus Scriptarum*, ed. Petrus Burmannus, 5 vols. (Leyden 1727), Ep. 835-836, II, 162-164.

with Montaigne and opened the *Essays* to public praise.[46] If Lipsius owed to the Frenchman his use of the first person and of intimacy with the reader, Montaigne probably was indebted to him for his admiration of Stoic morality and his growing pleasure in imitating Seneca.[47] Lipsius' earliest extant letter mentions how Montaigne loves ⟨44⟩ Seneca and scorns a flowery, empty style which cannot truly teach.[48]

It is useless to probe which friend showed the way to the other: both responded to the era. Their rationalism, curiosity mixed with incertitude, preoccupation with moral problems, love of Stoic isolation, and strange desire to reconcile submission to dogma with philosophic doubt were all results of this revolution in thought which was transforming the Renaissance into the modern world; at base their Anti-Ciceronianism was a way of expressing this development in terms of rhetoric. Lipsius embodies his epoch: his taste for a certain kind of Latinity was shared by many of his most original contemporaries; it became universal in the first half of the seventeenth century; allied in various ways with other tendencies and dispositions, it produced in different countries the characteristic prose modes of the age as well as impressing a certain direction on the great current of seventeenth-century prose.

[46] See his preface to *Essais* (Paris, 1635), sig. iiiʳ.

[47] For Montaigne's debt, see Villey, *Les Sources*, I, 177-183, 404, 406, 415; II, 65-66, 298-299, 400, 525-526. For relationships, see Paul Bonnefon, *Montaigne et ses Amis* (Paris, 1898), II, 178-180, 185n., and Amiel, *Un Publiciste*, p. 94.

[48] *Ep. Misc.*, II, 41, in *Opera*, II, 86-87. On September 30, 1588, he wrote to Montaigne that there was no man in Europe with whom he agreed more often.

Foreword to Essay Two

This famous essay is more indebted to classical scholarship than any other of Croll's articles, and especially to G. L. Hendrickson's work (as Croll fully acknowledged), but its universal acclaim is deserved. Not only has it saved many scholars much work, but, with more than Senecan perspicuity, it has served to relate ancient theories of style to Renaissance prose in a way which perhaps no other essay has yet rivaled. It provides the indispensable background for the earlier Lipsius essay and for the later more detailed studies of the other principal figures. Had Croll been content with short-cuts, he would have confined himself to Seneca and the other Silver Latin writers who, by his own admission, were the effective models for Lipsius and his collaborators. The first half of this essay, however, is a comparison of the Renaissance attempt to domesticate the *genus humile* with the history of this genre in Greek rhetoric. By showing the philosophical basis of the essay style in Plato, and the logical (as opposed to rhetorical) bias of the first two books of Aristotle's *Rhetoric*, Croll demonstrated the part which Greek precedents played in Renaissance theory, although European civilization was then predominantly anti-Greek. His account of the *genus humile* in Rome explains its late naturalization there—after Cicero—and emphasizes the scientific exploration of human nature to be found in Stoic writing: its interest in searching the crannies of an interior, subjective reality. In so doing, Croll recognized the great variety of individual forms which the *genus humile* was thereby likely to take, and confesses that the philosophical essay style was never really a plain style; though its rhetoric was more subtle and less ornate than the oratorical style, it nevertheless retained many aural qualities, even while aiming at the exact representation of thought. He also made a point of refuting the standard opinion of such scholars as W. C. Summers that sententious prose was generally the mark of a decadent age.[1]

[1] W. C. Summers, ed., *Select Letters of Seneca* (London, 1921), p. xvii; the whole introduction is a valuable analysis of Senecan style. See also Merchant, D'Alton, etc., as cited in *Lipse*, n.11.

Since this essay was written, there has been considerable discussion of Roman Atticism, and Cicero's relation to it. E. Castorina holds that Cicero himself began writing under Attic influence, and, after a middle period of hostility toward an unembellished oratory, ended his career by thinking of himself as the true Attic.[2] This theory has not been wholly accepted, but it suggests that the distinctions between Attic and Asian styles are harder to make than Croll allowed. (Williamson has shown, for example, that Erasmus distinguished between Gorgias and Isocrates in a way Croll did not.) A. Desmouliez, following Norden, claims that Attic style in Rome was part of an archaizing movement, connected with a trend to establish early Greek models in various arts, and that Cicero thought of himself as upholding the evolutionary principle in oratory which the Atticists, with their preference for Lysias and Thucydides over Demosthenes, ignored.[3] Classical scholars are at least agreed on the existence of more than one kind of Atticism in ancient Rome, and S. F. Bonner has concluded that the subject is not closed.[4] Croll's discussion over-simplifies the issue, and by minimizing the archaic element in Atticism he has traced a more regular history of the philosophical style than in fact exists. His conclusions for the seventeenth century, however, remain unaffected, unless it could be shown that "Attic" was then a complicated term, not merely a name for the *genus humile*. Croll understood clearly that Senecanism was a cult before it became a popular style, but his emphasis tends to fall as a rule on the progressiveness of the movement.

[2] *L'Atticismo nell'Evoluzione del Pensiero di Cicerone* (Catania, 1952).

[3] "Sur la Polémique de Cicéron et des Atticistes," *Revue des Études Latines,* xxx (1952), 168-185.

[4] "Roman Oratory," in *Fifty Years of Classical Scholarship,* ed. M. Platnauer (Oxford, 1954), pp. 363-368. The standard essay on Roman Atticism is U. v. Wilamowitz-Möllendorf, "Asianismus und Atticismus," *Hermes,* xxxv (1900), 1-52; see also P. Giuffrida, "Significati e Limiti del Neo-Atticismo," *Maia,* vii (1955), 83-124, an essay which describes the controversy as philosophical rather than stylistic; and José Guillén, "Cicerón y el Genuino Aticismo," *Arbor,* xxxi (1955), 427-457, which lists the principles of Atticism which Cicero praised. Roman historical style, which is closely related to the subject, has been discussed by A. D. Leeman, "Le Genre et le Style Historique à Rome: Théorie et Pratique," *RÉL,* xxxiii (1955), 183-208. Leeman distinguishes three kinds of Atticism.

An important article by Mlle. A. Guillemin has tended to confirm Croll's view of Seneca's style, especially in its emphasis on subtler forms of imitation, which were not committed to reproducing verbatim the characteristics of an original model, but above all she has indicated the great extent to which Seneca was influenced by the new theory of the sublime, and the *Treatise on the Sublime* in particular.[5] The sublime, Mlle. Guillemin asserts, was essentially the epideictic style which Cicero treated so inadequately; it was not hostile to other features of Senecan theory—clarity, the rejection of Asiatic *flores*, etc.—and neither did Seneca reject "abundance," although his was a copiousness which differed greatly from Cicero's. The significance of enlarging the range of effects possible in the Senecan manner is that one is helped to explain the enormous differences among the Senecan performances in the early seventeenth century. Croll himself was obviously puzzled by these variations, writing (in this essay) of the "monstrous births"—metaphysical sermons—engendered by the copulation of the philosophical style with oratorical magnificence; later he was to posit a "baroque" strain running through the three forms of Senecanism—Stoic (curt), libertine (loose), and political (Tacitean)—and finally was to label all the forms as subspecies of the baroque. In other words, he had an increasing sense of a much larger amount of embellishment and verbal wit in Senecan style than he had at first been prepared to admit.

His difficulty probably arose from his failure to make sufficient allowance for the differences between the sixteenth and seventeenth centuries, and he continued to write about the theorists of the plain style after the Restoration as if they had the same principles as Lipsius; to a certain extent he was right, but of course they were the excesses of the Senecan style which the plain stylists berated. Even in his treatment of the sixteenth century there is a dilemma.

[5] "Sénèque Directeur d'Âmes: Les Théories Littéraires," *RÉL*, xxxii (1954), 250-274. Tacitus' concern for psychological accuracy, which Croll saw as intrinsic to the Attic style, has recently been made the subject of an interesting essay by J. Cousin, "Rhétorique et Psychologie chez Tacite: Un Aspect de la 'Deinôsis,'" *RÉL*, xxix (1951), 228-247.

47

Croll recognized that Senecan style, though it aimed at rendering the movements of the mind exactly and without ornament, was in fact a "highly imaginative portrayal" of the writers' relations with truth, and was thus perforce highly rhetorical. Yet he also recognized in the statements about clarity and concision an effort to achieve a plain style; he was the first to perceive that Bacon had his reservations about florid Senecanism, but could speak also of Lipsius, Bacon, Balzac, and Browne as having a "normal" style; he noted "concettismo" as a "rhetoric of thought" arising directly out of Senecan theory, and yet stressed the antirhetorical aims of the movement. One is struck first with the justice of all these observations, and the bravery with which he suppressed none of the evidence. But, knowing what we now do, one must argue that some factor of genuine plainness eluded him, and that his theory about "the modern spirit of progress," born with the Senecan style, did not help him to find it.

Perry Miller and W. J. Ong have made out an overwhelming case for the part which Ramism played in the ultimate triumph of a plain style,[6] and, with some reservations from Williamson, Richard Foster Jones has demonstrated that science reformed all *flosculi*, Senecan or Ciceronian, and did much to insure a style which would describe an exterior rather than an interior reality.[7] That these two influences, coming into their own during the seventeenth century, did much to bring about a reaction against Senecanism can hardly be disputed. However, even Ong does not deny Rosemond Tuve's thesis[8] that Ramism, by strengthening the hold of dialectic over imagery, encouraged the strong lines of metaphysical poetry. And if poetry, why not

[6] Perry Miller, *The New England Mind: The Seventeenth Century* (Cambridge, Mass., 1954), esp. pp. 300-362; W. J. Ong, *Ramus, Method, and the Decay of the Dialogue* (Cambridge, Mass., 1958), passim, but esp. pp. 212-213, 283-288. For an important critique of studies of Ramus's influence on seventeenth-century prose style, see Jackson I. Cope, *The Metaphoric Structure of* Paradise Lost (Baltimore, 1962), pp. 27-49.

[7] "Science and English Prose Style in the Third Quarter of the Seventeenth Century"; "The Attack on Pulpit Eloquence in the Restoration"; "Science and Language in England of the Mid-Seventeenth Century," all in *The Seventeenth Century* (Stanford, 1951), pp. 75-160.

[8] *Elizabethan and Metaphysical Imagery* (Chicago, 1947), esp. pp. 331-353.

the metaphysical sermon also, though Perry Miller has said roundly that it would have been impossible to be a Ramist and preach like John Donne? Moreover, by 1650 the Ramist New England divines were left defending their flowers of speech against the attacks of their plainer Anglican brethren. It seems clear, therefore, that Ramism, even though it slighted rhetoric, made a definite place for it as appliqué work (to use Ong's term), and that its tendency towards plainness had to be reinforced from another quarter; the forces, whatever they were, and they certainly included science, were strong enough to change the dominant Anglican mode from metaphysical to plain preaching. Reaction to Laudian excesses, in style as in politics, probably accounts for some of it, social pressures for more. Latitudinarian sermons were not at first especially plain, as W. Fraser Mitchell has shown,[9] but the simplicity of spirit and word of men like John Hales and George Herbert, harking back to a moderate Anglicanism which existed before Jacobean politics, was in the long run the greatest influence for plainness in England.[10] As Croll was well aware, and as Mitchell has made even clearer, the patristic reading of the high Anglicans was largely responsible for their marked deviation from a Senecan norm, but there was in existence from the Reformation, and gathering strength as the revolt against enthusiasm proceeded, a belief in the pure and simple milk of the Word, shared by many Puritans and some Anglicans alike. The manifesto for such plainness can be heard in Jewel's famous sermon against pulpit rhetoric. For all the sympathy many churchmen felt for Seneca's morals, his rhetoric was pagan and held in special esteem by the sceptics, official believers though they were. Such plainness

[9] *English Pulpit Oratory from Andrewes to Tillotson* (New York, 1962), pp. 276-307.

[10] On this tradition see John Tulloch, *Rational Theology and Christian Philosophy* (London, 1874), I, 1-75, and Richard Foster Jones, "The Moral Sense of Simplicity," in *Studies in Honor of Frederick W. Shipley* (St. Louis, 1942), pp. 265-287. On the plain style in journalism and politics during the first half of the century, see Hugh Macdonald, "Another Aspect of Seventeenth-Century Prose," *RES*, XIX (1943), 33-43. Trimpi gives a full account of the plain style and considers its philosophical commitments, moral and aesthetic implications, and chief exponents.

owes nothing to an idea of progress, and little to the motives which Croll ascribed to the initiators of the Anti-Ciceronian program. But even in enumerating these reservations about Croll's thesis, one is aware how his work makes it possible to arrive at them. Without this essay on Attic prose we should be much further away than we are now from an understanding of seventeenth-century style.

JOHN M. WALLACE

THE JOHNS HOPKINS UNIVERSITY

ESSAY TWO

"Attic Prose" in the
Seventeenth Century*

EDITED BY JOHN M. WALLACE

❖ I ❖

TWO TERMS present themselves to the literary historian
seeking a name for the new kind of style that came into general
use in Latin and all the vernacular languages at the end of the
sixteenth century.[1] "Anti-Ciceronian prose" has the merit of indicating the character of the controversy out of which the new tendency emerged victorious: it connects the successful movement led
by Lipsius, Montaigne, and Bacon with the frustrated efforts of
Erasmus, Budé, and Pico early in the sixteenth century. But it is
open to several objections. In the first place, it indicates only revolt,
suggests only destructive purposes in a movement that had a definite
rhetorical program. Secondly, it may be taken as describing a
hostility to Cicero himself, in the opinions of the new leaders,
instead of to his sixteenth-century "apes," whereas in fact the
supreme *rhetorical* excellence of Cicero was constantly affirmed by
them, as it was by the ancient Anti-Ciceronians whom they imitated.[2] And thirdly, it was not the term usually employed in

* Originally published in *Studies in Philology*, XVIII (April 1921), 79-128.
[1] The present paper is part of a more extended study [projected by Croll as an
independent volume] with the same title, the object of which is to show that the
successful Anti-Ciceronian movement inaugurated by Muret, Lipsius, Montaigne,
and Bacon, in the last quarter of the sixteenth century, gave a new direction
to European prose style and determined its characteristic forms throughout the
seventeenth century. For the history of this movement and the description of
the forms of style which it created, the reader must be referred to the other parts
of this study.
Various discussions of the Ciceronian movement of the Renaissance are familiar,
and in all of these the earlier phases of the opposition to it—led by Erasmus,
Pico, and others—receive due attention. On the other hand, the decisive Anti-
Ciceronian movement of the last quarter of the century has heretofore received
but cursory mention, as by Norden, pp. 778-779, Sandys, pp. 145-173, and
Izora Scott, pp. 106-111—all cited in *Lipse*, n.9.
[All bracketed editorial additions to Croll's notes in this paper were written
by J. Max Patrick. J.M.W.]
[2] Montaigne, "Des Livres," *Essais*, II.x, ed. J.-V. Le Clerc (Paris, 1865), II, 124,

51

contemporary controversy, and was never used except by enemies of the new movement. The only name by which its leaders and friends were willing to describe the new style during the century of its triumph, from 1575 to 1700, was "Attic."

For these reasons "Attic" is the preferable term, and should take its place in literary history as the name of the dominant tendency in seventeenth-century prose style in contrast with that of the sixteenth century. To use it at the present time, however, for this purpose, without a full and clear explanation of the meaning attached to it could only cause positive misunderstanding or utter confusion. For it is a word that has suffered vicissitudes. In current and uncritical literary writing of the last two centuries it has often been employed to designate a style conformed to the conversational customs of a well-trained and sophisticated society—the society of Paris in the eighteenth century rather than of Athens in the age of Pericles. This meaning, it is true, was imposed by a later age than the seventeenth century and might safely be disregarded, the more safely, indeed, because it does not correspond to any of the more important meanings recognized as sound by the best students of antiquity. But unhappily in the usage of classical scholars themselves the word does not now carry a single and definite meaning; and the most recent researches tend to add complexity rather than clearness to its history. For the truth is that it was never a formalized word of rhetorical theory in ancient criticism, such as can be used for definition; it always tended to be a nickname of compliment or eulogy, and was subject to the variations of meaning that we may observe in many similar words of the modern critical vocabulary. There was a disposition, it is true, to associate it in Roman criticism with one of the two great "characters of style" of which we will

---

is franker than any other of the leaders in expressing a dislike of Cicero. Yet he admires his *eloquence*. "There is no real excellence in him," he says, "unless his eloquence itself is so perfect that it might be called a real and substantive excellence." Of course part of the point of this is, however, in the implied doubt of the value of pure eloquence, in itself; for no Ciceronian would think of doubting it. [Croll's "quotation" appears to be a conflation of two passages on Cicero, the one as documented above, the other in "Considération sur Cicéron," *Essais*, I.xxxix (xl in modern eds.), ed. Le Clerc, I, 358: "Fy de l'eloquence qui nous laisse envie de soy, non de choses! si ce n'est qu'on die celle de Cicéron, estant en si extreme perfection, se donne corps elle-mesme." This passage is quoted in (Croll's own?) English trans., *APL*, III (p. 178); cf. *Muret*, n.10. The attitudes of Muret and Montaigne toward Cicero are compared by W. H. Alexander in "The Sieur de Montaigne and Cicero," *UTQ*, IX (1939-1940), 222-230.]

speak presently. But on the other hand it might denominate a *quality* of style, vaguely associated with Athens in the time of its glory, which neither of the "characters" could afford to neglect and which might appear equally well in either. Or again it could be used in its exact geographical sense, of any author who lived at Athens, without reference to either the quality or the character of his style.

All the trees in this forest have again been studied close up by recent scholars; and we are now no more competent to give a comprehensive definition of "Attic" than the ancients themselves were. Evidently any one who wants to use the term at the present time for the purpose of identification must explain what he means by it. If this involved an attempt to discuss the many questions still in controversy among the classicists, or to adjust the relations of the various ancient meanings of the word that have been mentioned, it would be too pretentious an undertaking for one who is not a trained classicist. But we are not concerned here with any of these thorny problems. Our business is to understand "Attic" as the seventeenth-century critics did; and they at least had a clear idea of what they meant by it, and used it to define the stylistic purposes of their own age. It meant in their critical vocabulary one of two kinds of characters of style made familiar to them in modern and vernacular use by the imitation of antiquity since the beginning of the Renaissance, and corresponding, as they saw, roughly but definitely enough with the two leading "characters," or *genera dicendi*, distinguished by ancient criticism.[3] This limitation of meaning will serve as a clue to guide us through all complexities.

Classical scholars may not, therefore, feel highly rewarded by the present survey, and it is not in their interest that it is undertaken. Yet it may have some value even for them. For the word "Attic" had a lively, contemporary interest in the seventeenth century that it has never had since, and was used by men whose own writings were, by intention at least, direct continuations of ancient Latin literature. Their knowledge was limited in its range as compared with that of the most accomplished modern classicists; but as far as it went it was both sounder and more vivid than that of any later generation. It is possible that their use of the term we are considering will help to simplify a problem which has been greatly confused by the investigation of details; and it is certain that it is truer to

---

[3] Of course in the matured theory there are *three* characters. See explanation below on pp. 59-61 and 77-82.

ancient usage than that which has been current in popular criticism since the eighteenth century.

✧ II ✧

The seventeenth century, then, regarded the history of ancient prose style chiefly as a story of relations and conflicts between two modes of style, which—for the sake of the utmost simplification— we may characterize at once (in modern terms) as the oratorical style and the essay style, and may describe by the kind of ornament most used in each. The oratorical style was distinguished by the use of the *schemata verborum*, or "schemes," as we may call them, which are chiefly similarities or repetitions of sound used as purely sensuous devices to give pleasure or aid the attention. The essay style is characterized by the absence of these figures, or their use in such subtle variation that they cannot easily be distinguished, and, on the other hand, by the use of metaphor, aphorism, antithesis, paradox, and the other figures which, in one classification, are known as the *figurae sententiae*, the figures of wit or thought.[4] But of course such characterizations are mere caricature, and serve only as convenient labels. The form and history of the two styles must be fully considered.

The first is of earlier origin: it is the style in which prose first came to be recognized as a proper object of artistic cultivation among the Greeks. According to the sketchy and untrustworthy reports of ancient literary historians, Gorgias was its "inventor"; but this may mean no more than that he first formulated and systematized for teaching purposes the "schemes" which serve to ornament it, and especially the three most important of these, which still go by his name in rhetorical theory: and it is almost certain that even these figures originated long before Gorgias' time, in certain liturgical or legal customs of the primitive Greek community.[5] The next state in its history is associated with the name of

---

[4] The division of the figures into *schemata verborum* and *figurae sententiae* is here adopted because it represents the opposition of styles that we are concerned with. There were, of course, other classifications in antiquity, based on other principles.

[5] They are 1) *Isocolon*, approximate equality of *length* between members of a period; 2) *Parison*, similarity of *form* between such equal members as in the position of nouns, verbs, adjectives, etc.; 3) *Paramoion*, likeness of sound between words thus similarly placed. Descriptions of them may be found in Richard Volkmann, *Rhetorik der Griechen und Römer*, in *Handbuch der Klassischen Altertums-Wissenschaft*, ed. I. von Müller, 3rd ed. (Munich, 1901), II, iii, 40-49; Friedrich Landmann, *Der Euphuismus, sein Wesen, seine Quelle, seine Geschichte*

Isocrates, a disciple of Gorgias, to whom is always attributed the elaboration of the form of the rhythmic "period" and the subordination to this, in their proper artistic relation to it, of the Gorgian schemes. Isocrates was the most important of all that class of teachers to whom Socrates and Plato have given a much worse reputation than they deserve. The sophistic scheme of education included a great use of oratory because it was founded on a study of politics; the individual man was conceived as a kind of mirror reflecting the character and interests of his town or state, and his literary education was wholly determined by the customs of the forum and the public uses of rhetoric.[6]

In spite of all opposition from the philosophers this type of education spread generally throughout the Greek world, in the colonies perhaps even more widely than in the home cities, and was disseminated in the Hellenistic period throughout the greater part of the Mediterranean world. And with it, of course, went the "sophistic" rhetoric everywhere, now exfoliating in *cultus* and flamboyancy under the influence of provincial tastes, now degenerating into a merely puerile and academic employment of the schemes, or again assuming the normal grandeur of its proportions and the purity of its design, but preserving through all variations the essential features of its form as they had been perfected by Isocrates. In fact the conventionalized oratory of the sophistic schools must be considered not only the most conspicuous contribution of the Greeks to the prose style of Europe, but also the standard and normal form of their own prose, of which all other forms are variations, and to which it always returned as to the true rhetorical point of departure. Nor did it perish with the passing of classical Greek culture. It lived again in the Roman rhetoric which culminated in the oratory of Cicero, and survived, to enjoy still longer and stranger destinies, in the teaching of the Christian schools of the Middle Ages.[6a]

(Giessen, 1881); Clarence Griffin Child, *John Lyly and Euphuism* (Erlangen, 1894); Croll, *Sources*, printed in full below; or better in a number of the medieval treatises collected in Karl F. von Halm, ed., *Rhetores Latini Minores* (Leipzig, 1863), of which see index. They may be briefly described as the chief figures by which oratorical concinnity is effected.

[6] Edward M. Cope in the introd. to *Plato's Gorgias Literally Translated* (London, 1883) gives a clear statement of the character of sophistic education. [See H. M. Hubbell, *The Influence of Isocrates on Cicero, Dionysius, and Aristides* (New Haven, 1913); T. K. Whipple, "Isocrates and Euphuism," *MLR*, XI (1916), 15-27, 129-135; Williamson, *Senecan Amble*, pp. 20-37 and passim.]

[6a] [M. B. Ogle, "Some Aspects of Medieval Latin Style," *Speculum*, I (1926),

THE ANTI-CICERONIAN MOVEMENT

The form of Isocratean rhetoric need not detain us long here; we are concerned with it only in its relation with the style that arose in opposition to it, and the only point that it is necessary to emphasize here is the sensuous character of its appeal to its audience. Its "round composition" and the "even falling of its clauses" do not always satisfy the inward ear of the solitary reader. Heard solely by the reflective mind, it is an empty, a frigid, or an artificial style. But it is not meant for such a hearing. It is addressed first, like music, to the physical ear; and the figures with which its large and open design are decorated have been devised with a reference to the attentive powers and the aural susceptibilities of large audiences, consisting of people of moderate intelligence, and met amid all the usual distractions of public assemblage—as Cicero says, *in sole et pulvere*.

In their appropriate place they are the legitimate resource of a great popular art, and their fitness for their ends is vindicated by the fact that they reappear whenever the necessary conditions of popular eloquence are satisfied. But it is evident that their literary adaptability is strictly limited. They offer nothing that is pleasing to an intellect intent upon the discovery of reality; and a people like the Greeks, in whom philosophic curiosity was quite as strong an incentive to literary art as the love of sensuous forms, would not long resist the temptation to ridicule or parody them, and to study modes of expression deliberately contrasted with them. The beginning of the history of the essay style among them follows hard, as we should expect, upon that of the oratorical, in the lifetime indeed of the reputed founder of the latter.

170-189; Charles Sears Baldwin, *Medieval Rhetoric and Poetic to 1400* (New York, 1928) and *Renaissance Literary Theory and Practice: Classicism in the Rhetoric and Poetic of Italy, France, and England 1400-1600* (New York, 1939); Lee S. Hultzén, "Aristotle's *Rhetoric* in England to 1600," Cornell Univ. Diss., 1932; Richard P. McKeon, "Rhetoric in the Middle Ages," *Speculum*, XVII (1943), 1-32; J. W. H. Atkins, *English Literary Criticism: The Medieval Phase* (New York, 1943); Ernst R. Curtius, *European Literature and the Latin Middle Ages*, trans. W. R. Trask, Bollingen Series XXXVI (New York, 1953) from *Europäische Literatur und Lateinisches Mittelalter* (Berne, 1948); Wilbur S. Howell, "English Backgrounds of Rhetoric," *History of Speech Education in America* (New York, 1954), pp. 3-47, and the earlier chapters of his *Logic and Rhetoric in England, 1500-1700* (Princeton, 1956)—but see Walter J. Ong, *RN*, IX (Winter 1956), 206-211; Ong's concern, here and elsewhere, is with the special problem of the impact of Ramus on logic and rhetoric during the Renaissance; see his *Ramus, Method, and the Decay of Dialogue* (Cambridge, Mass., 1958); but see also R. J. Schoeck, *New Scholasticism*, XXXIV (1960), 537-545.]

In his dialogue named for the orator, Plato relates a conversation that is supposed to occur on a visit of Gorgias to Athens in about the year 405, when Gorgias was perhaps eighty years of age. Socrates had been invited to meet him at dinner and hear him deliver a new oration that he had prepared. Socrates avoided the proffered entertainment, probably with some malice; but, either by accident or design, met the dinner party on its way home, and was again invited to hear an oration by the master—this time at Callicles' house. Socrates went with the party, but asked whether Gorgias would not consent to converse with him instead of speaking to him. In the long conversation that followed, the philosopher succeeded by his unequalled dialectic art in making Gorgias and one of his disciples acknowledge that the true aim of education is not the art of persuasion, but how to see and like the truth, how to know right from wrong and love it; and gave an original turn to the whole theory of style by showing that it is at best a kind of cookery which makes things palatable whether they are good for us or not, whereas the study of morality is like medicine, which puts the soul in a state of health and keeps it there.

In this dialogue of Plato's, and in the *Phaedrus*, which treats the same theme, are laid the foundations of a new interpretation of the functions of rhetoric, wholly different from those of oratory, and of the practice of a style appropriate to these functions. But it is not fair to say that Plato and Socrates foresaw such an outcome of their controversy with the sophists, or would have been pleased by it if they had done so. Cicero complained that it was Socrates who first instituted the opposition between philosophy and oratory which, as he properly observed, is fatal to the highest development of the latter; and this statement seems to represent the attitude of Socrates in the *Gorgias* with substantial correctness. The purport of his argument is almost certainly that in the public life of a sound commonwealth, and, with still more reason, in the private activities of its citizens, there would be no use of an art of rhetoric of any kind. The Protestant, or Puritan, divorce of spirit and sense is apparent in his treatment of the subject, and he has apparently not thought of the possibility that a new theory of style could be erected on the foundation of his opposition to oratory and its forms.

History shows, however, that when you put rhetoric out at the door it comes in at the window, and the inevitable next step in the development of the ideas of Socrates and Plato was their systemization with reference to an art of prose composition. Aristotle effected this in the first two books of his *Rhetoric*, which have served as the starting point of all subsequent theories of style that have called themselves "modern." This book was a wholly new thing in the world; for the theory of rhetoric was here worked out for the first time, not on the basis of the susceptibilities of audiences, and the aural effect of language, but on the basis of the processes of reasoning and in strict relations with the science of logic. Speaking roughly, we may say that the *Rhetoric* treats for the first time the art of writing, as opposed to the art of speaking.[7]

This statement will have to be very carefully guarded, however; for there is an astonishing inconsistency in the work, which it will be useful to consider here for a moment. After treating style in the first two books as dependent upon the forms of thought, Aristotle discusses, in the third book, which is about style, a form which is not distinguishable from the Isocratean oratorical style, except that he lays an emphasis perhaps on shorter periods and treats the oratorical figures very simply. The explanation is probably to be found in the fact that the two parts were composed for different purposes at different times. The first is the work of a philosopher seeking to explain the part that rhetoric is observed to play in the life of man, and is not meant to have anything to do with the practice of the art; the second is a purely objective description of the form of style which he saw in actual use, the only describable, conventionalized form then in existence.[8] Of course this explanation does not get rid of the essential inconsistency of his two modes of treatment. Nothing can do that; for it is involved in Aristotle's theory, and we encounter here for the first time a phenomenon that meets us at every point in the later history of the intimate or essay style, namely, the slipperiness of all rhetorical theory when it tries to establish itself on anything other than the sensuous character of language and the social conventions that give it opportunity and effect. When it aspires to be the art of presenting things or thought in their essential character and their true lineaments, rhetoric at once begins to lose its identity and be dissolved into one or another

---

[7] For the relation between the ideas of Plato and those of the *Rhetoric* see Cope, *Gorgias*, pp. xxv-xxviii, and G. L. Hendrickson, "The Origin and Meaning of the Ancient Characters of Style," *AJP*, XXVI (1905), 249-252.

[8] On the inconsistency spoken of see Hendrickson, "The Origin," p. 251, n.2, and pp. 252-255. Norden, *Die Antike Kunstprosa*, I, 125-126, speaks of inconsistencies of the same kind between the *Rhetoric* and other works of Aristotle.

of the sciences. It is an art, in short, and every art is a social convention.

But we need go no further into this subject at present; what concerns us is that Aristotle's *Rhetoric* exactly represents the state of unstable equilibrium which had necessarily followed Plato's attack upon oratory. A new use of prose style had now attained general recognition as a form of art—in brief the use of style for the purposes of philosophy and as closely related to the art of dialectic; and on the basis of this new conception of the purpose of prose discourse Aristotle had erected the theory of the art of rhetoric. But in the meantime the older, traditional, oratorical customs had not yielded to the vigor of Plato's attack, but on the contrary were as flourishing as ever, and were universally recognized, even by Aristotle, as displaying the form of style which, in a purely rhetorical sense, is the ideal and abstract best. In other words, theory and the tradition of practice were in conflict, and Aristotle had done nothing to reconcile them.

The recognition of this difficulty was what determined the next step in the development of Greek rhetorical theory. The followers of Aristotle resolved it in a purely empirical way by recognizing a division of prose style into two distinct characters or genera, which henceforward played the leading role in all the rhetorical criticism of antiquity. At a later stage in the development a third "character" was added and appears in all Latin criticism; but in the most recent and much the best treatment of the subject this addition is considered as a makeshift which tends to confuse the principle on which the original division was based.[9] We shall have to speak of it in its place; but the main facts of modern stylistic history, as of the ancient, are best represented by a consideration of the two characters which first make their appearance in Theophrastus and are more clearly defined in later successors of Aristotle.

The first was known as the *genus grande* or *nobile*. It was the rhetorical style of the Gorgian tradition, and the adjectives used to describe it indicate the character it was originally supposed to have. When it was practiced independently of the social and political conditions upon which it depends for its greatest success, its

[9] In all that concerns the history of the three characters of style and the relations between the *genus grande* and the *genus humile* in ancient theory, I follow the convincing article by Hendrickson cited in the preceding notes, and its companion, "The Peripatetic Mean of Style and the Three Stylistic Characters," *AJP*, xxv (1904), 125-146.

elaborate form and ornamental figures, studied merely for their own charm, gave it a character of *cultus*, or empty ornateness; and it was so portrayed at certain periods by its opponents. But the true nature of the *genus grande* is to be broad and general in its scope, large and open in design, strong, energetic, vehement. Tacitus ridicules its degenerate practitioners as minstrels or dancers, in allusion to the musical beauty of their rhythms;[10] but Cicero in more than one passage compares the true orator with the tragic actor, in allusion to the breadth and passion of his portrayal of life.[11]

The newer style, which had appeared in opposition to this, was known as the *genus humile* or *submissum* (*demissum*), but its quality is better indicated by the more descriptive appellations often given to it, or to branches or varieties of it: *lene*, *subtile*, insinuating, flexible, subtle. A style of this general character would naturally have many particular forms. It might, for instance, become a deliberately rude, formless, negligent style—*décousu*, as Montaigne says of his own—in order to express contempt for *cultus*, or even for rhetoric itself, and a love of "honest" simplicity; on the other hand, it might emulate the colloquial ease and *mondanité* of good conversation, in intended contrast with the vulgar pomp of public oratory, and be distinguished as elegant, graceful, *nitidus*; or again it might declare its superiority to popular tastes, as in the hands of the Stoics, by affecting a scornful and significant brevity of utterance. All of these and other species of the genus were recognized by the ancients as actually existing, or as having existed at different times and places, and were distinguished by appropriate terms.[12] But the genus as a whole is properly characterized by its origin in

---

[10] *Dialogus de Oratoribus*, XXVI: *Plerique jactant cantari saltarique commentarios suos.* It is interesting that the reformers of style in the Renaissance compared the corrupt medieval form of the *genus grande* to minstrels' elocution. See my introduction to Lyly's *Euphues*, section v, glossed "Passage from Wilson's *Rhetoric*."

[11] For example, in *Brutus*, LV.203: *Grandis et, ut ita dicam, tragicus orator.*

[12] See, for instance, the classification by Demetrius, *De Elocutione*: graceful, plain, and arid; all of these being species which, in a different classification from Demetrius', would form parts of the *genus humile*. [For Demetrius' main passages on the plain style, see the Loeb ed., *On Style*, trans. W. R. Roberts (Cambridge, Mass., 1953), 190-222; also his observations on epistolary style, 223-239.] See also Diogenes Laertius, "Life of Zeno" [VII.59, quoted in *Lipse*, n.26], and Quintilian, *Institutio Oratoria*, XII.x.20-26. [Trimpi treats the *genus humile* at length, using Demetrius' statements and Cicero's account of the Attic orator "as the norm for the plain style in classical prose" (p. 8).]

philosophy. Its function is to express individual variances of experience in contrast with the general and communal ideas which the open design of the oratorical style is so well adapted to contain. Its idiom is that of conversation or is adapted from it, in order that it may flow into and fill up all the nooks and crannies of reality and reproduce its exact image to attentive observation.[13]

As to its specific rhetorical forms nothing needs to be said here; they will be considered fully elsewhere. But a general point must be urged which is often, or usually, ignored by admirers of a *genus humile*, and even by those who practice it, though the neglect of it is a prolific source of aberration both in theory and practice. And this is the point that its rhetorical forms are modifications, adaptations of those of the oratorical style. The ancients were very slow to recognize any kind of literary customs other than oral ones; and even in the genres that were obviously meant for silent reading, such as the letter, the form of the style was controlled by the ear. This is a sound principle at all times, and for all kinds of style, and its operation cannot be escaped even though it is forgotten or denied. There is only one rhetoric, the art of the beauty of spoken sounds. In oratory this beauty displays itself in its most obvious, explicit, exfoliated forms; in the *genus humile* in much more delicate, implicit, or mingled ones. But the forms are ultimately the same, and whatever beauty of style we find in the most subtle and intimate kinds of discourse could be explained—if there were critics skillful and minute enough—in terms of oratorical effect.

The history of Greek and Roman style is chiefly the story of the relations of the *genus grande* and the *genus humile*. Theoretically the two kinds are not hostile or exclusive of each other; Cicero is always anxiously insisting that they are both necessary in their proper places and relations to the oratory that he dreamed of as the perfection of literary art. But in fact they almost always proved to be rivals; and different schools, even long and important literary periods, distinguish themselves by their preference for one of them, their dislike of the other.

[13] Quintilian's metaphor (*Inst. Or.*, XII.x.37) is beautiful. Advising the Romans to cultivate the grand style rather than the "Attic," he says: "Greek keels, even the little ones, know well their ports; let ours usually travel under fuller sails, with a stronger breeze swelling our canvas. . . . They have the art of threading their way through the shallows; I would seek somewhat deeper waters, where my bark may be in no danger of foundering."

✧ III ✧

It proved to be so again during the formative period of modern prose style. The literary movement which is the subject of the present discussion was a successful attempt to substitute the philosophical *genus humile* for the oratorical *genus grande* in the general practice of authors and the general favor of readers.

Both the customs and the spirit of sixteenth-century life demanded literary expression in oratorical forms. It was a period of social unity, or at least of social unities. Brittle, temporary, illusory, these unities were; yet they were effective and brilliant while they lasted, and created the congregational and social customs which are favorable to a spoken literature. Even the religious controversy, so destructive of European society in the long run, had the opposite effect at first. For it consolidated large masses of people in devotion to a common cause, and gathered them together in popular assemblies which listened with a new motive for attention to discourses in the traditional forms of popular oration.

More important than all partisan loyalties, however, was the new feeling of national unity which made itself felt almost everywhere during this century. Whatever divisive forces were latent in the religious controversy were controlled and subordinated by centripetal tendencies in the political world; and the bitterest sectarian foes were compelled to share, with at least a semblance of concord and common loyalty, in the dazzling social and public life that centered in the courts of princes and in the cities that swarmed about them and took them as their models of conduct and manners. We hear remarkably little, during this period, of solitary and contemplative existences, of local characters, or of the self-dependent individualism of the country house. Everyone was present, either in fact or in idea, at court, and the most striking opportunities for literary distinction were offered at the constant gatherings, public or semi-public, more or less formal, which attended its various ceremonies and progresses and procedures. The occasions for the public display of stylistic art in the presence of the sovereign or one of his (or her) greater satellites were many: in the minor circles of courtiers and ladies-in-waiting they were innumerable. We should doubtless be greatly astonished, if we were able to recover a complete picture of the court life of the time, to observe how many of the uses of books like *Il Cortegiano*, Guevara's *Libro Aureo*, the

Arcadia, and *Euphues* were oral rather than literary. It is probable that these books—and there is no reason why we should not add Ariosto's and Spenser's epics—were habitually read aloud in assemblies of which we can now form but a faint picture in our minds, and were indeed composed chiefly with a view to such performance. When we add that solitary reading with the eye was only beginning to be a customary form of entertainment, we are prepared to understand why the literary education of the Renaissance was almost wholly conducted by means of the practice of oratory.

The various forms of prose style that resulted from this training need not be distinguished here. They were as various, of course, as the elements of the literary tradition in which the Renaissance was living. They were partly (indeed chiefly) medieval, partly classical, partly popular or folk forms. But it is enough for our present purpose to observe that all of them, by whatever channels they had come to the culture of the sixteenth century, had their ultimate origin in the Gorgian, or Isocratean type of oratory that we have been discussing in the preceding section. That this is true of the style taught by the orthodox humanists is well known: their aim was to teach their pupils to "write Cicero." But it is also true of the many kinds of style due to the survival of medieval educational customs and social modes: the forms of preaching style, for instance, that were prevalent until after the middle of the century, both in Latin and the vernacular; the style employed in letters composed for social display or amusement; the aureate style affected by those accustomed to Renaissance courtly ceremony, as in the show speeches of knights in tournaments, or in begging or complimentary addresses to sovereigns; and the literary *cultismo* practiced in many moral treatises and romances, as by Guevara, Sidney, and Lyly. However unclassical all these may be in their effect upon our ears and taste, they have one character in common: they are all arrived at by the elaboration of the "schemes," or figures of sound, that have been described as the chief ornaments of the Isocratean oratory. And that is all that is necessary in order to fix them in their place in the one great European tradition of oratorical style.

Against the literary tyranny of this tradition, and more particularly against its sixteenth-century efflorescence, the representatives of the modern spirit of progress were in revolt during the last quarter of the century. The temporary unities of the Renaissance were evidently breaking up; and the literary customs that had flowered upon them responded immediately to the tokens of their decay. The historian versed in the poetry of this period can detect the coming of the severer air of the seventeenth century in the new distaste that declares itself everywhere for the copious and flowing style of Ariosto and Spenser, and the "tedious uniformity" of Petrarchanism: the student of prose style is made aware of it at an even earlier date by the eager malice with which some of the new leaders recognize the artificiality of the oratorical customs of their time.

It was Muret, it seems, that remarkable prophet of seventeenth-century ideas, who first tossed this straw into the wind. In one of the latest and boldest of his academic discourses he asserts that the reasons for the practice of oratory in the time of his rhetorical predecessors, Bembo and Sadoleto, are no longer of any effect in the present age, because the real concerns of political life, and even the most important legal questions, are no longer decided in the public audience chambers of the senates and courts, but in the private cabinets of ministers of state and in the intimacy of conversation.[14] It was a cynical observation, perhaps, but a true one, justifying Machiavelli's wonderful realism at last, and foretelling the Richelieus, Bacons, and Cecils of a later generation.

Like his fellows in the new rationalism Muret arrived at his ideas by the first-hand study of facts. But he was like them too in that he desired to support his case by classical authority. The source of the passage just alluded to seems to be the discussion at the opening of the *Rhetoric* in which Aristotle explains that the justification of oratory is to be found in the imperfection and weakness of judgment characteristic of an uneducated public, incapable of distinguishing truth from error by the tedious processes of reason. Aristotle was perhaps the only ancient author whose authority was great enough to stand against that of Cicero on a question of this kind, and this famous statement in the *Rhetoric* was eagerly seized on by the anti-oratorical critics of the seventeenth century: its echoes are heard from Muret and Bacon to Pascal and Arnauld. But the same idea came to the Anti-Ciceronian leaders from other ancient sources; and it is to be observed that they find a more specific appropriateness to the circumstances of their own time in the magnificent de-

---

[14] Oration of 1582, introducing his course on the *Epistolae ad Atticum*, in *Orationes* (Leipzig, 1838), II, 140-151; see also his double oration of 1580, defending himself for the public teaching of Tacitus, which had made him the object of open attack and secret intrigue, II, 108-131.

scription of the decline of Roman oratory during the Empire which Tacitus puts into the mouth of Maternus in his *Dialogue*.[15] This passage played a great part in forming Muret's ideas; but the first clear intimation of its vital relation to modern life is found in Montaigne's essay on "The Vanity of Words" (I.51). After some introductory words suggested by the *Gorgias* of Plato, and the passage of Aristotle already mentioned, Montaigne goes on to say that oratory has flourished most in states where "the vulgar, the ignorant, or the populace have had all power, as in Rhodes, Athens, and Rome," and in periods of turmoil and civil strife, as at Rome during the Republic; "even as a rank, free, and untamed soil," he continues, "beareth the rankest and strongest weeds."

> Whereby it seemeth that those commonweals which depend of an absolute monarch have less need of it than others. For that foolishness and facility which is found in the common multi-tude, and which doth subject the same to be managed, per-suaded, and led by the ears by the sweet-alluring and sense-entrancing sound of this harmony, without duly weighing, knowing, or considering the truth of things by the force of reason: this facility and easy yielding, I say, is not so easily found in one only ruler, and it is more easy to safeguard him from the impression of this poison by good institution and sound counsel.

Is he looking back toward the Roman Empire or forward to the regime of absolutism beginning to be established in his own time? One cannot tell. In the literature of the period that was then be-ginning, these two historical phenomena are always presenting themselves side by side. For example, in a passage of Étienne Pasquier, plainly suggested by the same discourse in Tacitus' dialogue: "Tels fanfares sont propres en une Democratie, à un orateur du tout voué et ententif à la surprise du peuple par doux traits et emmiellement de sa Rhétorique. Ce qui ne se présenta onc-ques entre nous."[16]

---

[15] Chs. XXXVI-XLI. Hippolyte Rigault, Ch. I of *Histoire de la Querelle des Anciens et des Modernes*, in *Œuvres Complètes* (Paris, 1859), I, 1-17 has made an admirable use of this dialogue as one of the starting-points in antiquity of the modern idea of progress. An interesting paper might be written on the effect of the Anti-Ciceronian agitation on the growth of this idea.

[16] "Lettres," I.2 in *Œuvres* (Amsterdam, 1723), II, 5 (1st letter in *Œuvres Choisies*, ed. Léon Feugère, 2 vols. [Paris, 1849]). [As quoted by Croll, the passage contained minor errors which we have corrected, making it coincide with the

Political motives, however, were not the ones that weighed most with the Anti-Ciceronian leaders. Their scientific interests and above all their universal preoccupation with moral questions played a still greater part in determining their rhetorical program. The old claims of philosophy to precedence over formal rhetoric, long ago asserted by Plato, are revived by them in much the old terms, and the only justification they will admit for the study of style is that it may assist in the attainment of the knowledge of oneself and of nature. "The art of writing and the art of managing one's life are one and the same thing" is the motto of Montaigne and all his followers. "As for me," writes Lipsius to Montaigne in 1588, "I mightily scorn all those external and polite kinds of studies, whether philosophical or literary, and indeed every kind of knowledge that is not directed by prudence and judgment to the end of teaching the conduct of life."[17] Bacon deprecates the harsh treatment of rhetoric by Plato and labors its justification in *The Advancement of Learning*; but he treats it as a subordinate part of dialectic or logic, as Aristotle does, and in certain portions of its subject-matter as identical with moral or political philosophy.[18] La Mothe le Vayer is more express and clear than any of his predecessors. They have all praised the new genres, the letter and the essay; but he professes at the beginning of his discussion of rhetoric to treat of written style alone, *la*

---

text in Estienne Pasquier, *Choix de Lettres sur la Littérature, la Langue, et la Traduction*, ed. D. Thickett (Geneva, 1956), p. 78. Pasquier's pointing to Henri III's unsound policies is shown in Th. Glaser, "Deux Discours Manuscrits d'Estienne Pasquier," *Revue de la Renaissance*, VIII (1907), 1-28.] Andreas Schott develops at length the relations between the decline of oratory and the political conditions at the fall of the Republic, in the prefatory letter (to Lipsius) of his edition of the elder Seneca (Geneva, 1613).

[17] *Ep. Misc.*, II.41 in *Opera Omnia* (Antwerp, 1637), II, 86.

[18] *Of the Advancement of Learning*, in *Works* (1868), III, 409-411, ed. Wright, II.xviii.1-5 (cf. *De Augmentis Scientiarum*, VI.iii): "For although in true value it is inferior to wisdom . . . yet with people it is the more mighty." Its function is to "contract a confederacy between the Reason and Imagination against the Affections"; and again: "Logic handleth reason exact and in truth, and Rhetoric handleth it as it is planted in popular opinions and manners." The chief defect that he notes in the study of rhetoric is that too little attention has been paid to the study of *private* modes of discourse. In this art orators are likely to be defective, "whilst by the observing their well-graced forms of speech they leese the volubility [i.e. lose the subtlety or flexibility] of application." He then proceeds to supply this defect in part by making a collection of aphorisms and antitheses on the moral and political life of man, which he greatly extended in the *De Augmentis*, observing that whether this belongs to politics (prudential wisdom) or to rhetoric is a question of no importance.

rhétorique des livres, a style to be read, not heard: all that has to
do with speaking he repudiates.[19]

This is the general attitude of the leaders of opinion in the first
half of the century. In the second half it is not changed, but, on the
contrary, is more clearly defined. Pierre Bayle speaks of the *faux
éclat* of oratory. "Ces Messieurs-là [les orateurs] ne se soucient
guere d'éclairer l'esprit . . . ils vont droit au coeur, et non pas droit
à l'entendement: ils tâchent d'exciter l'amour, la haine, la colere."[20]
Bayle displays the scorn and intolerance that have always been
characteristic of the scientific rationalist; but with proper deductions
his opinions may be taken as characteristic of the age of La Bruyère,
Arnauld, Fénelon, and Malebranche, of the Port-Royal community
and the Royal Society of London. The temporary success of Puri-
tanism and Quietism, the rapid progress of scientific method, and
the diffusion of Cartesian ideas, all in their different ways helped to
create a taste for a bare and level prose style adapted merely to the
exact portrayal of things as they are. The severest theorists indeed
can hardly be brought to recognize a difference between logic and
rhetoric; while even the most liberal would exclude the characteristic beauties of oratorical form from the legitimate resources of
literary art. Persuasion is indeed the object of rhetoric. But the legitimate means of attaining this end, they constantly assert, is not by
the sensuous appeal of oratorical rhythm, but, on the contrary, by
portraying in one's style exactly those athletic movements of the
mind by which it arrives at a sense of reality and the true knowledge
of itself and the world.[21] Fénelon is the harshest critic of Isocrates

---

[19] *Considérations sur l'Éloquence Françoise de ce Temps* (1638), in *Œuvres*
(Dresden, 1756-1759), II, i, 193-195. He also has a treatise *Sur la Composition, et
sur la Lecture des Livres* (II, i, 319-391). Whether a work had ever been written
before on this subject I cannot say.

[20] *Œuvres Diverses* (The Hague, 1727), III, 178, col. 1. Cf. I, 644-645 on the
"Faux Raisonnement de Cicéron" and his *Dictionnaire*, s.v. "Pitiscus."

[21] Antoine Arnauld, *La Logique ou l'Art de Penser*, ed. L. Barré (Paris, 1874),
Part III, Ch. 20, p. 284: "la principale [partie de l'éloquence] consiste à concevoir
fortement les choses, et à les exprimer en sorte qu'on en porte dans l'esprit des
auditeurs une image vive et lumineuse, qui ne présente pas seulement ces choses
toutes nues, mais aussi les mouvements avec lesquels on les conçoit." Cf. Fénelon,
Dialogues sur l'Éloquence, "Second Dialogue, Pour Atteindre son But, l'Orateur
Doit *Prouver, Peindre*, et *Toucher*," *Œuvres*, ed. Louis Aimé Martin (Paris, 1870),
II, 668-679. And again: "La vive peinture des choses est comme l'âme de l'éloquence." [Wilbur S. Howell relates the rhetorical theories of Arnauld and Fénelon
in the Introd. to his trans. of Fénelon's *Dialogues on Eloquence* (Princeton, 1951);
I. von Kunow discusses ideas on style in "Sprach und Literarkritik bei Antoine
Arnauld," *Romanische Forschungen*, XXXIX (1921), 67-200.]

and his school—he was aware that this included Bossuet—that the century produced;[22] and Malebranche proposed to correct the too-imaginative prose of the age of Montaigne and Bacon by applying to it its own rationalistic criticism with a rigor that Montaigne and Bacon never dreamed of.[23]

In short, though this was the period when the Isocratean model was revived by Bossuet, the critics were all on the side of the severer style, and most of them were either hostile or indifferent to oratory in all its forms. The doctrine of the *genus humile* was taught everywhere.

Up to this point we have not mentioned the word "Attic," which is the object of the discussion. We have considered only the two great modes of style, the grand and the familiar, and the relation of the ancient rivalry between them to the theory of modern Anti-Ciceronianism. This, however, is the proper approach to our subject. For in the controversies of the Anti-Ciceronians "Attic style"

[22] See a passage near the beginning of the first dialogue, and a more interesting one near the end of the second (*Œuvres*, II, 658, 675-679), in which Fénelon seems to apprehend not only the connection between Bossuet and Isocrates, but the Isocratean character of medieval Latin preaching style. [Gonzague Truc gives a good general account of French pulpit oratory from the Middle Ages in *Nos Orateurs Sacrés* (Paris, 1950); See also E. C. Dargan, *A History of Preaching* (New York, 1905-1912); C. H. E. Smyth, *The Art of Preaching: A Practical Survey of Preaching in the Church of England 747-1939* (London, 1939); H. Caplan, "Classical Rhetoric and the Medieval Theory of Preaching," *Classical Philology*, XXVII (1933), 73-96; J. M. Neale, *Medieval Preachers and Medieval Preaching* (London, 1856); G. R. Owst, *Literature and Pulpit in Medieval England*, 2nd ed. (Oxford, 1961) and *Preaching in Medieval England* (Cambridge, 1926); H. Caplan and H. H. King, "Latin Tractates on Preaching: A Book List," *Harvard Theological Review*, XLII (1949), 185-206, and "French Tractates on Preaching: A Book List," *Quarterly Journal of Speech*, XXXVI (1950), 296-325; Joseph Vianey, "L'Éloquence de Bossuet dans sa Prédication à la Cour," *Revue des Cours et Conférences*, XXX, v-x (Feb. 15-Apr. 30, 1929): in the first of these articles Vianey shows how Bossuet adjusted his arguments and subjects to the needs of a courtly, *libertin* audience; the third treats the means—clarity, vivacity, anecdotes, emotional passages—used to attract and keep attention; the fourth appraises Bossuet's style, including sentence architecture, increased use of short sentences and maxims, etc. See the excellent bibliography in J. W. Blench, *Preaching in England in the Late Fifteenth and Sixteenth Centuries* (Oxford, 1964). See also Muret, n.48.]

[23] See the passages of *La Recherche de la Vérité* cited in n.66, below. [István Sötér, in his *La Doctrine Stylistique des Rhétoriques du XVIIe Siècle* (Budapest, 1937), distinguishes three stages in the art of expression: triumphant Ciceronianism; then a period dominated by simplicity, *bienséance*, and moderation; finally a stage characterized by the new issues of *je ne sais quoi* and *esprit*. Jean Cousin attributes French classicism to the influence of ancient rhetoric and Stoic philosophy in "Rhétorique Latine et Classicisme Français," *Revue des Cours et Conférences*, XXXIV, i-ii (Feb. 28-July 30, 1933). For related studies see *A Critical Bibliography of French Literature*, ed. David C. Cabeen and Jules Brody, Vol. III, *The Seventeenth Century*, ed. Nathan Edelman (Syracuse, 1961), pp. 281-284.]

means to all intents and purposes the *genus humile* or *subtile*, "Asiatic" describes the florid, oratorical style of Cicero's early orations or any style ancient or modern distinguished by the same copious periodic form and the Gorgian figures that attend upon it. "Attic" is always associated with philosophy and the *ars bene vivendi*, "Asiatic" with the *cultus* of conventional oratory. This is not the usual modern method of relating the two terms. Probably the fault now most commonly associated with Asianism is one to which the Anti-Ciceronians of the seventeenth century were themselves peculiarly liable when they used the characteristic forms of their art for oratorical purposes. We think of the tumor, the exaggerated emphasis, the monstrous abuse of metaphor in the preaching of the first half of the century in all the European countries; or of qualities dangerously related to these in the non-oratorical prose writings of Donne, Gracián, Malvezzi, and other masters of the "conceit"; or even of tendencies of the same kind that we may observe in writers so normal as Lipsius, Bacon, Balzac, and Browne. There is a kind of Asianism, in short, that arises from a constant effort to speak with point and significance, as well as from an excessive use of the ornate figures of sound, from too much love of expressiveness as well as from the cult of form; and inasmuch as this vice was more familiar to the reformers at the end of the century than the other, and was the one that was in immediate need of correction at that time, it has taken its place in our traditions as typical Asianism. But the Anti-Ciceronians were not aware that they were falling into error through an excess of their own qualities; they called themselves "Attic" because they avoided certain traits of style which they disliked, and did not observe that they sometimes ceased to be Attic through avoiding and disliking them too much. It is true therefore that their use of the terms was a one-sided and inadequate interpretation of their meaning in ancient criticism.[24] But on the other hand, it is fair to remark that so is the present use, and indeed that the seventeenth century was far more nearly in

[24] In antiquity, however, there was much the same variation of usage as that described in the text. The opponents of Cicero always tended to identify Asianism with the oratorical *cultus*, just as the modern Anti-Ciceronians did; but of course the prevalent doctrine was that there are two ways of becoming Asian; *aut nimio cultu aut nimio tumore*; either by studying too zealously the *orationis cultus* (as Bembo, Lyly, and many sixteenth-century writers did) or by exaggerating the *sententiarum venustas* (as Montaigne and Lipsius did, and Browne in the seventeenth century). See Hendrickson, "The Origin," p. 287, where the appropriate passages from Diomedes, Cicero, and St. Augustine are cited.

accord with the ancient ideas of the character of Attic prose than we are. Through the influence of eighteenth-century tastes we have come to associate it with the laws of taste and good form imposed by a slightly frivolous, or at least not very intellectual, social custom; and have lost sight of the fact that it had its original in philosophy rather than in the manners of "the world," and preserved its philosophical associations in antiquity through all its transmutations. This fact the Anti-Ciceronians of the seventeenth century never forgot. It was the basis of their distinction between Attic and Asian prose.

The evidence on this point is clear and decisive, and begins with the earliest phases of the sixteenth-century Ciceronian controversy. Erasmus, however, is the only witness that we shall need to cite from the first period. Throughout the *Ciceronianus* "Attic" denotes opposition to the copiousness of Cicero, and fondness for a scientific or philosophical brevity, marked by the same tendency toward ingenuity and point which accompanied the *genus humile* in ancient times. Speaking of the humanist Lazare de Baïf, one of the interlocutors says: "He prefers to be pointed [*argutus*], it seems, Attic rather than Ciceronian."[25] William Grocyn "was always inclined to the epistolary pointedness, loving laconism and appropriateness of style;[26] in this genre certainly one would call him nothing but Attic; indeed he aimed at nothing else, and when he read any writings of Cicero would say that he could not endure his fulness of expression."[27] Linacre, again, "surpasses an Attic in the repression of his feelings . . . ; he has studied to be unlike Cicero."[28] Scaliger, answering Erasmus, bullies and berates him for calling Cicero "redundant and Asiatic."[29] Improperly of course; for Erasmus is using these opprobrious words only in echoing Cicero's own criticism of his earlier orations, and is careful to point out the

[25] Desiderius Erasmus, *Opera Omnia* (Leyden, 1703-1706), I, col. 1012A.

[26] *Proprietatem sermonis*: on the technical meaning of this term in the theory of the *genus humile* see below, pp. 88-90.

[27] Erasmus, I, cols. 1012D-E.

[28] Erasmus (I, col. 989F), paraphrasing Horace's description of the brief style that tends to obscurity, calls it Atticism, though Horace has nothing to suggest this. [Cf. G. L. Hendrickson, "Horace, *Sermones*, i.4, A Protest and a Program," *AJP*, XXI (1900), 121ff. and "Satura—the Genesis of a Literary Form," *CP*, VI (1911), 129ff.; M. A. Grant and G. C. Fiske, "Cicero's *Orator* and Horace's *Ars Poetica*," *Harvard Studies in Classical Philology*, XXXV (1924), 26-34.]

[29] Julius Caesar Scaliger, *Pro M. Tullio Cicerone, contra Desiderium Erasmum Roterdamum, Oratio I* (Toulouse, 1620), p. 12, and elsewhere, in *Adversus Desiderium Erasmum Orationes Duae* (Toulouse, 1621).

variety of styles in his works. Still Cicero is prevailingly a copious
and ornate orator. Controversy is never nice and discriminating;
and Cicero continues "Asian" to the end of Anti-Ciceronian history.
Lipsius, for example, writes in 1586; "I love Cicero; I even used to
imitate him; but I have become a man, and my tastes have
changed. Asiatic feasts have ceased to please me; I prefer the
Attic."[30]

"Attic," however, by this time was beginning to be more fully
defined, and all its ancient associations re-awakened in defence
of it. Erik van der Putten (or Puteanus), evidently a follower of
Lipsius, publishes a rhetoric of "Laconism," in which he marshals
an array of "brief" ancient writers, Thucydides, Cato, Tacitus,
especially, who are properly called Attics, he says, because they
are so reticent, so incisive, so significant. But this term is inadequate to express their true glory; they may better, he thinks, be
called the Spartans.[31] Later Balzac in the Preface to his *Socrate
Chrestien* (1652), makes the same distinction. "Que si nostre zèle
ne peut s'arrester dans nostre cœur: Qu'il en sorte à la bonne heure!
Mais qu'il se retranche dans le stile de Lacedemone: Pour le moins
dans l'Atticisme: Au pis aller, qu'il ne se desborde pas par ces
Harangues Asiatiques, où il faut prendre trois fois haleine pour
arriver à la fin d'une periode." Further on he is more exact, and
speaks of the "Attiques de Rome, qui contrefaisoient Brutus, et
n'imitèrent pas Ciceron," meaning Seneca and his school.[32]

Great progress in critical discrimination and historical knowledge has evidently been made since the sixteenth century. This
progress continues in a later generation; and the clearest witness
of all is Père Bouhours. He has the prose of the century in perspective: its faults and dangers are vividly before his mind, and

---

[30] *Ep. Misc.* II.10, in *Opera*, II, 75 [cited in French translation by Croll in
Lipse, II (pp. 20-21)].

[31] *De Laconismo* (Louvain, 1609). In 1607 Lipsius was succeeded in the chair
of rhetoric at Louvain by Van der Putten; he was one of the disciples who
caused contemporaries to speak of Lipsius in the terms that Quintilian used of
Seneca, as "the man upon whose faults a sect was founded." Ideas adapt themselves to the size of the minds they find a lodging in, and it is not Lipsius' fault
altogether that *concettismo* of one kind or another makes its appearance so soon
in the style of his followers. Van der Putten thinks (pp. 78-79) that there is too
much *copia* in Demosthenes and the other Attic orators!

[32] Guez de Balzac, *Œuvres*, ed. Louis Moreau (Paris, 1854), II, 14, 16. [Cf.
Lipse, IV, par. 1, nn.33 and 36; Williamson, *Senecan Amble*, pp. 349-350; Gaston
Guillaumie, *Jean-Louis Guez de Balzac et la Prose Française* (Paris, 1927); Fer-
dinand Brunot, *Histoire de la Langue Française des Origines à 1900*, Vols. III-V
(Paris, 1927-1939).]

he sees that they are immediately connected with the imitation of the ancient models of the acute and subtle *genus humile,* Tacitus, Lucan, Seneca: yet, he says, I am still an Attic in my tastes; and what he means by that is exactly shown in a passage from an earlier work, every sentence of which is important for our purpose. He is speaking of the French language, and says that what he admires most in it is "that it is clear without being too diffuse [*étendue*]. (There is perhaps nothing that is less to my taste than the Asiatic style.) It takes pleasure in conveying a great deal of meaning in a few words. Brevity is pleasing to it, and it is for this reason that it cannot endure periods that are too long, epithets that are not necessary, pure synonyms that add nothing to the meaning, and serve only to fill out the cadence [*nombre*]. . . . The first care of our language is to content the mind [*esprit*] and not to tickle the ear. It has more regard to good sense than to beautiful cadence. I tell you once again, nothing is more natural to it than a reasonable brevity."[33] The form of the opposition between "Attic" and "Asian" in the seventeenth-century mind is more exactly expressed in the various phrases and turns of this passage than in any other that we shall be likely to find.

❖ IV ❖

The aim of the literary historian is the utmost simplification that is consistent with the actual variety of the facts he deals with; and in the preceding pages we have been trying to make our generalization broad enough to include all the significant facts of seventeenth-century prose style. But on the other hand, the uniformity of any large set of phenomena is only interesting in relation with their diversity. The *genus humile* had a history in antiquity running through seven or eight centuries, and during that period developed various phases of theory and various forms of style, most of which were known to the leaders of Anti-Ciceronianism and played their different parts in the drama of rhetorical controversy in the seventeenth century. To distinguish these phases, and the character and extent of the influence that each of them had in the

[33] Dominique Bouhours, *Les Entretiens d'Ariste et d'Eugène* (Amsterdam, 1671), p. 69. [The ed. by René Radouant (Paris, 1920) contains three of the six *entretiens* and treats relevant scholarship. Alexander F. B. Clark surveys Bouhours' influence on English writers and critics on pp. 262-274 of *Boileau and the French Classical Critics in England, 1660-1830* (Paris, 1925), with a useful bibliography; see *Muret,* n.26.]

period we are studying, is no less important than to observe the general tendency that is common to them all; and this will be the purpose of all the rest of our discussion.

The earlier Greek phases of this history—the only ones that we have considered up to this point—were of minor importance in determining the actual forms that prose style took in the seventeenth century; and if we only wanted to know what models it could imitate we might confine our attention to the Stoic school of rhetoric that triumphed over Ciceronian oratory in the first century of the Roman Empire. But, on the other hand, the critics whose business it was to defend and explain it were well acquainted with its purer sources in the classical period of Greek culture; and they very often, one might say usually, defended or concealed their real use of the inferior "Atticism" of Seneca and Tacitus by claiming the sanction of greater names than these. Unless we can interpret the disingenuousness of men laboring under the imputation of literary heresy we shall constantly be puzzled in reading their manifestoes. Three names associated with three phases of the history of *genus humile* in the classical Greek period occur with some frequency in their writings, those of Plato (or Socrates), Aristotle, and Demosthenes; and in the present section we will take up briefly each of these phases, with reference to its place in seventeenth-century prose criticism—reserving for the proper point the explanation of the paradox of describing the style of Demosthenes as a phase of the *genus humile*.

(a) Plato

Of the first not much needs to be said. The nature of the controversy recorded in the *Gorgias* and *Phaedrus* was of course known to the Anti-Ciceronian leaders; and they knew perfectly well, moreover, that the Isocratean, or Gorgian rhetoric was of essentially the same kind as the Ciceronian rhetoric taught by the orthodox humanists of the sixteenth century. It would have been strange if they had not used the name of Plato in propagating their new taste for a philosophical and intimate prose, or had not detected the similarity of the aims of their opponents to those of the ancient sophistic rhetoricians. It was in fact their occasional practice to apply to these teachers and their seventeenth-century successors the old name of "sophists."[34]

[34] See Balzac, "Paraphrase ou la Grande Éloquence," *Œuvres*, I, 278-289; the

There was an additional motive, however, for the revival of this ancient controversy, which will strike the modern reader as a curiosity of literary history. The new "Attics" were nine-tenths Stoic in their morals, as they were in their rhetoric. But Stoicism was stigmatized as heresy—especially when it called itself "Christian"—at every distributing center of Catholic orthodoxy; at Rome itself it was under constant surveillance. In these circumstances the name of Socrates was a convenient disguise, partly because it was not hard to wrench his philosophy into a Stoic form, and partly because his conduct at his trial and the manner of his death had long given him a place among those who had fallen as martyrs of the struggle against conventional sentimentality. Quevedo occasioned no surprise when he linked the names of Socrates, Cato, and Job in his Stoic hagiology;[35] and Balzac's title *Le Socrate Chrestien* could easily be read in its real sense of *le stoique chrétien*.

For these reasons, then, we occasionally meet with the names of Plato and Socrates in the propaganda of the new school. But as far as the form of its style was concerned the earliest masters of Attic had but little influence upon it. In the first half of the century it is almost safe to say that they had none. In the second, on the other hand, there were several ambitious revivals of Hellenism, both in England and France, and the name of Plato is often heard as that of a writer and a model to be imitated. Thus the Chevalier de Méré proposes a purely Greek literary program: Plato in prose and Homer in verse are the preferred models, and next to these (since one must do lip service, at least, to oratory) Demosthenes.[36]

---

works of Naudé, passim [and, handwritten in a copy of this essay presented to T. M. Parrott, now in Princeton University Library, Croll adds:] also Muret, Oration of the Year 1572. [For a summary of French knowledge of Plato in the seventeenth century, see Thérèse Goyet, "Présence de Platon dans le Classicisme Français" in Association Guillaume Budé, Congrès de Tours et Poitiers, 3-9 septembre, 1953, *Actes du Congrès* (Paris, 1954), pp. 364-371; also Ferdinand Gohin, *La Fontaine: Études et Recherches* (Paris, 1937), pp. 19-62.]

35 See Mérimée, *Essai sur . . . Quevedo*, pp. 283-287. [Cf. *Lipse*, n.45.]

36 The "Atticisme mondain" of Antoine Gombaud, Chevalier de Méré is very exactly described and placed in its true relations by Fortunat Strowski, *Histoire du Sentiment Religieux en France au XVIIIe Siècle: Pascal et son Temps*, 3 vols. (Paris, 1907), II, 248-269, III, 179-187. [Croll was considerably influenced by the work of Strowski whose treatment of Stoicism in Vol. I is partly superseded by Julien-Eymard d'Angers, "Le Stoïcisme en France dans la Première Moitié du XVIIe Siècle. Les Origines (1575-1616)," *Études Franciscains* (1951), no. II, 287-297, 389-410 (1952), no. III, 5-20, 133-154. D'Angers and M. H. Guervin list other studies on French Stoicism of the same period in *XVIIIe Siècle: Bulletin de la Société d'Étude du XVIIIe Siècle*, XIX (1953), 241-243; XXI-XXII (1954), 510; XXIX (1955), 353, n.2. See also works listed in *Lipse*, n.2.]

But there is some disingenuousness in this and similar professions. The actual style of de Méré does not differ in kind from that of St. Évremond, for example, which was formed in the "libertine" school of the first half of the century and "corrected" by the new *mondanité* of the second. Like other representative critics of his century, de Méré calls himself an Attic; but he had already discovered the eighteenth-century formula in which Atticism is identified with the "agreeable" style of *l'honnête homme*; and this is a style very different from Plato's.

With less emphasis the same statement can be made of the style of Fénelon in his *Dialogues*. Though it superficially resembles the model it imitates, its Platonism is but a thin disguise of the romantic and Christian poetry that we are familiar with in his other prose writings. Indeed there is but one prose style of the seventeenth century that will stand a comparison, either in kind or quality, with that of Plato: the prose style of the *Lettres Provinciales*; and Pascal is neither deceived nor disingenuous about the sources of this. He acknowledges that it has been formed by the imitation of the same Stoic models that were in favor in the first half of the century.[37]

The most important part played by Plato was to perpetuate the idea of an "Attic" style, with new and somewhat different associations, in the second half of the century, at a time when the Latin models of such a style, heretofore in favor, had begun to be discredited.

(b) Aristotle

The part played by Aristotle was much greater. Of course neither his *Rhetoric* nor any other of his surviving works could serve as a model for stylistic imitation, as the works of Plato could. Yet it is probably correct to say that certain forms of seventeenth-century prose style are chiefly due to the attempt to apply directly, in practice, ideas concerning the relation between logic and rhetoric

---

[37] "La manière d'écrire d'Epictète, de Montaigne, et de Salomon de Tultie [that is, of Pascal himself in the *Lettres Provinciales*], est le plus d'usage," etc. Blaise Pascal, *Pensées*, ed. Léon Brunschvicg (Paris, 1904), I, 30. See also Pascal's *Entretien sur Epictète et Montaigne*. [Presumably Croll refers here to the *Entretien de Pascal avec M. de Sacy*. See Joseph Bédier, "Établissement d'un Texte Critique de l'Entretien de Pascal avec M. de Saci" in his *Études Critiques* (Paris, 1903), pp. 21-80. But P. L. Couchoud argues convincingly that the conversation never occurred and that Sacy's secretary, Nicolas Fontaine, composed the dialogue by recasting an *Étude sur Epictète et Montaigne* by Pascal, Sacy's acknowledgment of receiving it, and Pascal's letter in reply ("L'Entretien de Pascal avec M. de Saci a-t-il eu Lieu?" *Mercure de France*, CCCXI, Feb. 1, 1951, 216-228.)]

gathered from the first two books of the *Rhetoric*. This is probably true of styles so different in their associations as that recommended by the Royal Society of London and often used by its scientific contributors and that imposed upon the writers of the Port Royal Community by their teachers. Both of these are characterized by a deliberate plainness which Aristotle would have been far from recommending for literary use; but they both seem to rest finally on Aristotle's resolution of the forms of rhetorical persuasion into forms of syllogistic reasoning.

The importance of his influence upon the forms of style was as nothing, however, when compared with that of his influence on the *theory* of the Attic school. The advocates of a style suited to philosophical thought needed a classical authority for their support as unquestionable and orthodox as that of Cicero, and Aristotle's *Rhetoric* provided them with what they needed. The rhetorical aphorisms and discussions in Seneca's letters expressed their ideas, it is true, in popular and telling ways. They served the purposes of Attics who did not need to profess any great amount of classical learning or any profound knowledge of rhetorical theory. But Muret, Bacon, Hobbes, and the teachers of Port Royal—the men whose task was to lay the philosophical foundations of seventeenth-century style—were all Aristotelian at first hand, while many others, Lipsius, Descartes, and so on, obtained their ideas from the same source, though perhaps less directly. To show adequately the relation of each of these philosophers to the *Rhetoric* would be a task far beyond our present limits; but at least it may be taken for granted that seventeenth-century Anti-Ciceronianism, like all other historical movements of protest against the excessive study of rhetorical form, derives its *ultimate* authority from the first two books of that work.[38] Even its third book proved useful. For its descrip-

[38] Muret's dependence upon Aristotle has been mentioned on an earlier page. One of the characteristic expressions of his irony was his choice of the *Rhetoric* instead of a Ciceronian subject for his course in 1576-1577, when he had been badgered into a temporary renunciation of the new antirhetorical studies of the rationalists. See Charles Dejob, *Marc-Antoine Muret* (Paris, 1881), pp. 293-296. Dejob fails to interpret Muret's career in an intelligible fashion because he does not understand the "Attic" movement and its intellectual implications.

Aristotelianism manifests itself clearly in the subordinate relation of rhetoric to dialectics and ethics in Bacon's *Advancement* and in the Port-Royal Treatises. On this point see Paul Jacquinet, *Francisci Baconi de Re Litteraria Judicia* (Paris, 1863), pp. 48-51. [See also Williamson's chapter on "Bacon and Stoic Rhetoric," *Senecan Amble*, pp. 150-185; K. R. Wallace, *Francis Bacon on Communication and Rhetoric* (Chapel Hill, 1943); R. S. Crane, *Wit and Rhetoric in the Renaissance* (New York, 1937); and Howell, *Logic and Rhetoric*.]

tion of the usual Isocratean oratorical forms was taken for what it was, a mere conventional recognition of existing customs; whereas its highly original treatment of Enthymemes was often employed for guidance in the art of forming aphorisms and *antitheta* in which the seventeenth century arrived at absolute perfection, and its treatment of the metaphor was often appealed to by the new Attics in defence of their favorite figure.[39] It is somewhat astonishing to find Aristotle quoted in justification of the devices of style by which *concettismo* achieves its dubious effect of power; but *concettismo* is, in fact, implicit in any "rhetoric of thought," such as Aristotle's was.

(c) Demosthenes

The third phase of Greek influence, namely that of Attic oratory, requires a larger discussion; for it involves the re-opening of the subject of the *genera dicendi*. Hitherto we have considered only two genera, or "characters," and this, as we have said, appears to have been the original form of the classification. The *genus humile* arose in opposition to oratory, as the appropriate language of intimate philosophical discussion; and the Gorgian kind of rhetoric which was then regarded as the only, or at least the typical, form of oratorical style, then properly assumed the name of the *genus grande* in contrast with it. But a kind of oratory arose at Athens during the fourth century which was not open to the charges brought against the Gorgian rhetoric by Socrates and Plato, which, on the contrary, had some of the same qualities that the masters of

[39] The raptures of the *concettisti* in praise of metaphor may be studied in Baltasar Gracián, *Agudeza y Arte de Ingenio*, in *Obras* (Madrid, 1674), I, *passim* [*Arte de Ingenio*, 1st ed. Madrid, 1642; see the ed. of Madrid, 1944]; in Cardinal Sforza-Pallavicino, *Trattato dello Stile e del Dialogo*, Ch. VII, in *Opere* (Milan, 1834), II, 594-597 ("si chiama reina delle figure") [*Trattato del Dialogo e dello Stile*, 1st ed. (Rome, 1646)]; and in Emmanuele Tesauro, *Il Cannochiale Aristotelico* (Bologna, 1693), Ch. VII, p. 179 ("il piu pellegrino e mirabile . . . parte dell'umano intelletto") [1st ed. 1654]. But Dominique Bouhours, the determined corrector of *concettismo*, is not less an admirer. See *La Manière de Bien Penser dans les Ouvrages d'Esprit* (Amsterdam, 1688), pp. 16-17. The whole theory of *concettismo* is derived from Aristotle, *Rhetoric*, especially II.xxii-xxiv (on enthymemes) and III.ii.8-15 (on metaphors). This point has been admirably brought out in the old work by Giovanni Ferri, *De l'Éloquence et des Orateurs Anciens et Modernes* (Paris, 1789), pp. 228-233, the only discussion I know of in which the preëminence of prose over poetry in any proper consideration of the seventeenth-century conceit is observed. [For a discussion of doctrines about conceits, with apt quotations from Gracián, Tesauro, Sforza-Pallavicino, Pierfrancesco Minozzi, Giulio Marzot, and modern theorists, see Joseph Mazzeo, *Renaissance and Seventeenth-Century Studies* (New York, 1964), Chs. II, III.]

the *genus humile* arrogated to themselves, an oratory disdainful of the symmetries and melodious cadences of the Isocratean model and professing to make its effect by the direct portrayal of the mind of the speaker and of the circumstances by which he has been aroused to vehement feeling. This later type of oratory was of course familiar to the post-Aristotelian theorists who adopted the bipartite division; but so strong was the tradition of the earlier type of oratory that they took no account of it in their theory. They merely wished to represent the dichotomy of style in its original and most striking form. When, however, the oratory of Lysias and Demosthenes and their school had at last taken so firm a place in the tradition that they could no longer be disregarded in the doctrine of the genera, a curious situation presented itself. For now a mode of style had to be recognized which was allied in its rhetorical form and procedure with the *genus humile*, yet was unmistakedly grander than the *genus grande* and had the same uses. Nothing but disorder could result from such an anomaly; and in fact the adjustment that was finally made was little better than a confused and illogical working arrangement. The "Attic" oratory of Demosthenes usurped the title of the *genus grande*; the *genus humile* remained undisturbed in its old functions and character; and a third genus was added to take care of the Isocratean oratory, and was given the name of the *genus medium* (*modicum, temperatum*, etc.), though this name does not appropriately represent either the historical or the formal relation of the Isocratean style to the other two. In the time of Cicero it had become customary to define the character of the three genera more fully by a reference to the effect of each upon the audience. The *genus humile* is best adapted to teaching or telling its hearers something; the *genus medium* delights them or gives them pleasure; the *genus grande* rouses them and excites them to action.[40]

It is true that this explanation of the development of the tripartite classification is not so clearly documented as we should like to have it. It is only probable. But it is the result of what seems the best investigation of the subject, and it at least *explains*. We may now add that the treatment of the three styles in the seventeenth century tends to confirm it, because it shows a similar solution of the prob-

[40] This interpretation of the relation of the three characters follows that of Hendrickson; see n.7 and n.9 above.

lem by men placed in a situation strikingly like that of the ancient theorists.

The aim of the founders of seventeenth-century prose style was to domesticate a *genus humile*. The movement inaugurated by the Anti-Ciceronian leaders, Bacon, Montaigne, Lipsius, was like that of Plato and Socrates and their followers in that it was meant to make and legalize a breach between oratory and philosophy, and to establish in general use a style meant to express reality more acutely and intimately than oratory can hope to do. And the form of oratory which was present to their eyes in the usage of their own age was, as we have seen, the same Isocratean form that the founders of the ancient *genus humile* had before them. But the seventeenth century could not sacrifice its love of grandeur and nobility to its love of philosophic truth any more than the Athens of the fourth century could. It was, indeed, an age that for peculiar reasons, affected solemnity, a kind of somber magnificence, in all the forms of its artistic expression. It was the immediate heir to the Renaissance, for one thing, and came naturally by a taste for pomp and grandiosity; but, furthermore, the peculiar political and religious temper of the time, especially as it came under Catholic and Anglo-Catholic influence, tended to strengthen these inclinations and to give them a special character. "Persuade the King in greatness," said Bacon in the confidence of his private journal; and the words might be taken as an index of the temper in which some of the most representative art of his age was produced. It was the age of the Baroque in sculpture and architecture; of the intense and profound Catholicism of El Greco; of the conscious Romanization of moral ideals; of the dogma and ceremony of absolutism; and of the elaboration, in sermon and essay, of a somber liturgy of Death.

Such an age could not be satisfied with the intimate and dialectic uses of prose alone. It needed them and made the most of them; but its rhetorical preceptors must also hold up before it the image of a great and noble oratory, greater and nobler even than the Ciceronian, but as free from Cicero's "Asianism," as "Attic," as their own philosophical essay style. They need not actually achieve this style, it is true, in their own practice; but even though it should prove to be far beyond its powers, the seventeenth century demanded the contemplation of such a model as the ideal form to

THE ANTI-CICERONIAN MOVEMENT

"persuade" it in greatness.[41] The name of Demosthenes therefore appears in the writings of the Anti-Ciceronian rhetoricians from the beginning of the century to the end as the symbol of the *genus grande* in the Attic manner. Bacon, in a letter written in the name of Essex, says that if one must study oratory, Demosthenes (not Cicero) is the model to be imitated.[42] Fénelon, opposing the Isocrateanism of preaching style—which had been revived in the eloquence of Bossuet and his followers—eloquently proclaims the superiority of the greater Attic orator.[43] And between these two great critics there are many that utter the same sentiment. But it was Balzac who made the name of Demosthenes his trade-mark or heraldic device. The sum and substance of his writings on the subject of style is that he aims to produce a union of Attic quality with the grand manner of a "heroic" oratory, to combine the virtue of Brutus' style, as he says in one place, with that of Cicero's, the naturalism, that is, of the one with the eloquence of the other. For the purposes of this program the authors who served as the models of his own style—Seneca, Tacitus, and Tertullian—were ill-adapted, and he publicly repudiated them—with a disingenuousness which was justified perhaps by a lofty purpose—as inferior and debased Attics, professing to find the only model of the true heroic style in Demosthenes, or perhaps in the late "Attic" orations of Cicero against Antony.[44]

Balzac took all this program with a grand seriousness worthy of it. It expressed a genuine will toward *la grande éloquence*. But

[41] Compare with this phrase of Bacon's one of Balzac's, wholly characteristic of him. In his later works, he says, he has written most on political themes, and his aim in these productions has been to express himself "de ce qu'il y a de plus magnifique et de plus pompeux en la vie active."

[42] *The Letters and the Life of Francis Bacon*, ed. James Spedding (London, 1861-1866), II, 25: "Of orators . . . it shall be Demosthenes, both for the argument he handles, and for that his eloquence is more proper for a statesman than Cicero's."

[43] *Œuvres*, II, 668. See n.21. [Georges Duhain compares Fénelon's translation of Demosthenes with other French renderings in *Jacques de Tourreil, Traducteur de Démosthène* (Paris, 1910).]

[44] Balzac, "Avant-Propos," *Socrate Chrestien*, in *Œuvres* (1854), II, 15-16, and *Paraphrase, ou la Grande Éloquence*, I, 284-289; also the attack of an enemy [Frère André] in Jean Goulu's *Lettres de Phyllarque à Ariste*, and François Ogier's answer in his *Apologie pour M. de Balzac*. [See *Lipse*, n.38. In the original publication, the following two sentences were misplaced at the end of the preceding note:] Lipsius, in his *Judicium super Seneca ejusque Scriptis*, prefixed to his ed. of Seneca, 1605, 1652, etc., anticipates Balzac's theory. See also the same use of Demosthenes' name and credit in Nicolas Caussin's chapter entitled *Anti-cicerones* in his *Eloquentiae Sacrae et Humanae Parallela Libri XVI*, II.xvii (Paris, 1619), pp. 79-80. [Cf. *Muret*, n.25.]

judged by his practice, or that of any one else of his time, it has as much significance as a flare of trumpets or a pyrotechnic display. The kind of Attic practiced in the seventeenth century could not combine with the magnificence of oratory to advantage, and the bizarre effects so common in the sermons and panegyrics of the first half of the century are the monstrous births that proceeded from the unnatural union between them. The taste of the age was not equal to the Athenian feat of being simple and grand at once; and when Bossuet turned from his early studies in Attic ingenuity and point to the reform of oratorical style, it was not the example of Demosthenes or Lysias that served his turn, but the old conventional oratorical model of Isocrates, and the medieval preachers.

The professed study of Demosthenes' oratory, in short, had but little practical effect upon seventeenth-century prose; and the same thing is true of all other Hellenistic programs of style in France and England during the period of Balzac and the generation that immediately followed him. Some of them were important as indicating new turns of thought and a widening of literary horizons; but none of them and not all of them taken together had a decisive influence on the form of vernacular style, or provided models that could be effectively imitated. Concerning the first half of the seventeenth century and the generation that preceded it a much stronger statement than this must be made. The truth about this period can only be expressed by saying that it was anti-Greek. The study of Hellenistic culture had become associated with the ornamental learning, the flowery science, of the humanists. "The wisdom of the Greeks," said Bacon, "was rhetorical; it expended itself upon words, and had little to do with the search after truth." This statement has a strange sound in modern ears; and in fact Bacon would have expressed the opinion of his age better if he had made it more carefully. We could not object if he had said that the Greeks were *speculative* and rhetorical; and the age of Bacon, Montaigne, and Descartes was equally averse to disinterested speculation and disinterested rhetorical beauty. The new rationalists were incapable, in short, of understanding the value of Greek culture; and even though they had been able to form a juster estimate of it, they would still have rejected it merely on the practical ground that it was too remote, too ancient, conveyed in a language too foreign to their own. It is thus that we are to explain the bravado of Burton and Descartes, and several other great scholars of the time, who professed that

81

they knew no Greek or had forgotten what little they had been taught.[45]

The culture of the period from 1575 to 1650 is almost wholly Latinistic; and we must seek for the models on which it chiefly formed its style in the forms of Latin prose which it considered Attic.

✧ V ✧

The history of Latin prose style during the classical period displays the same constant tendency to a rivalry and opposition between two great characters of style that prevailed in Greece; and indeed from the time that the facts begin to be clear enough for exact historical statement this rivalry is conducted under the direct influence of Greek theory and largely in imitation of it. But there was a difference, due to a difference in the characters of the two races, which manifests itself especially in the associations that attached themselves to the *genus humile*. In Greece, as we have seen, this "character" of style originated in philosophy and arose, later than the other, out of a protest against the emptiness and unreality of oratory. In Rome, on the other hand, it had its roots in the very beginnings of Roman life, and was originally the expression of the practical and *un*philosophical nature of the Roman

---

[45] Montaigne's reason for not reading Greek is characteristic of the period: "I am not satisfied with a half understanding" ("Des Livres," in *Essais*, II.x, ed. Le Clerc, II.115); see also "De l'Institution des Enfants," I, 233. [Croll probably had in mind "De l'Héllénisme au XVIIe Siècle," pp. i-lvi in *De l'Héllénisme de Fénelon* (Paris, 1897), by Léon Boulvé, who argues against the strong case for Greek influence made by Émile Egger, *L'Héllénisme en France* (Paris, 1869). Roy C. Knight is more thorough and brings the subject up to date in "La Grèce dans la Littérature Française au XVIIe Siècle," pp. 13-138 in his *Racine et la Grèce* (Paris, 1950); he counters Egger by emphasizing the superficiality of much in French Hellenism and by showing how modernization colored imitation of Greek models. Henri Peyre probably exaggerates the debt to antiquity in *L'Influence des Littératures Antiques sur la Littérature Française Moderne* (New Haven, 1941), pp. 36-46. See also R. R. Bolgar, *The Classical Heritage and its Beneficiaries* (Cambridge, 1954). Frank L. Schoell, "L'Héllénisme Français en Angleterre à la Fin de la Renaissance," *Revue de Littérature Comparée*, V (1925), 193-238 surveys Greek learning in England under Elizabeth I and James I.] On the Latinization of culture in this age see an excellent passage by Désiré Nisard, *Histoire de la Littérature Française* (Paris, 1883), I, 435-437; Ferdinand Brunetière, *L'Évolution des Genres* (Paris, 1890), p. 53; J. E. Spingarn, *A History of Literary Criticism in the Renaissance*, 2nd ed. (New York, 1908), p. 186. [See also H. Brown, "Classical Tradition in English Literature," *Harvard Studies and Notes in Philol. and Lit.*, XVIII (1935); Sandys, *A History of Classical Scholarship*; Douglas Bush, *Classical Influences in Renaissance Literature* (Cambridge, Mass., 1952); Bolgar, *The Classical Heritage and its Beneficiaries*.]

people. In its first phases it was certainly not a literary style at all, or at least owed nothing to formal rhetorical method; and the beauties that were later seen or imagined in it were merely the natural expressions of the soldierly and rustic character of the early Roman gentlemen, the accidental effects of art that sometimes arise spontaneously from a Spartan or Puritan contempt of art.

So at least we may suppose. Almost nothing remains to show what it actually was, and we cannot say with assurance how much of the character attributed to it was due to the philosophic theories of the days when Roman thought had already been profoundly affected by the Stoicism of later Greek culture. Probably there is general truth in the idea then prevalent that there had been a severe early Roman prose expressive of the national character; and whether there was or was not the belief in it had its effects upon the later prose, and the *genus humile* at Rome took from it associations of virility and sturdy practical purpose, associations with primitive and archaic forms of virtue, which always made it something different from its Greek counterpart even after Roman culture had been generally Hellenized. To these associations the *genus humile* owed part of its great success during the Empire, largely because they transported the men of that age to a different world from their own; and it had the same value once again in the seventeenth century to those who were reviving at that time "Roman" and Stoic conceptions of literary style. But even in a somewhat simpler and more classical period than either of these, in the pre-Augustan age of Cicero and Brutus, the *genus humile* was already supposed to have a peculiarly Roman and primitive character. In the style of the *Commentaries* of Caesar, as manly and efficient, men have always said, as his legionaries themselves, it was believed that the national genius still survived, though Caesar had in fact studied rhetoric assiduously in the schools; and in Brutus' treatise *De Virtute*—whose non-survival was the occasion of many Stoic tears in the seventeenth century—we might be able to behold an image of the early Roman through all the sophistication of a philosophical and rhetorical theory.[46]

We cannot in fact tell when or how the native tendencies of Latin style blended with foreign influences, or what forms of na-

[46] Norden *identifies* Roman "Atticism" with the archaizing movement. With all deference to his authority, the reader is compelled to feel he has made his point only *as regards the second century*, and has introduced new confusion into the history of the term "Attic."

tional prose they might have produced if they had been left to exfoliate in their own manner. What we do know is that Roman rhetoric became outwardly well Hellenized during the last century of the Republic, that the theory of the rhetorical genera was established in the same form that it had then come to have in Greek practice, and that henceforward the history of the *genus humile* in Latin prose—like that of its rival, the grand oratorical style of Cicero—has to be written chiefly in terms of Greek rhetorical theory. The Greek *genus humile* was not now, however, what it had been in the time of Aristotle; during the two centuries that had intervened it had undergone important changes in its technique and had acquired new associations, all of which are exactly reproduced in the Latin style that represents it. We must turn back to the point where we left off the account of its development and consider these changes.

We have seen that Aristotle first developed into a system the theory of style as it is determined by the processes of thought and that in the generations immediately after him a place was found in rhetorical teaching for a kind of style, known as the *genus humile*, founded upon this way of looking at rhetorical phenomena. We have now to observe that the great increase in the interest in philosophical studies in Greek communities during the third and second centuries was the cause of an increased attention to this *genus humile* and of interesting developments in its theory and practice, and that the occasions for the proper and healthy use of the more popular oratorical style were at the same time greatly reduced as a result of changed political conditions in the Greek world. Whether this change is to be regarded as a beneficent consequence of the restoration of order by absolute authority, as the Romans of the first century and most seventeenth-century observers considered it to be, or was, on the other hand, a lamentable indication of the decay of character that follows the loss of liberty, as Milton, for instance, undoubtedly thought it was, we will not stop to inquire. It is the fact alone that concerns us, and we will proceed at once to specialize it still further by noting that its importance did not consist so much in the spread of philosophical interest in general, as in the remarkable diffusion of the principles of the Stoic sect. This does not mean necessarily that Stoicism was in itself the most important philosophy of the age—though that also may be true—but only that it had clearer and more systematic theories than the other sects with regard to the form of a philosophical style, and was able to speak, at least on most points, as the general rhetorical representative of them all.

Aristotle describes two essential virtues of style: *clearness* and *appropriateness*. But his method of treating the theory of rhetoric in the first two books implies another of almost equal importance, namely, *brevity*; and in his immediate followers this virtue assumes actually a coordinate place with the other two in the description of the *genus humile*. Upon his analysis, modified in this way, the Stoic rhetoric depends; and the three qualities—clearness, brevity, and appropriateness—appear and reappear in it, usually in the order named, and with only such additions and subtractions as always occur in a traditional formula. Each of them, however, is interpreted in a particular way and takes on a special meaning in the Stoic system.[47] We will consider the three in order, and what they meant in Stoic practice.

(a) Clearness

Aristotle places clearness first. The Stoics often—though not always—give it the same titular position. But, whether they do so or not, it is never first in their affections. There were two features of Stoic thought that tended to reduce this virtue to a subordinate rank, or even to give a positive value to its opposite. Clearness is evidently the first merit of an exposition of objective reality, as in the statement of the facts and laws of natural science; Aristotle occasionally had such exposition in his mind, and, partly on his authority, there have been in modern times several attempts to erect the theory of style on the foundation of mere scientific clearness. But the kind of truth that the Stoics chiefly had in mind was

---

[47] The clearest statements of the form of Stoic style in antiquity are in Diogenes Laertius, "Life of Zeno," VII.59 [See *Lipse*, n.26]; Cicero, *De Oratore*, especially II.xxxviii.159 and III.xviii.65-66 (which Zielinski, with some exaggeration, describes as an exposition of Stoic theory), and Quintilian, *Inst. Or.*, XII.x.10ff. In the modern period, Lipsius' treatise on style, *Epistolica Institutio*, and La Mothe le Vayer's *Considérations sur l'Éloquence Françoise* [n. 19 above] rest directly on ancient Stoic authority. The clearest recent statement is by Hendrickson, "The Origin," pp. 257-261, 272, 284.

It should be said that in Diogenes Laertius another virtue, purity of language as determined by the usage of good society, precedes these three. This, however, proved so foreign to other ideals of the Stoic school that it was often omitted, and when it appears and is made prominent, as it is in the Roman Stoics of the second century, it is interpreted in such a way that it falls into virtual coincidence with the quality of appropriateness. Its history in the seventeenth century would make an interesting chapter, but must be omitted here.

moral and inward. It was a reality not visible to the eye, but veiled from common observation; hidden in a shrine toward which one might win his way, through a jostling, noisy mob of illusory appearances, by a series of partial initiations. This kind of reality can never be quite portrayed, of course, because ultimate knowledge of the mystery of truth is never attained. But it is at least possible to depict the effort of the athletic and disciplined mind in its progress toward the unattainable goal. And this effort of the mind was the characteristic theme of the Stoics, and the object of their rhetorical art. Though by the rigor of their theory they were bound to a cold passionless objectivity, they really aimed at a highly imaginative portrayal of their relations with truth; and even those who professed to strive for clearness, and in fact did so, could not resist the temptation to convey the ardor of their souls in brevities, suppressions, and contortions of style which are in fact inconsistent with a primary devotion to the virtue of perspicuity.

In the second place, the Stoic sage was always, by his own account, a foreigner in the world. His outward fortunes were bound up in every conceivable way with powers and conventions which were alien to his soul; and the form in which the problem of life presented itself to him was how to reconcile his inward detachment and independence with his necessary outward conformity to the world, or even with the desire—which he usually professed—to be of service to it. Obscurity, therefore, might be useful to him in two ways. Sometimes it was a necessary safeguard of the dangerous truths he had to utter; sometimes it was a subtle mockery of the puerile orthodoxies of society.

Clearness is a virtue, then, to which the Stoics pay lip service, which they more honor in the breach than the observance; and its value in the criticism of their prose consists chiefly in the fact that it enables us to distinguish two classes of writers among them. One consists of those who studiously defy it for the reasons just mentioned. Tacitus—*le prince des ténèbres*—Persius, and Tertullian are of this class, and their imitators in the seventeenth century, Donne (in his letters), Gracián, Bacon, Malvezzi, etc., may easily be distinguished by their cult of significant darkness. The other is of those who studiously cultivate clearness, not for its own merits, but as a wise corrective to the other qualities of Stoic prose, brevity and appropriateness, which they love better. Seneca and the seventeenth-century writers who directly imitate him, such as Lipsius and Bishop Hall, and Montaigne and Browne in some of their writings, are representative of this class.

(b) Brevity

Aristotle's second virtue is brevity, and this the Stoics liked so well that they sometimes actually put it first, in the place of clearness.[48] It is a quality that is almost necessarily involved in the attempt to portray exactly the immediate motions of the mind. In the history of all the epochs and schools of writing it is found that those which have aimed at the expression of individual experience have tended to break up the long musical periods of public discourse into short, incisive members, connected with each other by only the slightest of ligatures, each one carrying a stronger emphasis, conveying a sharper meaning than it would have if it were more strictly subordinated to the general effect of a whole period. Such a style is a protest against easy knowledge and the complacent acceptance of appearances. It was of course a style loved by the Stoics. But there was a feature of their discipline which gave a particular value to the virtue of brevity; for they made greater use than any of the other sects of the art of condensing their experience into "golden sayings," *dicta*, maxims, aphorisms, *sententiae*. Chrysippus, working perhaps on hints received from Pythagoras, gave directions for the manufacture of *sententiae*, and the use of them in moral discipline, directions which are familiar to modern readers through Bacon's reproduction and expansion of them in his *De Augmentis*, unhappily without due credit given to his predecessor.[49] It is not enough to say of Stoic style that it tends toward brevity. In its most characteristic forms it tends toward the *sententia*, which is as properly to be called its ideal form as the rhythmic cumulative period is that of the Ciceronian style.

[48] So, for instance, Lipsius, *Ep. Inst.*, Ch. VII, in *Opera*, II, 536: *Prima illa, prima mihi sermonis virtus est.*

[49] VI.iii, in *Works*, I, 674ff. [corresponding to *The Advancement of Learning* (ed. Wright), II.xviii.1-9; cf. Aristotle, *Top.* I.12ff., *Rhet.* I.vi.7] La Mothe le Vayer is more candid: see his *Considérations sur l'Éloquence Françoise* in *Œuvres*, II, Part 1, p. 196, etc. The source is Chrysippus as reported by Plutarch in his "Controversies of the Stoics" [i.e. "The Contradictions of the Stoic Philosophers," pp. 865ff. in Plutarch's *Morals*, trans. Philemon Holland (London, 1657)], but Aristotle's analysis of the enthymeme also contributed to the discussions of Bacon and La Mothe le Vayer. [Cf. n.39 above and *Muret*, n.33.]

(c) Appropriateness

The quality of appropriateness is not so easy to deal with, for it has been the subject of puzzled discussion, and has assumed a Protean variety of forms. Yet it is of the utmost importance in the interpretation of Stoic style. Aristotle does not clearly enough define what he means by it, but it is evident that he thinks chiefly of appropriateness to the character of the audience addressed and the nature of the occasion: a style should adapt itself to the social requirements of discourse, and not be, for instance, either too lofty or too mean for the kind of audience contemplated. Through the recognition of this virtue of style, it seems, he is able to introduce into his *Rhetoric* the description of the Isocratean model of oratory which occupies his third book.[50] But in this use of the word there was an obvious danger to the Stoics; for it might be used as an open door for the entrance of those modes of popular and sensuous appeal which they deprecated in public oratory and carefully excluded from their own private discourses. They gave to the quality of appropriateness, therefore, a meaning more suitable to the theory of a style which was to concern itself intimately with experience.

The statement of it by Lipsius will serve to present their view briefly.[51] Appropriateness, he says, has two aspects, appropriateness to thing and to person. The former we will consider first for a moment. It is evident that taken in its strict sense appropriateness to the thing has nothing to do with rhetoric. If (as Lipsius defines it) "everything is said for the sake of the argument" (or subject), and "the vesture of sentence and phrase exactly fits the body of the thing described," thought and discourse are exactly identical, and there is only one science of both, which we may call logic or dialectic, or what-not. The proper outcome of the doctrine of "appropriateness of the thing" is such a mathematical style as was contemplated by Bayle and some seventeenth-century Cartesians, a style admirable of course for scientific exposition, but limited to uses in which art has no opportunity. In short this phase of the Stoic doctrine of style exactly illustrates the instability of an anti-oratorical theory of style, which we have already noted in other connections. But, as we have also observed, practice never squares

---

[50] See Hendrickson, "The Peripatetic Mean," pp. 135-136 and "The Origin," p. 254.

[51] *Epist. Inst.*, Ch. x in *Opera*, II, 537.

exactly with a theory; and insistence upon the more literal truth of language has often served as a wholesome corrective or a partisan challenge in periods sated with the conventional ornaments of style.

Secondly, there is appropriateness to person; and this, says Lipsius, has two phases: appropriateness to the person or persons addressed, and appropriateness to the speaker or writer himself. In the former phase it may be taken as justifying the study of the abstract rhetorical beauties of oratory. So Aristotle seems to take it. But the Stoics lay all the emphasis on the other phase, namely, the exact interpretation in one's expression of the mode of one's thought; or rather they identify the two phases, the proper and effective mode of impressing one's hearers being, in fact, to render one's own experience in the encounter with reality as exactly, as vividly, as possible. And here we must return to what was said a moment ago concerning the character of Stoic morality, in order to show how this interpretation of appropriateness brings into play the rhetorical artifices which are characteristic of the Stoic style and were often so overdone in the periods that we are chiefly concerned with. If truth and reality were easily come at and declared themselves in the same unmistakable terms to all inquiring minds, their expression in language would be a comparatively simple task. The style appropriate to the thing would be almost the same as that appropriate to the mind of the speaker. But it is not so, of course. The secrets of nature are made known only to attentive and collected minds, prepared by a long preliminary training in habits of exclusion and rejection; and even to them but partially, and in moments of rare illumination. A style appropriate to the mind of the speaker, therefore, is one that portrays the process of acquiring the truth rather than the secure possession of it, and expresses ideas not only with clearness and brevity, but also with the ardor in which they were first conceived. It is no more a bare, unadorned, unimaginative style than the oratorical style is; it aims, just as oratory does, to move and please, as well as to teach, but is distinguished from oratory by the fact that it owes its persuasive power to a vivid and acute portrayal of individual experience rather than to the histrionic and sensuous expression of general ideas.

The figures it uses, therefore, are not the "schemes," or figures of sound, which characterize oratory, but the figures of wit, the rhetorical means, that is, of conveying thought persuasively. Antithesis is one of the chief of these, not however as a figure of sound, which it may be, but as a means of expressing striking and unforeseen relations between the objects of thought. Closely connected with this is the study of "points," or *argutiae*; for the effect of points or turns of wit is found to be due nearly always to an open or veiled antithesis. These two, antithesis and point, are the chief means employed in the art of aphoristic condensation, which, as we have seen, is the normal form of Stoic rhetoric. Of equal importance with these, and of greater literary value, is the metaphor. If Aristotle first expounded the uses of this figure, the Stoics of the late Greek period, and especially those of the Roman Empire, may have the credit of having first shown fully in practice its marvelous expressive powers. It is the greatest of the figures by which literature may interpret the exact realities of experience; and is as much the characteristic possession of the essay style as the musical phrase is of the oratorical.[52]

It has been necessary to enter into these details concerning the Stoic rhetorical technique because all subsequent practice of the *genus humile* was affected by it; in the Stoics of the late Greek period, of the first and second centuries of the Roman Empire, and of the seventeenth century we encounter the same traits of style.

We return now to the history of the *genus humile* at Rome.

How much progress the opponents of the Ciceronian type of oratory had made during the last century of the Republic in domesticating the devices of Stoic rhetoric which have just been described we cannot say with definiteness, because the remains of the literary activity of the circles of the Scipios and Laelius, and of Brutus and Pollio, are singularly few and fragmentary. It may be that the example of Cato and the image of the primitive Roman gentleman preserved a simpler and plainer character in their prose, and made them chary of adopting too freely methods of expression which had the double taint of foreign culture and philosophic sophistication. We cannot say with certainty. But we know that in its theory and general outlines the Stoic rhetoric was approved and imitated by them. Cicero's testimony makes this sure. For he calls the kind of rhetoric which was usually (but without his approval) set in contrast with his own almost indifferently by the names *genus humile* or *stilus Stoicus*, and the terms in which he describes it in his rhetorical treatises show that it had the same general features that the *genus humile* had assumed in Greece during the third and

[52] See n.39.

second centuries: its brevity, its significant abruptness, its tendency to sententiousness, and its preference of the "figures of thought" to the "figures of sound."

This form of style had, as we have seen, all the advantage of being associated in men's minds with the native Roman tradition. It was the "ancient" style in contrast with the Ciceronian model, which bore the imputation of Asianism and novelty. Why, we may well inquire, was it so slow in winning its way to a position of pre-eminence in Roman letters? When we read in Cicero's writings the names of the authors who represented it in his own time and the century before him we cannot fail to see that they are both more numerous and vastly more respectable and Roman than those of their literary opponents. Indeed if the name of Cicero himself is eliminated from the history of the grand style, a comparatively small number of important names remains to it. Yet this is unquestionably the style that won the greater successes during the pre-Augustan age and even in the Augustan Age itself, whereas the Stoic style did not attain its proper triumph until a later generation and after it had submitted itself to the process of regularization and conventionalization in the schools of declamation.

The explanation may be found in the uncompromising haughtiness of its pretensions during the earlier periods. It was *intransigeant* in two senses, both as Stoic and as "ancient Roman." Cicero's great success was due to his sympathy with popular tastes; and his own confidence and joy in the rightness of the rhetorical appeal which the people loved saves him from the imputation of insincerity. The Stoics, on the other hand, may have suffered from an excess of scruple. Their unwillingness to confess the aid of rhetoric or to study their characteristic modes of expression in the systematic and deliberate way in which they were later studied in the schools of declamation may have cost them their chance to be heard either in their own time or by later generations.

These are mere speculations concerning an interesting fact. What is clear and certain is that Stoic style entered on a new and brilliant phase of its history with the foundation of the "schools of declamation," which first made their influence felt during the Augustan Age, and later came to control the style of almost all Roman literature for more than two centuries.

If there is a common misunderstanding in the mind of the general reader of the character of the training in the schools of declamation, the blame must be imputed to the scholars who have written on the subject. The fault commonly attributed to the teachers in these schools is too great a fondness for rhetorical artifice and the love of it for its own sake; and this is a sound indictment. But without the critical specifications that might be expected to accompany it in the statements of scholars it is more misleading than helpful; for it might more justly be brought against the masters of the style that the new schools repudiated and supplanted than against those that accepted their training and practiced according to their precepts. A reader, for instance, who accepted the careless, denunciatory language of most modern historians on this subject—rather than their actual meaning—would suppose that Seneca wrote with more rhetorical exuberance and display than Cicero, that Tacitus' style reflected a less exact image of the actual world than that of Livy, and that Juvenal and Persius are characterized by an habitual use of the flaccid ornaments of conventional rhetoric![53] It is necessary, therefore, to point out that the purpose of the schools of declamation was to train their pupils in the practice of the *genus humile*—*de re hominis magis quam de verbis agitantis*. Their pretension was realism; their program the cultivation of all the means of individual expression at the expense of conventional beauty. It is true that they studied for this purpose the figures and devices that had been conventionalized by the rhetoricians of the Stoic schools of Greece; they even practiced them with a more conscious art and found in them new resources for purely literary and rhetorical pleasure. But these figures and devices were metaphor, antithesis, paradox and "point"—the appropriate means for the literary expression of ingenious thought and acute realism.

The name by which these schools were known has doubtless done much to create a prejudice against them; but the general custom of denunciation is due in a still greater degree to the fact that the period in which their influence culminated and produced its greatest results is conventionally treated as a period of literary decadence. That there was a general depreciation of moral values in the public and social life of the age of Nero and Domitian no one will deny; and it is probable that the literature of such an age reflects some of its evil conditions even in the character of works which are designed to correct them. But there is often an undue

[53] Gaston Boissier's *Cicero and his Friends*, trans. Adnah David Jones (New York, 1897) is very misleading in this way.

readiness to distribute the honors of degeneracy; and it is fair to recall that in great measure the literature of the Silver Age was a literature of protest. The first fruits of the schools of declamation came to maturity during the Augustan Age, in the writings of Ovid; and in the constant stylistic trickery, combined with the soft delicacy of sentiment and the absence of ideas that characterize these exercises in poetry there are grounds for the expectation of a literary decline. But the characteristic products of the next century are not at all in that vein. On the contrary they are nearly all the new births of a union between the forms of style taught in the schools of declamation—Stoic, as we have seen, in their origin, but not necessarily so in their application—and a genuine and powerful movement of Stoic philosophy, which derived its impetus from a revolt of the best ideas of the age against the corruption prevalent in society. The style of the schools of declamation gained a new value, a new meaning, from this happy alliance. In the writings of Seneca, Tacitus, Lucan, and Juvenal it served to recall the ideas of an age of Rome that seemed almost as primitive then as the Middle Ages do to us now, and reaped the advantages of that association with early native forms of prose which the Stoic style had always enjoyed. To this association, indeed, it partly owed its tremendous success. But on the other hand it might claim at the same time the honors of a "modern" style in a sense that that term has enjoyed in almost all periods; for its expressive and piquant forms lent themselves admirably to the needs of the new rationalists and their independent criticism of contemporary society.

✧ VI ✧

In the previous sections of this paper we have seen that "Attic prose" in the seventeenth century denoted the *genus humile,* or philosophical essay style, in contrast with the Ciceronian type of oratory; and have discussed the influence of the earlier Greek theorists and exemplars of this genus upon it. We have now to observe that the forms of the *genus humile* that were of practical use to it as models for its own imitation were the Roman forms whose history has been outlined in the preceding section.

This statement must be made still more specific, however. The prose that actually determined the forms of its style was that Stoic prose of the first century of the Empire—along with some later prose of the same school—which was alembicated in the schools of declamation. The traditions of the Republic on which "Silver-Age Latinity" rested, to which it always referred, were valuable, it is true, to the seventeenth century, and it is for that reason that they have been considered so carefully here. The example of Brutus, for instance, was of incalculable advantage to it both in morals and rhetoric when it wished to describe in the clearest and purest terms the ideal to which it aspired, or to express most unequivocally the motives of its opposition to an oratory of pure display; and we have seen that Balzac spoke of "the style of Brutus" as if it were a familiar form that could be studied at large in existing documents. The example of Caesar again served their purposes in the same way. That he did not actually belong to a particular school of philosophy or style made no difference. For his conduct and that of his legionaries were regarded as the counterparts in practice of the heroic virtue which Epictetus and Seneca portray in its moral and inward effects;[54] and his style, virile and *soldatesque*, like his life, would have been taken by Montaigne and Bacon as the model of their own, in preference to that of Seneca or Tacitus, if they had not been compelled by the spirit of their age to be rhetoricians *malgré soi.*[55]

But seventeenth-century writers could not imitate Brutus or Caesar or Cato in their own style. The explicit and inartificial candor of the Republic was the quality that some of them loved best, but none of them could emulate it in their own manners, because they were living in a different kind of an age and were wholly conscious of the difference. They felt sincerely, almost instinctively indeed, that they were living in a period of decline. There had been a culmination of energy and confidence in the sixteenth century; but the external unities of the Renaissance were dissolving, and the most striking phenomenon of the new age was the division

[54] In a sea letter to his father, the sailor-son of Sir Thomas Browne (*Works*, ed. Simon Wilkin [London, 1846], I, 143) is naïvely delighted with the spirit of the old Caesarian legions as portrayed in Lucan's *Pharsalia*: "This temper would have served [us] well," he says, "and had probably concluded the warre in our first fight with the Dutch."

[55] Daniello Bartoli ("Dello Stile," *Dell' Uomo di Lettere*, in *Opere* [Venice, 1716], III, 101), describing the "modern" style (a name often given to the new "Attic"), says "Its beauty does not rob it of its strength. It can make the same boast that Caesar's soldiers did, who were able *etiam unguentati bene pugnare.*" Bacon's Secretary names Caesar with Seneca and Tacitus as his master's favorite authors. Montaigne's almost poetic praises of him are well known.

between their outward and inward interests and allegiances which revealed itself to its wisest minds. As in the first century, authorities and orthodoxies were establishing themselves in the corporate political and spiritual life of the age which derived their sanction from its weaknesses rather than from its strength; and these the "good man," the "sage," felt himself bound to support or obey because they were the only safeguards against the evils which the divisions and corrupt tendencies of the time would bring in their train if they were left free to work out their natural results. But his true devotion was given elsewhere; his true ideals were not embodied in the external forms and symbols of the age; his real standards could not be made manifest by signs which would be visible to the crowd.[56] In such an age the true literary modes are those that serve the purposes of criticism, protest, individual intelligence. The *ideal* form of style to which it refers is of course the "natural" style which expresses naïvely the candor of the soul. But in fact the style it demands for its self-expression is one that has been wrought upon with subtle art to reveal the secret experiences of arduous and solitary minds, to express, even in the intricacies and subtleties of its form, the difficulties of a soul exploring unfamiliar truth by the unaided exercise of its own faculties.

It was not only its social and political state, however, that turned its literary tastes in the direction of the inferior Atticism of the Empire. An explanation that lies nearer the surface of things is found in the state of its artistic culture, the character of its literary tastes as determined by its historical position. It was still in the Renaissance, or at least was its immediate successor, and it had not yet cast away the love of rhetorical ornament for its own sake which had descended to the Renaissance from the Middle Ages. Its purpose indeed was to escape from this tradition, to represent things as they are, to be as little ornate and rhetorical as possible; but it could not express even this purpose except by means of artifice, mannerism, device. It was still somewhat "Gothic" in spite of itself; and the rhetoric elaborated in the schools of declamation offered it exactly the opportunity it needed to indulge what was

---

[56] This view is more rigorously asserted in Fulke Greville's neglected prose classic *A Letter to an Honourable Lady* than almost anywhere else (in *Works*, ed. A. B. Grosart, 4 vols., 1870, esp. Ch. III ff.). But it is implied in the voluntary retirement of Montaigne and Charron, Lipsius and Balzac, Greville and Browne, to mention only a few of the philosophical solitaries of the age.

most traditional, most unclassical in its tastes under the protection of classical authority.

For these, and doubtless for many other, reasons there was a revival of Silver-Age literature in the seventeenth century, or in the period from 1575 to 1675 which we are treating here as the seventeenth century. Many of the isolated facts which are included in this general statement and justify it have been noted of course by literary history. But the disingenuous or merely traditional orthodoxy which runs through the age has partly veiled the actualities of its taste and practice from the eyes of modern students. And it is partly at least for this reason that the period (1575-1675) between the Renaissance, properly so-called, and the neo-Classical age has never been clearly differentiated in literary history, although in the other arts, in sculpture, painting, and architecture, its character has been recognized and described. We shall not understand the seventeenth century, we shall not know the exact meaning of the eighteenth century, until we have come to realize more clearly than we now do that a century intervened between the eighteenth and the sixteenth in which Lucan had a more effective influence on the ideas and the style of poetry than Virgil did; in which Seneca was more loved and much more effectively imitated in prose style than Cicero had been in the previous generations; in which Tacitus almost completely displaced Livy as the model of historical and political writing; in which Martial was preferred to Catullus, and Juvenal and Persius were more useful to the satirists than Horace; in which Tertullian, the Christian representative of the Stoic style of the Empire—*notre Sénèque*, as he was called—exercised a stronger power of attraction over the most representative minds than St. Augustine, who is the Cicero and the Ciceronian of patristic Latin.

These are the great names. But the movement of imitation and rehabilitation extended the broad mantle of its charity over minor works which have not at any other time been well regarded by the modern world. Velleius Paterculus' odd mixture of anecdote and aphorism[57] and Pliny's unpleasing *Panegyric to Trajan*[58] played their

[57] In Trajano Boccalini's *I Ragguagli di Parnaso e Pietra del Paragone Politico*, I.23, ed. Giuseppe Rua (Bari, 1910), pp. 67-75, Velleius Paterculus carries Lipsius' works to Apollo to receive immortality, and leads the author himself into the presence, between "Seneca the moralist" and "Tacitus the politician." There is an allusion here to Lipsius' *Commentary* on Paterculus. Gracián the *concettisto* finds in Paterculus a storehouse of examples of his loved *Agudeza*.

[58] Dom Jean Goulu, the translator of Epictetus, published a long eulogy and

several parts, and not unimportant ones, in seventeenth-century prose history; and it would be possible to add interesting details concerning the taste of this period for other minor authors of the first century. But space must be reserved even in so general a survey for the mention of two Greek writers, by no means minor, who were at Rome during the period of Seneca and Tacitus and display in different ways the spirit of the Roman culture of their time. Plutarch's *Morals* and Epictetus' *Discourses*, known chiefly in translation, exercised an enormous influence upon the moral ideas, and only a little less upon the literary ideas, of the generation from Montaigne to Pascal.

The zeal of this revival was not more remarkable than its success. It is probably true that no other modern period has so thoroughly domesticated in its own literary productions the thought and the style of a period of antiquity; and the title of the Silver Age of modern literature as applied to the period of European literature beginning about 1575 would have considerably more in its favor than nicknames given by this method of nomenclature usually have.

To prove the soundness of assertions sweeping over so wide an area as this would of course be impossible within the limits of a single paper; and even the evidence concerning prose style, which is all that we are concerned with here, would only be convincing through its cumulative effect in a series of chapters. There is no more than room here to gather together a few of the passages in which the dependence of the age upon first-century models is most broadly depicted.

François Vavasseur, the French Jesuit rhetorician of chief authority in the middle of the century, may almost be said to have devoted his literary career to the exposition of the Silver-Age proclivities of his time and an attack upon them. His admirable treatise on the Epigram is meant to show, among other things, the superior excellence of Catullus over Martial, and that on the *Novum Dicendi Genus* is an accurate and sweeping description of the preference of the age for the Latin authors of the Decadence.[59] All this is echoed, but less clearly and with less candor, in the later opinions of Balzac,

---

analysis of the "Panegyric to Trajan." Lipsius made a commentary on it, and analyses and imitations of it were common in Italy and Spain. For an English imitation see Wotton's "A Panegyrick to King Charles." [See *Lipse*, n.17.]

[59] François Vavasseur, *Oratio Tertia Pro Vetere Generi Dicendi Contra Novum* (1636), in *Opera Omnia* (Amsterdam, 1709), pp. 201-209. [*Muret*, n.25.]

who probably learned more from Vavasseur than his critics have confessed. But Balzac is torn between his romantic tastes and his classical judgment; and the perspective is better preserved in two critics of the latter half of the century. In describing the taste of Priolo, the historian, for the ancient Anti-Ciceronians of the first century, Bayle allows himself to enlarge his theme into a discussion of the contrast between the three Augustans, Cicero, Livy, and Virgil, who have an eloquence of the same general kind, he says, and Seneca, Pliny, Tacitus, and Lucan, whose style he describes in striking terms of denunciation, and adds: "The French begin to be sick of the same distemper." One questions, after reading what he says of Mlle. de Gournai and Montaigne, and other writers of the earlier part of the century, whether he does not mean the word *begin* ironically.[60] Father Bouhours, at least, has no doubt of the cause of the distempers which have appeared for a century in French style. In his various critical writings he constantly draws a parallel between a certain class of ancient authors, in which Seneca, Tacitus, Lucan, and Tertullian are the chief names, and the authors of the century past. At different places he includes on the modern side of the parallel Montaigne, Lipsius, Balzac, the *concettisti* of Spain and Italy, especially Gracián and Malvezzi, and a great array of other writers of the seventeenth century. And in his best-known work he represents Philanthe, the voice of the common tastes of his time, as saying that he finds his opinions beginning to change: he does not despair of some day coming to prefer Virgil to Lucan, Cicero to Seneca.[61]

Poets and prose-writers are mingled in these citations indiscriminately; and in this respect they correctly represent the criticism of the time, which usually makes no distinction between them in discussions of style. There is no lack of witnesses, however, who are concerned wholly with questions of prose; rather there is an embarrassment of riches. We need not cite the polemics of Muret and

[60] Pierre Bayle, *The Dictionary* (London, 1737), IV, 778, s.v. "Priolo," n.L. See also the articles on Balzac, Goulu, and Javersac.

[61] Bouhours, *La Manière* (1688), end of 3rd Dialogue, p. 336. Cf. p. 388: "plus capable de préférer les pointes de Sénèque au bon sens de Cicéron, et le clinquant du Tasse à l'or de Virgile." [Alexander F. B. Clark, pp. 262-274 (see n.33), treats Bouhours' influence on English writers. There are useful bibliographical references in V. M. Hamm, "Father Dominic Bouhours and Neo-Classical Criticism," in *Jesuit Thinkers of the Renaissance: Essays Presented to John F. McCormick, S.J.* (Milwaukee, 1939), pp. 63-65. Bouhours' estimate of Gracián is explored in Adolphe Coster, "Balthasar Gracián (1601-1658)," *Revue Hispanique*, XXIX (1913), 666-685.]

Lipsius, who were engaged in a deliberate attempt to rehabilitate Seneca, Tacitus, and the whole school of Silver-Age Latinity, or of Montaigne, who was just as consciously the propagandist of the influence of Plutarch and Seneca. For these are controversialists whose testimony is prejudiced. The comments of later writers who have observed the current of their times serves our purpose better. In the Latin translation of his *Advancement of Learning*, published nearly twenty years after the English version, Bacon added a significant passage to his famous denunciation of Ciceronianism, which has wholly escaped the attention of critics. Here he describes another *styli genus*, characterized by conciseness, sententiousness, pointedness, which is likely to follow in time upon a period of oratorical luxury. Such a style is found, he says, in Seneca, Tacitus, and the younger Pliny, "and began not so long ago to prove itself adapted to the ears of our own time."[62] If this passage had not been concealed in Latin it would have had a greater influence upon our reading of the seventeenth-century prose. It is admirably confirmed by what Father Caussin said in France in 1619: he describes the new form of style in the same way, mentions the same ancient models, adding Sallust to the list, and says it is the style that *everyone now covets*.[63]

From the middle of the century an interesting array of parallels in ancient, Biblical, and seventeenth-century literature drawn up by the libertine scholar Gabriel Naudé must suffice. Naudé puts Seneca and Plutarch in the first rank of his preference, as a Montanist should; and with them Epictetus and Aristotle; the Wisdom of Solomon he thinks has the same value; and the chief modern authors of like quality are Montaigne, Charron, and Du Vair.[64]

After 1650 the knowledge of what has been happening in prose grows steadily clearer; the defects and errors of the first half of the century are under correction, but it is generally recognized that the same models are still preferred, the same "Attic" tendency prevails. Perhaps the most interesting comment of all, because of the genius of its author, is the fragment of Pascal's, cited on a former page, in which he asserts that the spirit of the time has all been favorable to

---

[62] Quoted in full in *Lipse*, n.40.

[63] Caussin, *Eloquentiae*, II.xiv-xvi, ed. 1619, pp. 73-78.

[64] *Bibliographica Politica*, p. 25 in *Grotii et Aliorum Dissertationes* (Amsterdam, 1645). See also his *Syntagma de Studio Liberali* (Rimini, 1633), pp. 55-56 et passim [and James V. Rice, *Gabriel Naudé 1600-1653*, Johns Hopkins Studies in Romance Lit. and La., Vol. xxv (Baltimore, 1939)].

an intimate style, which portrays things in their familiar form and as they are known at first hand, and that the style of Epictetus, Montaigne, and Louis de Montalte (that is of Pascal himself in the *Lettres*) is of this kind.[65] Pascal, it is true, derives his Stoicism, and the intimate style appropriate to it, partly from the Greek spring of Epictetus, but even he was more influenced by the style of his French translation, says Strowski, than by the original; and, as we have had occasion to observe, the Latin sources of neo-Attic were those that availed most for the uses of the seventeenth century. Malebranche, looking back over its history and criticizing it from the angle of a "mathematical" Cartesian, sees three great literary influences, all of the same kind, that have constantly been in operation. Tertullian, Seneca, and Montaigne are the members of this interesting trio; all of them, as he says, enemies of clear thinking and pure reason, because they have more fancy than judgment and dress the truth in colors of imagination.[66]

Finally, in the last year of the century, Shaftesbury sums up the history of Senecan imitation in his *Characteristics*. He describes accurately the form of the familiar essay in the manner in which Seneca had written it, and says: "This is the manner of writing so much admired and imitated in our age, that we have scarce the idea of any other model. . . . All runs to the same tune and beats exactly one and the same measure."[67]

It may be expected by the reader that in order to round off our argument we shall give illustrations of the use of the word "Attic" in the seventeenth century as applied specifically to the style of Seneca and Tacitus and their contemporaries. Many passages could be cited, of course, in which this attribution is implied; but those in which it is expressly stated would not be very numerous. For the age was aware, as our own is, that "Attic" had certain associations which made it seem inappropriate to authors so fond of rhetorical artifice as the Stoics of the first century were, even though it recognized that their philosophical and intimate manner gave them a general right to this appellation when they are contrasted with the

[65] See n.37.

[66] *La Recherche de la Vérité*, II.iii. Ch. 3 [the best modern ed. is in Vols. I-III of Nicholas Malebranche, *Œuvres Complètes* (Paris, 1958-), ed. Geneviève Rodis-Lewis], in *Malebranch's Search after Truth*, trans. Richard Sault (London, 1694), I, 411, chapter entitled "Of the Force of the Imagination of Certain Authors: Of Tertullian"; the next two chapters discuss Seneca and Montaigne.

[67] *Miscellaneous Reflections*, Miscellany I, Ch. 3, in *Characteristics*, ed. J. M. Robertson (London, 1900), II, 171. Cf. the first chapter also.

Ciceronian and Isocratean kind of orators. "Attic" in short named in their use a *genus dicendi* that was very general in its character and very inclusive, and they were reluctant, just as the ancients were, to apply it to particular schools of writers. But this need not greatly trouble us. It is not so important for our purpose to defend our use of the term "Attic" as it is to indicate the relation between ancient forms of style and those prevalent in the seventeenth century. And this relation is exactly expressed by saying, first, that "Attic" meant in the seventeenth century the *genus humile*, and secondly, that the form in which the ancient *genus humile* was actually imitated in its own practice was the form in which it appeared in the prose and poetry of the Silver Age of Latin literature, and especially in the prose of Seneca and Tacitus. The term "Attic" is, in truth, not wholly satisfactory; but it is the only one that seems to be available to describe the dominant tendency of the seventeenth-century style, and was also the only one generally used for the purpose in the seventeenth century itself.

Foreword to Essay Three

When Croll's essay on Marc-Antoine Muret appeared in 1924 its import was revolutionary. For centuries scholars had regarded his prose as an exemplar of Ciceronianism; they associated him with Julius Caesar Scaliger, in whose household he once resided, as an opponent of Erasmus and a persecutor of Ramus. But Croll, while conceding that Muret had begun as a model Ciceronian, demonstrated that he had led the reaction against it. More truly even than Montaigne, Muret led the way to Anti-Ciceronianism for Justus Lipsius, Quevedo, and Bacon. Croll not only demonstrated this forgotten, never well-understood truth; he had to explain how the misconception arose and prevailed. To correct it, he placed Muret accurately in the intellectual history of his time.

Even today, Muret's literary career is not well known: he left a few short volumes of Latin orations and epistles; and the usual tribute paid to him in biographical dictionaries is seldom more than a few lines. In contrast to the lofty stature which he enjoyed during his lifetime, he has almost dwindled from sight. Modern critical and historical attention focuses on authors who wrote and published more extensively than he did. His contribution was largely oral, and it was composed in Latin. Because he chose not to write in the vernacular, even the great lectures which he delivered as Professor at Rome are now neglected. Perhaps the very fact that he ended his career in that city has something to do with this oversight, for the modern student is likely to forget, in the light of the earlier glories of northern Italian humanism, that it was with the Counter-Reformation that Rome finally came into its day, a day in which, Croll points out, Muret played a particularly important part.

Much of the little which we are likely to know of Muret is associated with his earlier years in France before his conviction, at Paris and Toulouse, for alleged heresy and sodomy, and before he rebuilt the ruins of his career in the Italian climate. After summing up the rhetorical situation in twenty or more pages, Croll turns to Muret himself. The summary he accomplishes with great excellence, especially for a generation that has forgotten (or grown out of sympathy with) rhetorical theory, which, he points out, "expressed itself in a congeries of similar dogmas in all the chief subjects of sixteenth-century learning." We tend to forget that rhetoric was the central doctrine about which the edifice of sixteenth-century learning was constructed, and we think of it as mere organization or as a collection of figures of speech or, what is worse, as a burden of dry-as-dust exercises. To the Renaissance mind it was the stuff of life itself, and not the least merit of Croll's articles on prose style is that they interrelate controversies over rhetoric with political, religious, and social issues.

The analysis which Croll makes of Muret's prose is a somewhat cursory one; but even a hasty comparison of Muret's earlier pieces anthologized in the two volumes of *Scripta Selecta* (Leipzig, 1871, reprinted by Teubner in 1887) with the later ones, which were not published there, indicates that Croll's principles are correct. Muret's style clearly changes. But, as Croll observes, that fact somehow escaped the attention of the classical scholars best able to perceive it—though their failure was in part due to the unrepresentative nature of the pieces in *Scripta Selecta*.

It would be convenient to date Muret's change, his disillusionment about Ciceronianism, with his conversion from Protestantism to Roman Catholicism; but Croll, who is a stickler for accuracy in such matters, denies this notion. He shows that earlier there was evidence of what was to take place and that later, after Muret had adopted the "Attic" style, there are still instances in which he is highly Ciceronian, especially the lecture delivered in 1575, which he composed on orders from authority. But while these qualifications need to be made, on the whole Muret's course is clear enough, once Croll points it out, and we can easily trace his growing attention to Seneca, Tacitus, and Pliny and see him become the earliest leader of the Anti-Ciceronian movement. Thus Croll reversed an accepted academic opinion (based mainly on lack of attention) concerning Muret.

Croll also makes clear that Muret himself did not always know where he was headed. It would be too much to ask for the clarity of our historical perspective from a sixteenth-century writer; moreover, the philosophical implications of Anti-Ciceronianism, its Stoicism and tendency toward scepticism—Croll prefers the term "libertinism"—were by no means clear to Muret. It was in the works of his follower, Lipsius, that Stoicism appeared in clear outline; and in those of Montaigne the scepticism was unmistakable. Nevertheless, in literary history and in the history of ideas Muret's position is paramount, although no one of the twentieth century before Croll recognized so much. His eminence was, of course, recognized in his own day. Thus Croll's essay rehabilitates Muret, who had become a minor figure, and attempts to regain for him major status. At the same time Croll provides a summary of the development of "Attic" prose, which, as a piece with his other essays, constitutes the authoritative work on the subject to this day. The tribute paid by Williamson in *The Senecan Amble* remains a valid one: "For a proper understanding of the [Anti-Ciceronian] movement in general, the various studies of 'Attic Prose' by Morris W. Croll are indispensable."

One or two minor matters of considerable interest are also pursued in the essay. For example, Croll does not regard Muret simply as an advocate for the *genus humile*, as a writer who produced his greatest work in the epideictic rhetoric despite his recognition that henceforth deliberative rhetoric was to be vastly more important. Croll also traces to him the beginnings of a style that found virtues in obscurity.

ROBERT O. EVANS
UNIVERSITY OF KENTUCKY

ESSAY THREE

Muret and the History of
"Attic Prose"*

EDITED BY J. MAX PATRICK AND ROBERT O. EVANS

❖ I ❖

Introduction

IT IS doubtful whether any other great literary reputation of the
Renaissance has survived in so ambiguous and confused a state
as that of Marc-Antoine Muret, recognized in his own time and ever
since as the best writer of Latin prose in the second half of the
sixteenth century. The most important event in the history of
literary ideas during that period was the controversy concerning
the imitation of Cicero, and in that controversy and the various
conflicts connected with it Muret was more or less engaged at all
periods of his career. Yet modern literary history tells us nothing
intelligible of his part in it; or, to speak more exactly, it records
two conflicting statements. On the one hand, he appears as the
associate of Bembo, Sadoleto, Longueil in the stricter sect of the
Ciceronians, a more accomplished, and not less devoted, imitator of
the master. This is certainly the commoner view among those who
have any acquaintance with his name; for generations he has been
held up to the admiration even of school-children as the modern
Cicero.[1] How confusing it is then to find that he also holds a conspicuous place in the sketches—few and inadequate—of the move-

* Reprinted by permission of the Modern Language Association from *PMLA*,
XXXIX, 2 (1924), 254-309. Although publication of this essay took place after
"Attic Prose: Lipsius, Montaigne, Bacon" reached print, Croll indicates in the
first footnote of that article that it was "meant to follow one with the title *Marc-
Antoine Muret and Attic Prose* in a current number (1923) of *PMLA*"; accordingly the essay on Muret is here restored to the position originally intended for it.
    Originally the introductory section of the essay was not numbered and the
following sections here numbered II, III, etc. were numbered I, II, etc.
    The footnote numbers used below correspond to those in the original publica-
tion except for a few minor rectifications.
[1] See the quotations from German teachers prefixed to Antonius Muretus,
Scripta Selecta, Teubner ed., 2 vols. (Leipzig, 1887); S. Reinach, *Cornélie, ou le
Latin sans Pleurs* (Paris, 1914), Preface.

ment of opposition that finally triumphed at the end of his century over the great rhetorical scheme of education! From his letters and orations one or two passages have been cited which outdo the sarcasm of Erasmus' *Ciceronianus* and display a latitude of classical taste which even a modern critic cannot regard without dubiety.[2]

It is clear that this is a case requiring some particular explanation; the evidence will not tell a consistent story without careful interpretation. But when we turn to the scholars who have attempted a picture of Muret's career, we find neither agreement among them nor any single explanation that carries conviction to the mind of the reader. Mark Pattison, in a readable but superficial review of the subject, decides that he is one of those true Ciceronians who succeed in being like their master by not imitating him.[3] Yet this interesting conclusion will not stand the test of the most obvious facts in the case; for it is evident that in some of his orations he deliberately does imitate Cicero, while in others he is just as deliberately *not* imitating him, but self-consciously reproducing a style directly opposed to his. Charles Dejob, Muret's only careful biographer, has indeed marshalled all the facts of his life with admirable care, and provided the materials for their interpretation.[4] But he has placed himself too near his subject to see it in its historical relations, and his only explanation of the variations of opinion and purpose that appear in Muret's intellectual career is found in the extreme mobility of his temperament. This is an explanation that might indeed satisfy a reader's curiosity; but it would leave him with no further interest in the career of Muret.

It is a curious, not to say a disgraceful, fact that an author whose reputation depends—whether justly or unjustly—almost solely on the excellence of his prose form has not yet been placed in an intelligible relation with the progress of modern style. But the fault does not lie chiefly with the critics who have written about him. It lies in the failure of modern literary history to recognize the importance and the true character of the literary movement in which the explanation of Muret's career is involved—the movement of opposition to the Ciceronian dogma which swept everything before it in the last quarter of the sixteenth century and established the

[2] Quoted by Izora Scott. Cf. *Lipse*, n.9.
[3] *Essays by the late Mark Pattison*. 2 vols. (Oxford, 1889), I, 124-131.
[4] *Marc-Antoine Muret* (1881) [see *Lipse*, n.10]. Upon this accurate and useful work I have depended almost wholly for the facts of Muret's life.

forms of prose style both in Latin and in the vernacular tongues that prevailed throughout Europe in the seventeenth century. The modern scholar finds peculiar difficulties in the study of this subject, the most baffling of them all perhaps being his inability to pass in thought back and forth from the facts of Latin to the facts of vernacular style as easily as men of the age of Montaigne and Bacon were wont to do. But these difficulties explain rather than excuse his failure to recognize a phase of the history of prose style which must be understood before the transition from the Renaissance prose of the sixteenth century to the so-called classical style of the end of the seventeenth can be intelligibly described. Hitherto the opposition of Bacon, Lipsius and Montaigne to the imitators of Cicero has been but casually and perfunctorily described as a negative movement, designed to correct the extravagances of humanism and to complete the correction of taste begun by Erasmus fifty years earlier. It was in fact a movement of progress and discovery, which brought prose style into living connection with the intellectual movement of the period from 1570 to 1660 and with the parallel tendencies of the same period in the other arts, the sculpture and architecture of Bernini, the painting of Tintoretto and El Greco, the poetry of Donne and Marino, of Ben Jonson and Corneille.[5]

It is in connection with this later Anti-Ciceronianism that Muret's literary opinions are to be interpreted; and there are therefore two good reasons for studying them anew. The first is that by this means we may get such a view of a great intellectual and literary movement as may be had only in the period when its purposes are beginning to formulate themselves clearly. The second is that we may do belated justice to a critic and artist whose real aims and merits have been obscured by contemporary prejudice and the ignorance of later ages.

What is necessary to the accomplishment of these purposes is not a knowledge of new facts in Muret's career. Those that we have already at our command are enough. We only need to restudy them in their relation with the larger body of facts that belong to the life

---

[5] In "Attic Prose in the Seventeenth Century," I discussed the theory of this Anti-Ciceronian movement of 1575-1660, and especially its relations to its classical models and authorities. An object of the present study is to show its relations with the *movement of ideas* in its age. "Attic Prose: Lipsius, Montaigne, Bacon" carries the history into the generation following Muret. "Juste Lipse et le Mouvement Anticicéronien" now calls for revision at several points.

of the age in which Muret lived, with the history of the movement of ideas in a period when an old generation had not yet quite passed away, and a new one had not yet quite learned what its mind was to be. That is to say, we are compelled to look pretty widely round about our subject before we can look intelligently at it.

✧ II ✧

Ciceronianism and Anti-Ciceronianism

The history of thought in the sixteenth century, seen in its simplest outlines, is the story of the relations between two tendencies, both of which at the times of their sharpest opposition took the form of well-defined and self-conscious movements. The first was the tendency to give free, or freer, play in the knowledges that were then most critically placed, to the spirit of sceptical enquiry which had been the characteristic and novel part of Petrarch's message to the modern world, which had been indeed the only strictly new thing in it. It was in short the growth of scientific and positive rationalism, and we need define it no more exactly than this, for we recognize it at once as the movement which by its further developments in the seventeenth century has created what we call the "modern" world.

The other is not so easy to describe exactly or to estimate justly; first, because it is *not* what we call "modern," and, secondly, because, like all movements of conservatism, it mingled in more intimate and intricate ways with the various special interests of its age than the radicalism that opposed it, and presents to the historical student cross-lights and contradictions which it is much harder for him to pattern or arrange. We may sum it up perhaps as the tendency to summarize and systematize the gained knowledge of the world, both that which had been inherited from the medieval past and that which had been added to this by the Renaissance, and to express this by means of formulistic methods or abstracts which would serve the practical purposes of general education. More briefly described, it was the tendency to study the *forms* of knowledge, as the Middle Ages had done, rather than the facts of nature and history. But if it was conservative and often reactionary, it was also eminently literary and classical, and was the friend of the beauties and symmetries of Renaissance art. Ciceronian imitation was, as we shall see, the representative of all that was best and worst in it. This is a very inadequate description, it is true; but it will be more convenient to adjourn further discussion of it to the point where we find it in sharpest conflict with the various radical movements which it attempted—successfully for a time—to check or divert. Its real character can be made clearer at that point.

Meanwhile it is necessary, for our present purpose, to sketch the progress of the rationalistic tendency in the various fields of knowledge in which it showed most vitality during the century; and this need not be so elaborate an undertaking as it would seem; for we can conveniently take as our guides the "strong wits" of the seventeenth century. These bolder positivists of a later day, when the victory of their cause had already been won, were fond of making out catalogues or calendars of their heroes in the preceding century, and these lists, with other hints from their works, will serve to show us at least where to make the emphasis strongest, since it is precisely their view of the sixteenth-century conflict that we are most interested in.[6]

[6] The best studies of the Libertine movement will be found in F. Strowski, *Histoire du Sentiment Religieux*, Vol. I; François T. Perrens, *Les Libertins en France au XVIIe Siècle*, 2nd ed. (Paris, 1899); J. Roger Charbonnel, *La Pensée Italienne au XVIe Siècle et le Courant Libertin* (Paris, 1919). [See also the treatment of *libertins* in Henri Busson, *La Pensée Religieuse Française de Charron à Pascal* (Paris, 1933); Ch. II in Louis I. Bredvold, *The Intellectual Milieu of John Dryden* (Ann Arbor, 1934); René Pintard's detailed and indispensable *Le Libertinage Érudit dans la Première Moitié du XVIIe Siècle* (Paris, 1943) and Henri Gouhier's review of it and other books by Pintard in *Revue Philosophique de la France et de l'Étranger*, CXXXIV (1944), 56-60; Antoine Adam, *Histoire de la Littérature Française au XVIIe Siècle*. I. *L'Époque d'Henri IV et de Louis XIII* (Paris, 1948), pp. 285-329; Julien-Eymard d'Angers, *L'Apologétique en France de 1580 à 1670* (Paris, 1954), pp. 11-28; and R. H. Popkin, "The Sceptical Crisis and the Rise of Modern Philosophy," *Review of Metaphysics*, VII (1953-54), 132-151, 307-322, 499-510.] The roots of this movement in pure philosophy lie too deep for our present purpose but may be studied in Charbonnel, [Pintard, and Popkin]. Muret's real interest was in *popular* philosophy and *practical* culture. It should be added here that all the "strong wits" were not professed libertines. In the best of them—Montaigne, Lipsius, Sir Thomas Browne, etc.—scepticism and stoicism intermingle in always varying relations. Such catalogues as I speak of in the text will be found in Lipsius' *Institutio Epistolica* and often in his letters, and often in Gabriel Naudé, *Bibliographia Politica*, p. 25, and *Syntagma de Studio Liberali*, pp. 77-80, both published in *Grotii et Aliorum Dissertationes* (Amsterdam, 1645). Compare the famous gallery of portraits in a room in Guy Patin's Paris house, described by him in a letter of Dec. 1, 1650; see pp. 159-160, and n.46 below.

Accounts of the rise of rationalism during the sixteenth century and after will be found in the introduction to Villey [*Lipse*, n.4], and in Nisard's *Histoire* [*APS*, n.45], especially I, 428ff. and II, 66-70, which seem to me to give a better account of the relation of ideas to letters in the period than any of the later works. [Both are utilized in, and partly superseded by, Henri Busson, *Les Sources et le*

Politian's was the earliest name that had a current value among them, if we exclude those of certain sceptical philosophers whose works were too difficult to be known to the public at large or paraded for propaganda. Why they should have preferred Politian to Petrarch himself or to any other of Petrarch's successors during the fifteenth century we need not stop to inquire. He was slightly nearer to them in time, for one thing; his activities had been more public and conspicuous than those of any other fifteenth-century humanist of their type; and his militant opposition to the two "superstitions" of orthodox humanism, Platonism and Ciceronianism, justified the admiration of philosophers like Lipsius and Naudé.[6a]

His name, however, was overshadowed by that of Erasmus, who was generally considered by the seventeenth-century rationalists, from Montaigne and Bacon to Halifax and La Bruyère, as the greatest teacher and patron of their own method of acute realism. To limit the range of Erasmus' influence to a single subject of inquiry, or even to two or three subjects, would be a serious error. For the essence of his liberalism was his equal respect and enthusiasm for all kinds of learning; and the reason for his peculiar enjoyment of learned society in England was that there he could still observe the Renaissance in its first phase of unlimited and hopeful curiosity, scarcely touched as yet by the formalizing, the rhetorical, influences which he was combating with all his industry and wit on the Continent. Indeed it was Erasmus' spirit and temper rather than any of his particular doctrines that made him the hero of rationalism. For he had in perfection the manner that is constantly encountered in later protagonists of that school and was often studiously cultivated by the strong wits of the seventeenth century—a satirical and purposeful gaiety that was meant to reveal by contrast the pedantry of his opponents.

Développement du Rationalisme dans la Littérature Française de la Renaissance, 1533-1601 (Paris, 1922). See also René Bray's comprehensive *La Formation de la Doctrine Classique en France* (Paris, 1927, repr. 1951); R. Michéa, "Les Variations de la Raison au XVIIe Siècle: Essai sur la Valeur du Langage Employé en Histoire Littéraire," *RPFE*, cxxvi (1938), 183-201; Joseph E. Fidao-Justiniani, *Discours sur la Raison Classique* (Paris, 1937)—though all of these are chiefly concerned with the seventeenth century.

Croll parallels his account of the progress of rationalism in *APL* pp. 195ff.]

[6a] [For the views of Politian (Angelo Poliziano), see his correspondence with Paolo Cortesi in Izora Scott's introd. to the trans. of Erasmus' *Ciceronianus* in *Controversies*, pp. 14-22; J. W. H. Atkins, *English Literary Criticism*: *The Renascence* (London, 1955), pp. 8-34.]

Yet we should have but a faulty idea of the character of his influence if we failed to note that his successors during the century that followed his death looked to him chiefly for instruction in a particular subject of knowledge, and that not one of the subjects that modern scholars oftenest associate with his name. Moral philosophy was the dominant interest of the sixteenth century, and even in the seventeenth it was more important than the new scientific studies; it was virtually the exclusive theme of Lipsius, the founder of Neo-Stoicism, and of Montaigne, the teacher of philosophical libertinism; and it may be for this reason alone that these philosophers read a moral significance in almost every conspicuous phase of Erasmus' activity, even where we should not suspect that they would find it. His vast collections of the adages and apothegms of the ancients were chiefly of use to them in the discovery of a realistic method in the study of human nature; his especial diligence in the reading of Seneca and Plutarch's *Morals* had an effect—how much we cannot say—in determining the most characteristic tastes of Lipsius and Montaigne and a host of their contemporaries; his dislike of oratory, his preference of the more intimate modes of discourse, meant to them primarily a new emphasis on the inner and individual life of men in contrast with the plausible and public forms of their social existence; and, finally, his discourse on the method of writing familiar epistles helped to reveal to them the chief instrument of moral instruction and casuistical discipline through which the seventeenth century was to practice the "heroic virtue" of self-dependence. Whether his own century estimated him more justly and correctly than later ones have done we need not stop to inquire; but we must at least recognize that Erasmus has more profoundly affected the modern world by teaching a rationalistic method in the study of morals than by any other part of his varied labors.

Budé and Vives were perhaps the two humanists of his own time who best understood Erasmus' spirit. In the interests of both of them, however, the subject of political and social science, which had been subordinate in Erasmus' mind to private morals, occupied a high, or even the highest, position; and their names may therefore be conveniently used to introduce another important phase of the development of sixteenth-century rationalism. The most conspicuous names in the reform of political study in the sixteenth century are of course those of Machiavelli and his disciple Guicciardini. In a later generation than their own their acute and sceptical method, reinforced by a new study of Tacitus, was to prove the chief instrument of one of the most radical movements in the history of modern rationalism. But it was both too bold and too difficult to produce this effect at once, and it was not perhaps until Lipsius had made Tacitus familiar by his famous 1575 edition that the period of its great success really began.

Meanwhile, during the earlier generations of sixteenth-century scholarship the cause of progress in political science was chiefly associated with the outcome of the struggle—so typical in every way of the conflict of ideas in the Renaissance—between the approved medieval method of the Barthollist Commentators and the effort of some of the greatest and bravest scholars of the century to show that the Institutes of the Roman Law are really historical documents, to be studied in the light of particular conditions of life in the Roman republic. The actors in this drama who were most admired by the positivists of the seventeenth century were Frenchmen of three successive generations, Guillaume Budé, Jacques Cujas, and the French-Swiss, François Hotman; and even in Muret's time the pre-eminence of the first two was so well recognized that the new historical study of Law was spoken of as the French method.[7] It is true that Alciati deserved at least an equal place in their esteem for his service to their cause. But they were accustomed to choose their heroes with as much attention to their temperaments as to the value of their ideas; and in both Budé and Cujas they recognized the quick mobility of mind, the venturesome satirical

---

[7] [At the end of this section, in n.16, Croll provided information which is more pertinent at this point. He explains that wherever possible he used the Teubner volume of Muret's *Scripta Selecta* (see n.1 above), and he adds, "For material not there included, I refer to the two volumes of Orations, Letters, and Poems, published at Leipzig in 1629, *juxta editionem postremam Ingoldstadianam.*" Presumably these volumes were another imprint of the ed. published by M. J. Rhenii, *Volumina Duo Orationum cum Tribus Libris Epistolarum. Item Hymni et Poemata et Alia Ejusdem . . . quae in Ultima Ingoldstadiana Editione Habentur* (Leipzig, 1628). Croll continues, "The publication of Muret's works after his death seems to have been in the hands of German Jesuits. Unfortunately the modern edition of Muret's collected works, ed. by Frotscher [*sic*] has not been available." *M. Antonii Mureti Opera Omnia*, ed. C. H. Frotsher (Leipzig, 1834) is nevertheless cited in the originally published n.7, where he also refers to the "1629" ed. In the footnotes below we retain Croll's refs. to the 1629 ed.]

See a letter addressed to Muret in 1578 by the German "Nation" at Padua (1629 ed., Ep. lxxv; ed. Frotsher, ii, 212); also a letter dated 1564 from Martinus Belliviceius, a former colleague at Padua (1629 ed., i, Ep. i, 45).

wit that have always been dear to the intellectual radical. Were they not also, like most of their successors, Northerners?

Morals and politics—*sapientia* and *prudentia*—were the subjects of thought in which the cause of rationalism made most progress during the sixteenth century. This would have been so, if there had been no other reason, merely because private and public morality were the chief subjects of interest, even to scholars, during that century. But a second fact of almost equal importance was that these subjects could be pursued with little danger of interference from the established authorities of the intellectual world. They were near the circumference of the intellectual system, no more than its outer defences, and the attacks of the radical modernist spirit of the age could be tolerated more easily at these points than when they were directed closer to the citadel of orthodoxy itself. And this Pierre de la Ramée found out to his grief when he promulgated to the world his new—or, as he said, his old—logic, which, he declared, had not been invented by Plato, or by Aristotle, or by Petrus Ramus, but by nature herself. He was challenging, or could be made to seem to be challenging, the authority of Aristotle. The authorities of the Sorbonne, representing all the orthodoxies, rallied to the defence of a fading tradition, rejoicing perhaps that at last the issue was thus sharply drawn. They had the temporary success which those who hold power may always enjoy, and the convenient death of Ramus among the crowd of undistinguished slain on St. Bartholomew's Eve may have seemed to his friends and enemies alike a symbol of the failure of the movement for free thought in the Renaissance.

To us, of course, that event seems rather the signal of the beginning of its triumph. For in the year 1572 Montaigne was already contemplating his philosophic retirement from the world—the symbol of a new age; Lipsius had returned from his visit to Rome with the new program of positive radicalism born full-armed in the moment of his meeting with Muret; and Bacon was beginning his studies at Cambridge. Within two generations of that date rationalism had won all its decisive victories—in moral philosophy, politics, and the natural sciences; an acrid and virile realism had displaced the fluent eloquence of the sixteenth century in all the arts; and the beginning of the modern age of reason waited only for the unifying influence of the Cartesian philosophy.

Seen from the vantage point of a modern historical student, this victory seems of course inevitable; it must have seemed certain to an intelligent spectator even in the last decade of the sixteenth century. But at any earlier period it was far from certain; and during the middle and the third quarter of the century the forces that stood in the way of radicalism and progress enjoyed more powerful and intelligent support than ever before and recovered the ascendancy of which Erasmus' singular influence had at least seemed to deprive them for a time. During this period the leaders of orthodox humanistic opinion in both Protestant and Catholic circles, Ascham, Melanchthon, and Sturm in the North, the organizers of the new Catholic education in the South, were first of all practical men, more interested in training pupils who should worthily represent the political and religious causes to which they themselves were so devoted than in promoting the triumph of pure reason or disinterested scholarship. The liberalizing influence of Erasmus, Budé, Vives, and Cujas was not lost upon these leaders; they were more intelligent and humane conservatives than the orthodox scholars of Erasmus' own generation. But the use they made of their broader wisdom was to reason more broadly and wisely for a policy of reaction which was hostile to all the purposes of Erasmus, to formulate a more humane program of imitative and formal education, which doubtless had its immediate usefulness, but was fatal for the time to the progress in positive knowledge which the rationalists of the Renaissance believed that the modern world could achieve.

It would be easy—but not wise—to dismiss this conservative movement as an aberration in the history of modern education. A movement which has entered into history *cannot* be dismissed; and to do justice to this one we have to observe carefully a distinction of great importance in Renaissance culture. If we mean by the Renaissance the beginning of the modern mastery of fact, the progress of positive and sceptical modes of reasoning in the thought of Petrarch, Erasmus, Montaigne, and Descartes, of course the movement we are considering was a counter-Renaissance, a surrender of the disinterested purposes of the Revival of Learning to the immediate educational needs of an age. But the Renaissance was also a revival of *letters*, an attempt to create cultured habits in the minds of modern men by contact with the literary forms of ancient art; and of this part of its tradition Ascham and Sturm and the more orthodox party among the Jesuit teachers professed honestly and truly to be the devoted representatives, while their opponents, the radicals, they constantly and correctly asserted to be its enemies. (It must be observed that the later history of the rationalist movement exactly bears them out in this contention: from Montaigne to Descartes there is an anticlassical tendency in this movement, which shows itself most clearly in the scorn of Greek studies which is characteristic of it. It may justly be regarded, in this respect, as a counter-Renaissance.) In their view the Renaissance, the rapid advance in learning, that is, of the past hundred years—for it is necessary to remind ourselves that the word *Renaissance*, with its implications of sudden and utter change, is a modern coinage—had brought with it a serious public peril, the peril of the disorganization of educational programs and a consequent failure in the task which to these conservatives seemed most important, namely, the diffusion of the new culture among the laity of the upper classes. The free range of intellectual curiosity, the unlimited extension of what we should call the "elective system" in learning, was doubtless a safe enough process as far as the class of professional scholars was concerned. But education is not for them. It is for the ordinary sensual human beings who have the means of paying for it, and in the sixteenth century it needed to be brought especially, so these conservatives argued, within reach of the desires and tastes of a class of nobles and gentlemen who were still lingering, for the greater part, in the gross ignorance and provinciality of the fifteenth century. The way to win such a class, they said, was not to address their minds to the exact truth of reason or the immediate study of things as they are. The truth of nature is too diffuse and various for their needs; it is dull and inornate; and it does not act directly and quickly enough upon the barbarism of inherited manners and customs. The only education that would meet their needs—and this is more or less true of any class that must acquire a culture alien to it—was one that would give them a palpable design, a single and sensuous pattern, which might finally teach them—when they had learned to conform their speech, their manners, their external lives to it—the method of apprehending the truth itself. Surely, said Thomas Wilson the English rhetorician, if we learn the gesture of the ancients, we shall not fail at last to have minds like theirs too.[8] Yes, literature, they thought, had to be the staple subject,

[8] *The Arte of Rhetorique, 1560*, ed. G. H. Mair (Oxford, 1909), p. 5. [The Scholars' Facsimiles and Reprints series provides the 1553 text, ed. Robert Hood

practically the unique subject, of education for their time; literature, too, in the easy and teachable form of oratory.[9]

It was a reasonable enough argument. There was nothing in it that was not humane and intelligent; and as a general or abstract theory of education we dare not treat it with contempt unless we are prepared to put out of court the only principles upon which a classical education can be defended. The judgment of history upon its proponents in the sixteenth century must depend solely upon whether it decides that they had read the character of their age correctly. If it was indeed an age that had reached such a maturity in the positive sciences that it could afford to pause and consider a balancing of its accounts; or, on the other hand, if it was so weak and immature that it could not hope to advance by its own inventive power but must rest content with the imitation and revival of a more glorious past; in either of these cases a study of the external forms and conventions of culture was what was required. But if, on the contrary, it was an age full of new and unbreathed energies, on the eve of great discoveries and expansions, and capable of coping with the ancients themselves in the criticism of life, then of course the reactionary teachers cannot escape the condemnation due to those who misread the signs of their times. And the modern world is not slow to render its judgment. Had the sixteenth-century rhetoricians succeeded in their purposes the progress of the seventeenth century in natural science and the study of life would have been postponed we cannot tell how long, and the Cartesian philosophy would never have been born in the womb of Time. If their success had been permanent they would have done for the culture of the upper classes of European society in succeeding centuries

---

Bowers (Gainesville, Fla., 1962). Russell H. Wagner's Cornell dissertation, "Thomas Wilson's *Arte of Rhetorique*," 1928, has not been printed. For a good short account, see Howell, *Logic and Rhetoric*, pp. 98-110.]

[9] The following words of a rhetorician to a philosopher are worthy of being pondered by all who are interested in education: "Now, what you write about ideas I am very loth to question, seeing that you are a learned man and have great reputation. But how can you think that there is an idea of style innate in your mind? As for me, I can only declare that I saw no form of style, no image of discourse in my mind until I had formed one there by attentively reading the ancients for many years and by practising long. Before I did this, I used to look into my mind and seek as from a mirror some shape from which I could fashion what I wished. But there was no image there. And when I tried to write, I was borne along at random without law or principle of judgment. None of those things that you mention, no idea, no image, guided me." (Pietro Bembo to Pico della Mirandola, Rome, Calends of January, 1513.)

what the philosophers of China had already done centuries before for the culture of *their* aristocratic patrons.

And even that does not tell the whole truth. The sixteenth century was in a state of rapid and confused transition—at least this was so in the northern countries—from medieval to modern civilization. It had, strictly speaking, no definable character of its own, and but one thing is clear about it, that it could not rest where it was. It must go forward or back, and whatever in its culture and ideas did not impel it towards the future was sure to strengthen its links with its past. The advocates of a program of pause and recollection in such an age were sure to promote other results than those they had in view. However humane and intelligent their own culture might be, they were doomed to witness the revival in their pupils and imitators of ancient habits of superstition justifying themselves by modern pretensions, of the old medieval indolences disguised by the great classical names of the Renaissance. And this was in fact a phenomenon that was generally observed by the teachers of the more progressive policy. When Bacon and Montaigne, for example, looked about them and took stock of the learning of the sixteenth century they remarked with justice that almost every impulse of the new age had been re-conformed to a medieval habit or formula. The new study of Plato had only produced a new, a more frivolous, Platonism; the enlarged knowledge of Aristotle's method had given new vigor to the old Aristotelianism of the Universities; the new investigations of the history of Roman Law had enriched the orthodox Barthollism of the schools with a few specious ornaments; the more critical reading of the science of Pliny and Plutarch had had no other visible effect than to re-establish medieval pseudo-science in a new position of literary respectability; the revival of the pure Latinity of the best ages had issued in the new authoritarianism of the Ciceronian cult. They might be pardoned if they believed that another hierarchy of orthodoxies had arisen out of the ashes of the Renaissance.

Ciceronianism, then, was not an isolated phenomenon, a mere aberration of Renaissance taste; it was the representative in rhetorical theory of a tendency which expressed itself in a congeries of similar dogmas in all the chief subjects of sixteenth-century learning. To show this relation has of course been the object of the preceding survey. And we must now observe that it was much the most conspicuous of all these dogmas of orthodoxy, and was chosen more frequently than any of the others to appear in the controversial arena as their common champion.

The explanation of this fact is not difficult. In the first place, merely because it was a *rhetorical* doctrine, Ciceronianism ideally represented the aims and interests of the conservative orthodoxies. For rhetoric was the form of learning toward which they all consciously or unconsciously aspired. The method that characterized them all, Barthollist, Platonist, Aristotelian, was in a broad sense the method of rhetoric, in the sense, that is, that they all tended toward the study of the *forms* of their various sciences rather than toward the direct observation of the facts; they all busied themselves, as their opponents constantly affirmed, with words rather than with things. Well, there is, as we have observed, a great deal to be said, at least educationally, for the study of forms. But it was only the Ciceronian who could profess this doctrine with perfect confidence and consistency; for his was the only learning—unless it be music—which is directed solely toward the art of expression through a conventional form, and the model he offered for the imitation of his pupils was admittedly the most perfect single instrument of education that the world has in its possession. It is not surprising that the principle on which educational conservation rested in that period expressed itself in the words of a rhetorician and Ciceronian. "Ye know not what hurt ye do to learning," says Roger Ascham, with a boldness that may still make one stare, "that care not for words, but for matter."[10]

A second reason, but a little less important than this, for the preeminence of Ciceronianism is to be found in the love of authority and a single standard of reference which still flourished in the medieval mind of the sixteenth century. All of the orthodoxies, it is true, drew their profit from this inherited habit of mind; but none of them in the same degree as the Ciceronian cult, because it alone

---

[10] *The Whole Works of Roger Ascham*, ed. J. A. Giles, 3 vols. in 4 (London, 1864-65), III, 211. [Trimpi, p. vii, notes how, "in the most general terms, the emphasis shifted from expression to content," from this "Ciceronian comment of Ascham," which he quotes, "to Bacon's Senecan reversal of the proposition when he lamented that 'Men began to hunt more after words than matter.'" Cf. Trimpi, p. 33. On Ascham see Lawrence V. Ryan, *Roger Ascham* (Stanford, 1963), esp. pp. 259-279.] The rhetorical tendency of *all* learning is admirably illustrated in the introductory discourse of Lorenzo Valla's *De Latinae Linguae Elegantia* (Paris, 1541). "Who," he asks, "are the men who have been great philosophers, orators, jurists, in short, great authors? Why, only those who have striven to speak well. . . . If we will only strive heroically enough, the Roman speech, and along with it every branch of learning, will revive and flourish in its old splendor."

could claim the full sanction of the Renaissance. The authority of Aristotle in philosophy, the authority of Rome in religion had suffered in various ways because they were evidently survivals of a medieval mode of thought that had now for a considerable time been subject to attack and suspicion. They were, even in the least damaging view of them, habitual and routinary. Ciceronianism alone could offer the freshness and charm of modernity combined with unity and simplicity of doctrine.

It is hard for us of the present day to understand the customs of an age in which a rhetorical doctrine made common cause with philosophical and religious orthodoxies, sharing the benefits of their sanctions, and lending them in turn the support of its literary prestige. That this was in fact, however, the relation between Ciceronianism and the other dogmas of learning in the sixteenth century is proved by all the evidence that is necessary. The reader of the correspondence of Lipsius, for instance, will find it impossible to explain in any other way the curious air of mystery and danger in which the Belgian scholar envelops his Anti-Ciceronian, or "Attic," principles. Though he had been converted to these principles before 1570 he did not dare to profess them openly until after 1585.[11] And if we desire a specific illustration of the kind of dangers he dreaded, we need look no further than the indictments drawn up against Ramus by the doctors of the Sorbonne, in which the rhetorical doctrine of his *Ciceronianus* marches *pari passu* with his Anti-Aristotelian logic and his ecclesiastical heresy. The Jesuit teacher quoted by a modern historian, in fact, merely stated a common opinion more incautiously than most when he said that the authority of Cicero in rhetoric, of Aristotle in science, and of Rome in religion would stand or fall together,[12] and of the same substance is Ascham's constant plea that the radical opponents of Ciceronian imitation are undermining the defences of the semi-Protestant establishment of Henry and Elizabeth.

It is just as clear, on the other hand, that Anti-Ciceronianism

---

[11] See *Lipse*, II, pp. 15-17. Even in the 1580's, Lipsius' two letters to Montaigne show caution and concealment.

[12] "As in the study of theology we follow the divine Thomas Aquinas, and in philosophy Aristotle, so in the humanities Cicero must be regarded as our peculiar and pre-eminent leader. . . . But some, misguided by a willful and self-formed taste, have gone astray, preferring a style totally different from that of Cicero; such an erratic course is quite at variance with the genius of our institutions and hostile to the spirit of prompt obedience" (quoted by W. S. Monroe, *Comenius and the Beginning of Educational Reform*, New York, 1900, pp. 7-8).

was associated with the radical and rationalistic tendency in whatever fields of controversy it manifested itself, though there are not here the same signs of concerted *action*—there seldom are in a radical movement—that one may observe among the defenders of the traditional dogmas. The names of the scholars most frequently mentioned in the preceding pages have been chosen, without reference to their rhetorical opinions, as those of the positivist teachers who made the strongest impression on the minds of their successors. It is interesting, therefore, to find that they were all Anti-Ciceronian in theory and practice, and that nearly all of them took some part in the agitation against the Ciceronian dogma. This statement needs no defence in the case of Erasmus. His *Ciceronianus* was almost the Bible of the later movement; for it not only showed the method which was to be employed by all subsequent leaders in the attack upon orthodox style; it was also a model of the easy and fearless competence in the criticism of the ancients which it was their duty to oppose to the deferential purism of the Ciceronian.

Vives and Ramus played a somewhat important role of course in the rhetorical conflict; but the broad scheme of education outlined by the first, founded expressly on the subordination of rhetoric to less academic subjects, was well known to the leaders of liberalism,[13] and the excellent and temperate treatise of the second, named like Erasmus' dialogue, exerted a steady influence throughout the last quarter of the century.

[13] Best described in his *De Tradendis Disciplinis*, 1531. [See the translation by Foster Watson, *Vives: On Education* (Cambridge, 1913) and his ed. of *Vives and the Renascence Education of Women* (New York, 1912); Trimpi, Ch. ii; Atkins, *English Literary Criticism: The Renascence*, pp. 35-65; and *Joannis Ludovici Vivis Opera Omnia* (Valencia, 1782), especially *De Ratione Dicendi* (1533) in Vol. ii. Montaigne's debt to Vives is discussed by William F. Smith in "Vives and Montaigne as Educators," *Hispania*, xxix (1946), 483-493.

The "treatise of the second" mentioned later in the same sentence is probably Petrus Ramus (Pierre de La Ramée), *Dialecticae Libri Duo, A. Talaei Praelectionibus Illustrati* (1560); an ed. by Roland MacIlmaine was published in London in 1574 and one with a commentary by George Downame in 1669. See Frank Pierrepont Graves, *Peter Ramus and the Educational Reformation of the Sixteenth Century* (New York, 1912); René Radouant, "L'Union de l'Éloquence et de la Philosophie au Temps de Ramus," *Revue de l'Histoire Littéraire de la France*, xxxi (1924), 161-192; Norman E. Nelson, *Peter Ramus and the Confusion of Logic, Rhetoric, and Poetry*, University of Michigan Contributions in Modern Philology, No. 2 (Ann Arbor, 1947); Pierre Albert Duhamel, "The Logic and Rhetoric of Peter Ramus," *MP*, xlvi (Feb. 1949), 163-171; Wilbur S. Howell, "Ramus and English Rhetoric: 1574-1681," *QLS*, xxxvii (1951), 299-310, and his *Logic and Rhetoric*, pp. 146-281; Walter J. Ong, S.J., "Hobbes and Talon's Ramist Rhetoric in English," *Transactions of the Cambridge Bibliographical Society*, i (1949-1953), 260-269.]

The "French" school of legal studies and Roman jurisprudence does not occupy a large place in modern histories of sixteenth-century literature, because modern historians are disposed to divide the fields of learning very sharply, and especially to treat science and letters as distinct provinces of human culture. In this respect, however, the sixteenth century itself differed from them, and it is a habit of thought which we shall have to correct if we are to understand the important role that was played by unliterary scholars like Cujas and Budé in the history of modern prose style. It may have been chiefly because they were so realistic and positive in their intellectual purposes that these scholars showed themselves hostile to the rhetorical formalism of the Ciceronian school: they were Anti-Ciceronian, that is, for the same reason that Erasmus and Ramus were. But there was also a reason peculiar to them, which is worthy of a moment's consideration because it opens up a curious and almost unexplored region of literary history. The historical studies of these legalists made them acquainted with some of the most curious forms of written language that the records of the past have to show—the law French of the Middle Ages, for instance, and the special forms it took in England, the legal medieval Latin, more despised by Renaissance Latinists than any other style of the Gothic ages, and, finally, the primitive ancient Latin of the laws of the Twelve Tables. By contrast with the impoverished and regularized Latin of their Ciceronian schoolmasters, there was a rich feast for their fancy, their curious, erudite humor, in the language of these ancient documents—not only in its novel old words, though they took a keen pleasure in these, but also in its licentious, wandering sentence form, phrase added upon phrase in delightful disregard of the rules of classical form. Anti-Ciceronianism thus had a special character and a peculiar charm for these antiquarian scholars, because it meant to them, not a more liberal classicism, or the substitution of one kind of classical model for another, but rather the freedom of individual fancy from academic control; in their own prose they expressed their tastes with exuberant license; and before the end of the century their writings, especially their letters, were being used as models of that "libertine" type of Anti-Ciceronian prose which is at present so much in need of a historian.[14]

[14] The excellent work of Louis Clément, *Henri Estienne et son Œuvre Française* (Paris, 1898, 1899) has a brief discussion of the influence of law Latin on the French and neo-Latin vocabulary, and the ideas on this subject derived by Estienne

And there is another chapter in this story of the connection between literature and the law. In their study of early Roman institutions the masters of historical jurisprudence were of course compelled to study Plautus; and of this necessity they made a literary opportunity. A taste for this author became known as one of their characteristic eccentricities, and finally a kind of shibboleth by which their followers claimed the right of initiation both into the new legal method and into the school of extreme Anti-Ciceronianism. His antique and "rustic" vocabulary was one of the sources from which Muret, Henri Estienne, and Lipsius enriched the modern Latin which the Ciceronians had so impoverished; and he takes his place beside Rabelais and Plutarch and Montaigne among the heroes and models preferred by many writers of libertine prose in the seventeenth century—for example, Gabriel Naudé and Robert Burton.[15]

The scholars whose opinions we have been considering were primarily moralists, social philosophers, legalists, or logicians; not one of them was a professed rhetorician. To explain their common interest in a rhetorical controversy we need not suppose anything resembling a deliberate agreement among them, or even a transmission of ideas from one to another. There is a golden chain wherein the sciences (like the virtues) "linked are y-fere," and they

---

from Guillaume Budé. Concerning Cujas' influence in the movement for freer vocabulary, see below. Budé's *Forensia* (1544), his *Notes on the Pandects*, and his *De Studio Litterarum* (1532) will have to be studied carefully by anyone who should wish to consider the subject.

[15] The following will be useful in the investigation of Plautus' part in the Anti-Ciceronian triumph: Henri Estienne, *De Plauti Latinitate*, appended to his *De Latinitate Falso Suspecta*, 1576; Lipsius, *Quaestiones Epistolicae*, 1577, introd. epistle [also v. 26: "*Idem in hoc scribendi genere est, necessario potest, quam pulchro. At in verbis fui, quam debui, antiquior. Jam enim is sermo aures meas tetigit. Et Plautum, inquiunt, potius sapit quam Ciceronem. Utinam verum dicerent! nam hoc volui.*" See also *Lipse*, II, esp. pp. 16-17, 23-25. Trimpi, pp. 66, 74-75, quotes praise of Plautan style from Lipsius' *Epistolica Institutio* and letters, and, p. 65, cites the high estimates of Plautus held by Jonson and Varro]; Sir Thomas Browne's letter addressed *Amico Opus Arduum Meditanti*, in his *Works*, ed. S. Wilkin (London, 1836), IV, 291-293; Gabriel Naudé, *Syntagma de Studio Liberali* [*APS*, n.64]; Balzac, letter (in Latin) in his *Epp. Sel.*, published with Vavasseur's *De Ludicra Dictione* (Leipzig, 1722). [The influence of Plautus, chiefly but not exclusively in drama, is treated in Marie Delcourt, *La Traduction des Comiques Anciens en France avant Molière* (Paris, 1934). For the influence of the Latin sentence on sixteenth-century style, see Charles Bruneau, "La Phrase des Traducteurs au XVIe Siècle," in *Mélanges . . . Henri Chamard* (Paris, 1951), pp. 275-294.]

are quick to feel anywhere the presence of a spirit hostile or friendly to their mutual purposes. In the sixteenth century, rhetoric was the *nodus* in which their interests were all knit up. As the Ciceronian doctrine was the representative of all the educational orthodoxies, so the opposition to it was the form in which a liberal and rationalizing spirit in any of the sciences could most effectively express itself.

It has been necessary to treat these two great tendencies in sixteenth-century thought at so much length because without a clear understanding of them and especially without a clear understanding of their connection with the rhetorical controversy, it is impossible to interpret Muret's career intelligently. Through failure to grasp the true implications of Ciceronian and Anti-Ciceronian doctrine, it has been possible, as we have seen, to represent the variations of his opinion and practice as the mere whims of a volatile temperament. But in fact the history of his ideas is a steadily unfolding drama of consistent change. Beginning a Ciceronian, establishing in his youth a European reputation which led his patrons to regard him as the probable successor of Bembo, he diverged from this expected course, in the face of much opposition, by a series of steps which can be accurately distinguished, until in middle age he had become a declared Anti-Ciceronian and a pioneer in the development of the rhetorical and intellectual program of the triumphant Anti-Ciceronianism (or "Atticism") of the seventeenth century. His later life was spent in confirming, defining, extending this program. It was a progress, like that of his age, from conventionality to intellectual realism; and his position in it was at the front, often far in front, not among the slowly increasing numbers of the rank and file.

The story of this progress is written in all of his publications and academic labors, and even in some of the events of his career in the world; but it is written most conspicuously and clearly in the long series of orations which he delivered year after year in introducing the courses of reading in ancient literature through which he conducted his pupils; and upon these, interpreted by other evidence, we may safely depend in tracing the interesting course of his intellectual adventures.[16]

[16] See n.7 above.

✧ III ✧

Muret's Progress

At the age of twenty-five years, Marc-Antoine Muret was widely known both in poetry and prose as a better master of Augustan Latinity than any other member of the rising generation of humanists; and his tastes and associations seemed already to have committed him irrevocably to the Renaissance program of rhetorical education. He had been adopted as the intellectual "son" of Scaliger, Erasmus' bitterest literary antagonist; he was supposed to have taken an active part in the persecution from which Ramus was now beginning to suffer; and the fame of his own oratorical style had already signalized him, even beyond the bounds of his own country, as the Ciceronian of the future. In short his intellectual career seemed to be unalterably determined, when, at the age of twenty-eight, disaster overtook him and he began anew in a different scene. He was convicted at Paris and Toulouse of Protestant heresy and of sodomy; he was burned in effigy by public order at the latter city; and he fled from France to begin his career over again in the new Italy that was rising out of the moral and material catastrophes of the previous generation—the Italy of the Counter-Reformation.

We will not discuss the effects of this disaster upon his character and opinions. It may have confirmed in his mind a tendency toward the Machiavellianism of his later political doctrines; for his personal sufferings were in some ways characteristic of the general disturbances which occasioned so wide a diffusion of Machiavellian principles in the later sixteenth century. But biographers are, on the whole, too prone to read the inward life of their heroes in terms of manifest events of their external experience. The crisis in Muret's affairs does not coincide in time with the critical point in the change of his literary teachings and practice that we are to trace in the following pages. It neither caused nor hastened this change, as far as we can see; and it is possible that it tended rather to retard it.

After some weeks of curious and dangerous adventure in the north of Italy, he secured, with surprising ease, from the Venetian Senate, the appointment to the vacant professorship of eloquence at the University of Padua, and preluded his first courses of reading (in 1554 and 1555) with orations *De Laudibus Literarum* . . .

adversus quosdam earum Vituperatores, which have often been
cited in evidence of his blameless Ciceronianism. That he was
Ciceronian at this time they do in fact abundantly demonstrate.
Their perfect elegance of phrase, the conventional beauty of their
cadence, could be illustrated by the quotation of one or two of the
elaborate periods in which they are composed; but to display adequately their poverty of ideas, the suave emptiness of complimentary paragraph after paragraph—so strangely different from
the incisive utterance of the later Muret—would demand a larger
space than we have at our command.[17] The young scholar, in short,
had elected to begin his new career by being what his employers
unquestionably intended him to be, the successor of Bembo in the
Ciceronian tradition; and all of his public acts during the four
years of his incumbency serve to make clear this deliberate choice
of vocation.[18] The works he published at Manutius' press to justify
his new academic honors were either Augustan or impeccably
orthodox: one on Catullus, one on Terence; and he let it be known
that his public readings would be from Cicero's works in every
alternate year as long as he held his professorship.[19]

Is it possible to imagine that Muret was guilty of an elaborate
deception during these four Venetian years? Had he already broken
definitely in his own intelligence with the literary orthodoxy which
he was publicly defending? Was his desire to re-establish his ruined
reputation so strong that he was willing to conform, either in bitter
irony or in pure cowardice, with the opinions of a Senate which
had lately forbidden the reading of Erasmus and Budé in its university and conferred the title of *Ciceronianus* as the crown of
literary achievement? There are two considerations that might lend

---

[17] Muret, *Scripta*, I, Orat. i, ii; 1629 ed., I, Orat. ii, iii. The following is a period
from the 1555 oration:

A quibus ego quoniam ita dissentio, ut ex omnibus, qui se aliquid docere
profitentur, horum vel gravissimum munus esse contendam, neque ullos esse,
qui aut laborum plus perferant, aut majores in republica pariant fructus,
doctrinae denique a nullo hominum genere majorem aut copiam requiri aut
varietatem arbitrer: constitui hodierno die, Patres amplissimi vosqui caeteri
viri ornatissimi, eam mihi ad dicendum materiam sumere, et nobilissimam
studiorum partem, quantum id quidem in me positum erit, a contemptu atque
ab intolerabili ineruditorum hominum insolentia vindicare.

[The fourth last word was erroneously printed in 1924 as *eruditorum*.]

[18] Pietro Bembo, who had died seven years before, had been official historiog-
rapher of Venice.

[19] Dejob (Ch. vi) has strangely distorted the meaning of Muret's Venetian
utterances in a mistaken effort to find a consistency in his career. The only consistency to be found is a progressive change.

color to so unlikely a conjecture. One is the fact that when we find him, settled once more—after an interval of a few years, it is true—in a different kind of situation, he has already gone far from his first opinions. The other is that during his last year and a half in France he had already attempted to establish himself as a teacher of jurisprudence according to the new method of Cujas, and had been hailed by Douaren as a brilliant novice in its mysteries.[20] A man could not consistently be both a Ciceronian rhetorician and a disciple of Cujas! We will have occasion to consider the meaning of both of these facts at a later point. Neither of them however, must be taken as indicating insincerity in Muret's Venetian professorship. It was never his way to truck and huckster in the affairs of the mind; he was capable of an exquisite diplomacy in the accomplishment of his intellectual purposes; but his temperament was too lively and eager to let him conceal them for any great length of time. Indeed it would be possible, if it were worth while, to point out, even in these Venetian orations, the first faint beginnings of his later opinions.

Events happened, however, immediately after this which made him more susceptible to new ideas or encouraged a change which may have already begun, by removing him from the scene on which he had so unhappily committed himself to the policy of reaction. Enemies of Muret asserted, some years after his death, that the cause of his departure from Venice was his continued practice of the vice that had driven him out of France.[21] This is all obscure; and what we know is only that he was taken into the employment of the magnificent Hippolito II, Cardinal d'Este, during the year 1558, and went to reside in his Ferrarese palace. During the next five years he traveled once at least to Rome with his employer and accompanied him in 1561, in the capacity of official orator, on an embassy to his native country, whence he had fled seven years before, an outlawed Huguenot and libertine. Finally in 1563, by the appointment of Pope Pius IV, he became professor at the University of Rome—professor, we note, not of rhetoric this time, but of moral philosophy—and began the course of teaching and

---

[20] Dejob, pp. 48-50.

[21] See *Scaligerana* II [p. 267 in the alphabetized ed. (Cologne, 1695)]; also an unpublished biography of Muret by Guillaume Colletet, used by Dejob, p. 47. [Presumably this was one of the "Vies des Poètes François" which Colletet left in manuscript. See item 2682 in *A Critical Bibliography of French Literature*, III, ed. Cabeen and Brody.]

public discourse which was to occupy him without interruption until his retirement in the eighties. The salary of his post was small; but this was a matter of little importance, as his fellow-scholars enviously observed, because he enjoyed, during almost all of this period, the material luxuries and artistic splendors of Hippolito's palace at Tivoli.

His transplantation meant that Muret had at last reached the center and source of European Catholic culture during the period of the Counter-Reformation. After the disasters which she had suffered during the preceding generation, the city of Rome was undergoing a process of material transformation which exactly corresponds to the change that was taking place in her relation to the culture of Southern Europe. Before her misfortunes she had been the beneficiary of the arts and learning of the Renaissance; but she had not been the original source or teacher of them. Painters, sculptors, poets, and scholars had sometimes brought their various works to adorn the papal city; but the schools in which they had learned to produce them were elsewhere. And this condition was almost a necessary consequence of the non-Christian character of the Renaissance arts as they were practiced at the beginning of the sixteenth century. An art of Latin prose, for instance, which excluded the mention of the Christian titles and offices as one of the conditions of its excellence could not, openly at least, acknowledge the inspiration of the Holy See. But the Reformation had given a check to the cult of Paganism by making everyone vividly aware of it. The secular glories of the high Renaissance could never be renewed; the arts that should adorn the new age must be animated by the spirit of the Catholic revival; their motives and sanctions must proceed from a re-Christianized papacy, as the opportunity for the practice of them proceeded chiefly from the need of restoring the damaged splendors of the papal court.[22]

22 The best description of the effect of the Catholic revival upon the arts is in Marcel Reymond, *De Michel-Ange à Tiepolo* (Paris, 1912), Chs. i-ii. [A vast literature has grown up since 1924 on this matter: the view that seventeenth-century art is essentially related to the Counter-Reformation is implicit throughout Émile Mâle's *L'Art Religieux après le Concile de Trente* (Paris, 1932). For a time scholars tended to identify baroque art with the Counter-Reformation: this view is explicit in Werner Weisbach, *Der Barock als Kunst der Gegenreformation* (Berlin, 1921); see also the section on religious painting in his *Französische Malerei des XVII Jahrhunderts im Rahmen von Kultur und Gesellschaft* (Berlin, 1932). However, the difficulty of restricting the baroque to post-Tridentine Roman Catholicism, excluding Protestants such as Agrippa d'Aubigné, is causing modifications in this view and emphasis on the intimate connection between the

That the culture of the Counter-Reformation must be Christian and Roman was a point of common agreement among the leaders of Catholic policy. But this does not mean that there was unity of literary doctrine or educational program among them. On the contrary, the conflict between the formal classicism of the Renaissance and the "modern," or positivistic tendency of sixteenth-century thought is displayed just as clearly in the Catholic education of this period as in that of the northern countries; and indeed there is no body of writings in which it may be so advantageously studied as in those which proceeded from various representatives of Jesuit education. This is a point which needs to be insisted upon because the history of the literary tendencies of the succeeding century has been confused by the failure to give it the attention it deserves. A number of critics have attempted to show that the authority of the Jesuit teachers was chiefly thrown into the scales on the side of classical purism and the Ciceronian dogma;[23] and there is a huge array of facts and names to be cited in support of their contention. But, on the other hand, an equal weight of evidence has been urged by others in favor of the opinion that the Anti-Ciceronian movement, and particularly the *concettismo* that was one of its offshoots, owed their success to the influence of teachers of the same order.[24] The truth of the matter is that there was no more unity of intellectual purpose among the Jesuits than there was among the Protestant humanists of the North, and it would be as absurd to look for a common tendency among their various educational programs as to try to present a synoptic view of the doctrines of Roger Ascham and Francis Bacon. There was a faction among them, as

---

baroque and the general Christian ethos: see, for example, Imbrie Buffum, *Studies in the Baroque from Montaigne to Rotrou* (New Haven, 1957), pp. 134-135. See also Croll's "The Baroque Style in Prose" and the works listed in connection with it.

Recent studies incline to withdraw the term *baroque* to the later part of the period once covered by that term and to classify its earlier part as *mannerism*. See N. Pevsner, "The Architecture of Mannerism," *The Mint*, ed. G. Grigson (London, 1946); I. L. Zupnik, "The 'Aesthetics' of the Early Mannerists," *Art Bulletin*, xxxv (Dec. 1953), 302-306; W. Friedländer, *Mannerism and Anti-Mannerism in Italian Painting* (New York, 1957); Roy Daniells, *Milton, Mannerism and Baroque* (Toronto, 1963), especially Index, s.v. Counter-Reformation.]

[23] So, for instance, Norden, *Die Antike Kunstprosa*, ii, 779, n.1, where many Jesuit rhetoricians are cited; and B. Borinski, *Gracian und die Hofliteratur in Deutschland* (Halle a S., 1894), p. 54.

[24] See Arturo Graf, "Il Fenomeno del Secentismo," in *Nuova Antologia*, cxix (Sept.-Oct. 1905), 372ff. Graf himself thinks that Jesuitism had little to do with the *secentismo*.

there was in the North, that was devotedly attached to the conservative doctrine of classical imitation; and another that had felt the rationalistic impulses of the time and was groping its way toward the positivistic formula of the seventeenth century: *de re magis quam de verbis*. That the weight of official sanction was always on the side of literary orthodoxy is shown by a great variety of evidence. But, as in other societies, forces were openly at work in literary Jesuitry quite different from those that were officially acknowledged; and the historian of the positivistic movement in prose style has to observe that new phases of this movement constantly come to light within the Order or under its patronage: it is enough here to mention the rhetorical doctrines of Lipsius, Quevedo, and Gracián. In the first half of the seventeenth century, Father Caussin and Father Vavasseur represent that alliance of literary orthodoxy with authoritarianism in politics and religion which was approved by high Jesuit policy;[25] but, on the other hand, Father Bouhours, though he was the professed reformer of the vices of *concettismo* in the following generation, is just as clearly Anti-Ciceronian, or "Attic," as they are conservative and Augustan.[26]

When Muret arrived in Rome in 1563 the conflict of intellectual forces had not yet declared itself there. The teaching in the University and the other educational institutions controlled by the Papacy had been reformed in the sense that it had been brought into harmony with the new moral seriousness of the Counter-Reformation; but it showed no disposition to reform itself in any other sense. The new Jesuit discipline, which was already imposing

[25] See Caussin, *Eloquentiae . . . Parallela* [*Lipse*, n.37 and *APS*, n.44], which is largely an attempt to correct the prevailing Anti-Ciceronianism of the seventeenth century, and Vavasseur, *De Novo Dicendi Genere* [for the proper title, see *APS*, n.59], an oration of 1636, devoted, like Vavasseur's other rhetorical works, to the same purposes. Both writers had a considerable part in correcting the errors of *secentismo* and establishing the dominion of "good taste," though their use of the Latin language has concealed their true importance from most modern critics. [On *good taste* or *goût*, see Charles H. Wright, *French Classicism* (Cambridge, Mass., 1920), Ch. VIII; Bray, as in n.6; Elbert B. O. Borgerhoff, *The Freedom of French Classicism* (Princeton, 1950).]

[26] See the passage from Bouhours, *Les Entretiens*, quoted in the last paragraph of *APS*, III (p. 72); also the quotation from a Louvain Jesuit, Erik van der Putten, in the paragraph preceding this. [Bouhours' significance in the history of *goût* is discussed with bibliographical references by Victor M. Hamm in "Father Dominic Bouhours and Neo-Classical Criticism," in *Jesuit Thinkers of the Renaissance*: *Essays Presented to John F. McCormick, S.J.* (Milwaukee, 1939), pp. 63-75. Georges Doncieux, *Un Jésuite Homme de Lettres au XVIIe Siècle: le Père Bouhours* (Paris, 1886) is still worth consulting.]

itself upon the life of the University, displayed all the familiar signs of intellectual conservatism and academic orthodoxy. During the twenty years of his professorship it was to be Muret's mission to give voice to the new intellectual tendencies of the age at the very center of Catholic education and under the protection of Popes and Cardinals. He was not only a man of mobile intelligence, quick to adapt itself to new perceptions; he also had the active and challenging disposition which leads men to give immediate effect to their ideas in the world about them. The successive steps in the evolution of his own thinking are exactly indicated, therefore, by the controversies in which he was involved; and the history of his activity at Rome during the two decades from 1563 to 1583 is a kind of microcosm in which we can study the rise of positivistic culture in Europe from apparent defeat at the middle of the century to an almost universal triumph at the end.

He was appointed professor of moral philosophy, not of litera-ture; and in the three public lectures with which he inaugurated his courses in 1563-1565 he made clear the deliberateness of his breach with his rhetorical past by discoursing on "the praises," the "neces-sity" of *philosophia moralis*, and the "lauds of justice." The pattern of his style, it is true, is still moderately Ciceronian; in his exordiums he still displays the suavity and copiousness of the epideictic ora-tion; nor is there anything original or challenging in the ideas he expresses. These are productions made to order, with the deliberate purpose of illustrating the moral gravity and elevation that Pope Pius and his Cardinals wish the world to look for in the new art of the Counter-Reformation. Their only significance in Muret's intellectual development is to be found in their subject.[27]

Immediately after his series of readings on the *Nicomachean Ethics* was completed, however, Muret announced another delib-erate change in his intellectual pursuits which might convict him of the volatility which his biographer so readily invokes at hard places in his career, were it not apparent that it was the result of a process of change which had been going on slowly in his mind for a number of years. Muret, as we have already seen, had made an experiment in the teaching of jurisprudence and Roman law during his last years in France, and had rashly attached himself to the new school of Cujas and Douaren. There is even some slight

[27] Muret, *Scripta*, I, Orat. iv-vi; 1629 ed., I, Orat. vii-ix.

evidence to show that he maintained an interest in this suspected subject and in the study of Plautus, which often accompanied it, by discussions in an intimate circle during the years of his professorship at Venice.[28] It is not easy to relate this discordant note to the smooth harmony of his other intellectual interests at this period; and he himself apparently made no attempt to resolve the discord. We can only infer, therefore, that he was unaware at this time of the significance which he afterward came to see in the rationalistic jurisprudence of Andrea Alciati and Jacques Cujas. It appealed to his lively temperament because it was novel and exciting; it appealed to his love of adventure because it was slightly dangerous; but he had evidently not yet observed the connection between the new jurisprudence and the radical movement of the age in moral and political philosophy (perhaps no one had yet seen it quite clearly); and, in particular, he had not discovered a necessary relation between it and the literary tendencies of his day, which after all were his chief interest.

Since his Venetian days, however, his ideas had been undergoing a steady, and partly unconscious, development, and his fortunate encounter with certain works of Alciati and Budé soon after his settlement at Rome had the effect upon his mind of a revelation. The scales fell from his eyes, he says; he awoke to the full consciousness of his former ignorance; and the way he was henceforth to travel lay clear before him. The exact date of this illumination is not clear. But in 1567 he threw down his gauntlet. He announced the Pandects [the abridgement, in fifty books, of the opinions, writings, decisions of ancient Roman jurists] as the subject of his course, and in an initial discourse, composed, we observe, in a wholly new and Anti-Ciceronian manner, rashly asserted that he would henceforth teach no other subject but jurisprudence. He recalls now with pride his youthful adventure in this direction, which in the interval he had been willing to forget, and asserts that his audience is well aware of the causes that have detained him now for so long in the "softer studies" of rhetoric and moral philosophy. (Of course he implies that it was the will of his superiors; but does he not acknowledge that his own enlightenment has been recent?) These other pursuits, he says, have been the wanderings of Ulysses to the caves of the Sirens and the land of the lotus leaf. He has now returned to rugged Ithaca, enriched, it is true, by his adventures,

[28] See Belliviceius' letter, cited in n.7.

but resolved never again to wander from the country of his intellectual birth.[29]

The importance of this conversion, so defiantly announced,
is not to be measured by the value of Muret's contribution to the
science of Roman law; both he and his critics declare that this is
very slight. When his eyes were unsealed, the vision revealed to
him was not of new facts in legal history, but of the new spirit in
which, as he dimly foresaw, the pursuit of letters and learning
would be conducted in the age that was then beginning. The terms
in which he compares his old studies with his new one are such
as we constantly hear from the "strong wits" of the next generation;
and, though he returned before ten years had passed to the subject
of moral philosophy which he had been appointed to teach, it is
clear that from the moment he detected a significant relation between *sapientia* (private wisdom) and *prudentia* (public or worldly
wisdom), on the one hand, and *jurisprudentia*, on the other, he
became a conscious forerunner and founder of the seventeenth-
century positivistic learning.

The bad Latinity of the Barthollist legal commentaries—*illas
mixobarbaras cantiones*, as Muret himself calls them—was notorious; and it had even created a general supposition that the study
of style and the study of law were disjunct and irreconcilable. It
was incumbent upon a man of Muret's literary reputation to show
that this was a pernicious heresy. The necessary union of science
and art, then, may be more or less correctly stated as the subject
of all his four academic discourses of 1567, 1569, and 1571.[30]
This was an interesting and important doctrine, with all the charm
of novelty in the sixteenth century. But what is still more significant
in these discourses is that Muret is here gradually revealing in
public what he was more frankly admitting in private, that his
literary tastes and theories themselves had accommodated themselves to his new zeal for political science and jurisprudence.

[29] 1629 ed., I, Orat. xv: "On the History of his Intellectual Pursuits and the
Necessity of Uniting Eloquence and the Other Subjects of Study with Jurisprudence."

[30] 1629 ed., I, Orat. xv-xviii. These orations and the oration of November,
1565 (described below) are the most significant for the history of Muret's ideas,
being written in an un-Ciceronian style with a spirit and zest which he had not
displayed before. Their omission from *Scripta Selecta*, by which he is now chiefly
known, gives a disproportionate value to the perfunctory orations of 1564 and
March, 1565, and the commanded discourse of 1575 on "The Excellence of
Literary Studies."

This change had, it is true, occurred before his public profession of law. After the three "public" discourses of 1564 and 1565, in which he spoke officially, as we have seen, for the court of Rome, he had delivered another in November of the latter year to a smaller, essentially a "private," audience of his pupils in introducing a second term of readings in Aristotle's *Ethics*; and to any of his hearers who were intelligent enough to understand what Muret meant, the contrast with the epideictic orations which had immediately preceded it must have greatly heightened the effect of this remarkable deliverance.[31] He not only describes admirably the alliance of moral philosophy and political science (*sapientia* and *prudentia*), which was to become, partly through the mediation of his disciples, the educational formula of seventeenth-century rationalism; he also shows what were to be the ideals of the new kind of style which was to accompany this educational program, and even illustrates the methods by which many of his successors in the next age were to teach themselves and others the practice of it. After describing *prudentia* ("policy," as Bacon calls it; political science, as we might say; though perhaps the recent term *Realpolitik* would be more exact) he goes on to say that "we acquire from nature, or at least may easily learn, certain maxims or sentences concerning good and evil, things to be desired and things to be avoided: of which sort are: 'the social laws that bind men together must be observed'; 'justice must be observed'; 'we must abstain from injuring others'; 'to repel force with force is both law and righteousness'; and others of the like sort, which are the rudiments, or as it were the seeds, of the arts necessary to life. From these rudiments springs at last the art that is schoolmistress of life—*prudentia*." The passage is founded wholly upon Aristotle, partly on the *Ethics*, but partly also upon the discussion of the use of "positions," or commonplaces, in the *Rhetoric*, which served as authority for the cultivation of the fixed form of the aphorism, or *pensée*, in the seventeenth century.[32] Who

---

[31] 1629 ed., I, Orat. x, "On the Knowledge of Oneself and on All the Faculties of the Human Mind."

[32] It could be said without much exaggeration that the whole subject matter of Bks. I-II of Aristotle's *Rhetoric* is propositions (κοιναὶ προτάσεις), or Commonplaces; for propositions are the elements of logic or dialectic; and Aristotle's purpose is to establish rhetoric in an intimate, insoluble connection with dialectic. It is for this reason that his treatise was taken as the foundation of Anti-Ciceronian theory in the seventeenth century. On this point see *APS*, pp. 75-77. The passages on which Muret particularly depends, in the passage quoted are I, Ch. 3, sect. 8-9, and perhaps II, Ch. 21 (on the maxim or γνώμη). [The reference here seems

can fail to think of the famous passage in the *Advancement of Learning* in which Bacon, using Aristotle as his monitor, advises the study of the "colours of good and evil" and of *antitheta rerum*, as a great aid in that "politic part of eloquence in *private* speech" which he opposes to the "well-graced forms of speech" of "the greatest orators," and professes that he is indifferent whether this new kind of literary practice ought to be considered a branch of "policy" or of rhetoric?[33]

The style itself of this oration of 1565—its broken period; its deliberate rhetorical roughness, every phrase a thought; its original metaphors, themselves thoughts—what is it but the pure Baconian positivism in rhetoric? A reader familiar with his earlier orations might suppose that Muret is here speaking merely as a *savant* indifferent to the effect of his style, except that a moment later he calls attention, in a challenging manner, to his *quotidiana verba*, his *inornatum dicendi genus*, and appeals, in his peroration, to those, if there be any, who can be captivated by an exact treatment of things "arduous and remote from a vulgar comprehension," who can find a pleasure in discourse that it not grand and *sublimis*, but concerned with matters of daily use and adapted to the needs of real life.

It is clear that in 1565 Muret had already renounced the *genus sublime* and the *genus ornatum* (or *medium*) of ancient rhetorical theory; his literary formulas were already those of the *genus humile*. The effect of his public espousal of the law in 1567 was to commit him more definitely in the same sense; and in his oration of 1569, on the method of teaching law, we find him more "Attic" than he has ever dared to show himself before. The style he now proposes as a corrective to the barbarism of the legalists has the three qualities

---

particularly to be to *Rhetoric*, II.20-21; cf. the discussion of virtue and practical wisdom in *Nicomachean Ethics*, VI.13.]

[33] Bacon, *Works* (1867), III, 411; *Advancement*, ed. Wright, II.xviii.5; in the corresponding passage in *De Augmentis*, VI.iii (*Works*, I, 673ff.) the discussion is extended by the addition of fifty pages meant to supplement Aristotle's *Rhetoric*, I.vi-vii. [Cf. *APS*, nn.18 and 49.] See also *De Aug.* VIII.i-ii (*Works*, I, 746ff.) on Civil Knowledge Touching Negotiation or Business; in the corresponding section of *Advancement* (ed. Wright, II.xxiii.1 ff.; *Works*, III, 445ff.), Bacon employs an extraordinary number of English names to describe what in Latin versions are called *axiomata*, *aphorisma*, or *sententiae*: sentences politic, axioms, aphorisms, precepts, positions (Cf. Aristotle's *Topics*, I.2, I.21, and elsewhere [in *Rhetoric*, II.xxiii he enumerates 28 topics]; all of these English terms and their Latin equivalents are in effect renderings either of Aristotle's κοιναὶ προτάσεις or of his γνῶμαι. Of course almost all of Bacon's own works illustrate the method of writing by aphorisms or "commonplaces."

of the Stoic rhetoric; first, the purity of idiom that can be studied in the conversation of cultivated people; secondly, terseness; thirdly, aptness or expressiveness. The dishes he eats from, he says, need not be of gold; they need not be adorned with jewels and emblems. (He alludes here, in his new metaphorical manner, to the richness of oratory.) He can eat of earthen vessels, provided the viands are fine; but these vessels must be well rubbed (*tersa*), clean (*nitida*), trim in appearance.[34]

Two years later, in 1571, he has made still further progress, spurred on clearly by opposition. He had resolved, he says,[35] to begin his course of legal readings without a prefatory discourse; his friends and patrons protest, however, against so violent a break with custom, and he has yielded on the main point. "But," he says, "that I should take as my theme something, however remote from and alien to our subject, something popular and plausible, in which to display merely verve and copiousness of style (*vim ac copiam dicendi*)—that they should have leave to obtain this of me, I could not obtain leave of myself to grant them. Hardly could I persuade myself to do this when I was young and devoted myself to the rhetorical studies that justify such things. If I should show myself anxious *now* to frise and rouge my style after the manner of boys and sophists, I could hardly escape the reprehension of serious and resolved men." "I mean to discourse, therefore," he continues, "not in the oratorical manner, but in a scholastic, domestic (*umbratili*), and composed manner of our own, not meant to excite but to teach, not planned to catch the clamors of applause, but rather to win the respect of silence and attention."—These are the terms constantly employed by students of Attic in the seventeenth century, and are derived by them from the same critics in antiquity.

In the preceding section of this paper, a connection was traced between the new study of jurisprudence and the Anti-Ciceronian cult of unfamiliar, new or old words.[36] There is evidence to prove that in this phase of the movement Muret played the part of a mediator between the scholarly legalists and the taste of the general public. The fondness he indulged for Plautus is made manifest in his letters and *Variae Lectiones* of all periods; that this was long cherished as a heretical hobby of his unacademic hours is also clear.

---

[34] 1629 ed., I, Orat. xvii.
[35] 1629 ed., I, Orat. xviii.
[36] See above, II, paragraph following ref. to n.13.

When he cites Plautus therefore in the same breath with Cicero, Caesar, and Terence as masters of Latinity in his revolutionary oration of 1569, he is fully aware of the meaning of his words; and we are not surprised at the fact that the first step taken by Lipsius after his conversion from Ciceronianism by Muret (in 1568) was a public profession of his pleasure in the rustic words and the ingenuous style of the old comedian.[37] But we are able to connect Muret's fondness for Plautus directly with his devotion to Cujas and his interest in jurisprudence. There is a letter,[38] from a former colleague at Padua, implying that in a circle of his friends there his project for an edition of Plautus and his study of Cujas' method had been discussed side by side, as if they were closely related; and there is a passage in his *Variae Lectiones* (XI, 17) concerning Cujas himself, in which Muret expresses his delight at the old words with which the legalist has enlivened his pages, and congratulates him on his effort to correct by this means the tendency of Ciceronian purism to impoverish the vocabulary of modern Latin. As Dejob has pointed out,[39] the word *pauperare*, used here by Muret, occurs only in Plautus.

Muret's adhesion to the new rationalistic program of studies did not involve in his own mind a renunciation of his old interest in literature; on the contrary he regarded it as a movement of rhetorical as well as intellectual progress. But the opponents of modernism could not or would not see it in that light. He was under constant pressure to return to the teaching of the subject with which the world even yet persists in associating his name; and when a lectureship in rhetoric fell vacant in 1572[40] he was urged to accept the appointment, without, however, as it would appear, giving up his professorship in philosophy. He yielded on the advice of his patrons and announced as the subject of his first course of reading, Cicero's *Tusculans*, and as the topic of his initial discourse, "the Method of Arriving at Distinction in Eloquence." It seemed a victory for the reactionaries, but if they indulged the hope of his return to orthodoxy on the strength of these promises they had not made sufficient

---

[37] In the Preface to his *Epistolicae Quaestiones*, 1577. On the significance of this see *Lipse*, p. 16.

[38] 1629 ed., I, Ep. xlv.322-323.

[39] 1629 ed., I, 242.

[40] Through the honorable dismissal of an old Professor, Caesareo Cosentino, whose noonhour lectures had long been the scene of notable undergraduate disorder.

allowance for the ironies that Muret was capable of.[41] For this discourse proved to be not only a diatribe against the Ciceronians, but the most telling attack yet delivered upon the conventional academic method of rhetorical teachings.[42]

The general tenor of his remarks on this occasion will not surprise any one who has read the orations in 1565, 1569, and 1571; but the discourse is epoch-making in the history of modern style because here the greatest rhetorician of the second half of the century for the first time openly arrays himself by the side of Erasmus and Ramus; and it is full of interest to the careful student of Muret's career because it shows his advance in several respects toward the complete Atticism of the seventeenth century. In the first place, it contains the first intimations of the leaning toward utter individualism in style, and even toward the "libertinism" of Montaigne, which Muret often displays throughout the rest of his career, though his orthodox past usually holds him back from a free expression of it. "It is no better than an eloquence of Picts and parrots," he says, "to echo and reverberate words you have already heard, nor ever to say anything that is really and peculiarly your own." Muret never rejected in terms the Renaissance doctrine of Imitation; probably he never determined clearly whether he had broken with it in fact; but such words as these show how little hold it retained upon his affections or his imagination. In the second place, he made clearer than before the connection between his literary ideas and his enthusiasm for *prudentia*, or political philosophy. The ancient teachers of style, he says, were masters of the history of institution and laws, were skilled students in the art of government, and prided themselves in the name—not of rhetoricians or sophists—but of politicians (*politici*).

Thirdly—to complete the picture of this striking work—Muret here places the study of rhetoric firmly upon the foundation of Aristotle's treatise, where it was to rest during the century of "Attic" prose which was to follow. Aristotle's *Rhetoric* is a difficult work to

[41] A letter written to a former pupil, Francisco Bentio, indicates the spirit in which Muret went at his new task. After relating the circumstances of his appointment, he says that the additional money has prevailed with him. He will return for a time to those *congerrones* of his youth, Horace and Cicero—*et mihi quodammodo repuerascere videbor*. He adds that those who had expected to hear him continue his exposition of the Pandects are raising a tumult (*Scripta*, II, 65).
[42] *Scripta*, I, Orat. vii; 1629 ed., I, Orat. xxi.

interpret historically; the modern historian finds inconsistencies in it that are hard to explain. But Muret and his successors disregarded these; to them the work meant one thing, an inexpugnable authority, equal in magnitude to that of Cicero himself, to which they could appeal in their effort to divorce prose-writing from the customs of epideictic oratory and wed it to philosophy and science. It is so that Muret interprets the work in this oration. Its teaching is, he says, that rhetoric is "a something that arises (or floats up) out of the mixture of dialectic and politics,"[43] and he cites the passages in which the study of it is brought into connection with the processes of reasoning and feeling and with the proper methods of carrying on a demonstration. Muret, then, derives his *theory* of style here from the first two books of the *Rhetoric*; his doctrines concerning *practice* are drawn from the same work. But here he picks his way carefully, disregarding, as the seventeenth-century "Attics" did, Aristotle's full treatment of the conventional style of oratory in Book III and basing his doctrine on the connection between dialectic and rhetoric elaborated in Books I and II and Chapter 17 of Book III. "As the dialectician," says Muret, "uses two instruments of proof, the syllogism and induction; so the orator, the twin and true comparative of the dialectician,—his exact similitude in a dissimilar *genre*—has two also, each of which corresponds to one of these: the enthymeme, which corresponds to the syllogism, and the *exemplum*, which corresponds to induction. . . . Without a copious supply of enthymemes and *exempla* adapted to every subject matter no one can support the name of an eloquent writer." In these passages is foreshadowed a new method of rhetorical training founded on the use of the *Index Rerum* and the Common-place book, the method of "colours," "positions," and *pensées*, practised by countless seventeenth-century writers, and learned by them, partly from Aristotle, partly from the prose writers of the Roman Silver Age.

The delivery of this public discourse determined Muret's intellectual and literary position unalterably. During the decade of active life that remained to him he was only to carry out toward their logical conclusions the principles he had now arrived at. But before we continue the story of this progress, we must notice a phase of his literary career which has done more than anything else to shadow his reputation and confuse the judgment of posterity

---

[43] See Aristotle, *Rhetoric*, I.ii.7 and I.iv.5. Bacon frequently refers to this doctrine of Aristotle's [e.g., *Advancement*, ed. Wright, II.xviii.5].

concerning his service to modern literature. His position at Rome was more than that of a professor. He was also the official orator of the Roman court; and, as it happened, his activities in this function attained their greatest fame during the years 1571-1572, just at the time, that is, when he was making clear his final emancipation from the rhetorical formalism of the Renaissance. During these years he was called on by his patrons to use the art for which he was famous throughout Christendom in the adornment of three great occasions of public ceremonial: the celebration of the victory of Lepanto in the church of *Ara Coeli*, the funeral of Pope Pius V in St. Peter's in the Vatican, and the reception, probably in the Vatican palace, of an envoy-extraordinary sent by the king of France to lay his fidelity at the feet of the new Pope, Gregory XIII. Muret responded exuberantly to these opportunities to celebrate the glories of reformed Catholicism; and on the third occasion even went out of his way—it would seem—to glorify the massacre of St. Bartholomew's Eve in the most ornate and fulsome rhetoric that the odious art of panegyric could provide him with.[44]

The moral aspect of these performances does not interest us here. Our only concern with them is to show their right relation with the intellectual and literary tendencies that we have been studying and their curious effects upon Muret's literary reputation. Both in their form and in their substance they appear to be in direct conflict with the positivistic movement on which Muret was now embarked. Inasmuch as they are in the oratorical genre, and in a peculiarly inflated and grandiose variety of it, they are hard to reconcile with the professions of one who was teaching the form of an intimate and philosophical *genus humile*; and they have in fact tended to confirm his reputation as a Ciceronian in the minds of those who can conceive of only one type of oratory. Inasmuch as they are apologies of absolution and persecution, they seem to run counter to the liberal stream of modern thought. With the sceptical liberalism of the eighteenth century, which developed out of the "libertinism" of the seventeenth century, they are in fact at complete variance. But we are interested here only in Muret's relation to his immediate successors, the "strong wits" of the seventeenth century; and the orations we are speaking of are in both respects, that is, both in the character of their ideas and in the character of their

---

[44] 1629 ed., I, Orat. xxii (Jan. 1572 Old Style, 1573 N.S.). The others mentioned are Orats. xix-xx (Dec. 1571 and May 1572).

style, representative of one of the most important tendencies of that school.

Almost all of the liberal and sceptical thinkers of the seventeenth century were believers in external conformity. Montaigne and Bacon, Browne and Balzac, for instance, supported the religious and political orthodoxies of their time, though their inward convictions and principles were almost wholly independent of them; and they were all advocates of absolutism in the administration of public affairs. These philosophers, it is true, also believed in a policy of toleration, and most of them played some part in promoting the growth of this modern principle in the mind of the seventeenth century. But there was another mode of thought on this subject, directly opposed to theirs, and on the whole more characteristic of the positivistic movement of ideas in their time. The "strong wits" of the century had in a special degree the weakness characteristic of their kind in all ages, namely, an undue contempt for the conventional sentiments and tender prejudices of the minds that they considered commonplace. They were convinced realists, and applied the principle of "thorough" as firmly in their political and social philosophy as Strafford and Richelieu did in the political practice of two kingdoms. The heroic thinker, the heroic statesman, was in their opinion he who was willing to march rough-shod over the feelings of the weaker part of mankind, or the scruples of his own mind, straight toward a clear-seen goal; and if persecution was necessary to the accomplishment of his ends and the advancement of civilization—well, persecution is justified by the incompetency of mankind in all great matters and large programs.[45]

Muret's eulogy of St. Bartholomew's could give no offense to thinkers of this kind; on the contrary, when it was taken in connection with the rumors of his secret "atheism" which circulated underground in the seventeenth century, it might especially qualify

[45] Concerning this phase of libertine thought, see Paul-Alex Janet, *Histoire de la Science Politique* (Paris, 1872), Bk. III, Ch. II, "L'École de Machiavel"; Charbonnel, Ch. IV, pp. 389-437; Perrens does not deal much with political ideas; see n.6. Fra Paolo [Paolo Emilio or Paulus Aemilius of Verona, author of *De Rebus Gestis Francorum* (1517?)], Lipsius, Gaspar Scioppius [see n.59, below], Naudé, and Gracián are good representatives. Bacon, in spite of what is said of him above, was strikingly Machiavellian, and Descartes somewhat less so. [On political thought see John William Allen, *A History of Political Thought in the Sixteenth Century* (London, 1928); Pierre Mesnard, *L'Essor de la Philosophie Politique au XVIe Siècle* (Paris, 1936); Henri Sée, *Les Idées Politiques en France au XVIIe Siècle* (Paris, 1923). See also the essays on Machiavelli in Joseph A. Mazzeo, *Renaissance and Seventeenth-Century Studies* (New York, 1964).]

him for their admiration. There can be no doubt, for instance, that it won him his place among the *libri homines* of the past venerated by Gabriel Naudé, Guy Patin, François de La Mothe le Vayer and the circles of learned libertines that gathered about them in the middle of the seventeenth century; and it is not improbable that the praise of St. Bartholomew's, which was one of their favorite themes of discourse, was suggested to them by this very work of Muret's. It may not be possible to prove that Lipsius took his notorious formula *Ure et seca* from the same source; but it is certain that the idea it expresses sprang from the general complex of ideas that he derived from his master.[46]

As regards the form in which Muret expressed these dangerous doctrines, it is to be observed, in the first place, that the positivists of the seventeenth century by no means rejected the use of public oratory. On the contrary, though they acknowledged a secret or open contempt for its necessary insincerity, they constantly recommended the study and practice of it as an important instrument in controlling the affairs of the world.[47] The style, however, that they employed was not of the Ciceronian form, but of a form exactly opposed to that, namely a condensed style full of points and aphorisms for which they often professed to find the model in Demosthenes' orations, but which they in fact derived from the study of Roman prose of the first century, and especially from Pliny's *Panegyric to Trajan*. It was a style developed, in fact, from the practice

---

[46] Janet, pp. 95-98; Charbonnel, pp. 53, 58, 617-620; Naudé, *Considérations Politiques sur les Coups d'État* (1639), III, 379-392. [La Mothe, Naudé, and Patin are incisively treated by Pintard and others listed in n.6 above. See also Julien-Eymard d'Angers, "Stoïcisme et Libertinage dans l'Œuvre de François La Mothe le Vayer," *Revue des Sciences Humaines*, LXXV (1954), 259-284; Jean Grenier, "Le Sceptique Masqué: La Mothe le Vayer," *Table Ronde*, XXII (Oct. 1949), 1504-1513; Florence Wichelgren's more conventional, *La Mothe le Vayer, sa Vie et son Œuvre* (Paris, 1934); and the evaluative introduction and critical bibliography in Ernest Tisserand's ed. of La Mothe's *Deux Dialogues Faits à l'Imitation des Anciens* (Paris, 1922); also R. H. Popkin, "Theological and Religious Skepticism," *Christian Scholar*, XXXIX (1956), 150-158. Selections from Patin's works are topically arranged in *Guy Patin*, ed. Pierre Pic (Paris, 1911); the treatment of his ideas is broader than the title suggests in Francis R. Packard, *Guy Patin and the Medical Profession in Paris in the Seventeenth Century* (New York, 1925). Cf. *Lipse*, p. 8, and *APS*, n.64. See also Josephine De Poer, "Men's Literary Circles in Paris, 1610-1660," *PMLA*, LIII (Sept. 1938), 730-780.]

[47] Bacon's opinion is exactly representative. Concerning "that science which we call Rhetoric, or Art of Eloquence," he writes, "For although . . . it is inferior to wisdom . . . yet with people it is the more mighty" (*APS*, n.18). See also his letter to Fulke Greville (signed with Essex's name and cited in *APS*, n.42), advising him about his studies.

of the Stoic *genus humile* of antiquity, but vitiated, as this style is likely to be when it is used for purposes of public oratory, by the tumor which Cicero recognized as one form of Asianism. The style of Muret in the three orations we are considering is exactly in this form; and it is strange indeed that none of the competent classicists who have written of Muret's style should have pointed out its complete contrast with the oratory of his Ciceronian period.[48] How far it is true that these orations set the model of style for the panegyrics of the seventy-five years following—until Bossuet returned to the normal Isocratean model of oratory—it is impossible to say until the history of this form shall have been adequately studied. At least they have the same traits that prevailed throughout that period; they are certainly among the earliest examples of the art of panegyric in which these traits are displayed; and they derive them from the imitation of the same work that was so minutely studied in the succeeding generations, Pliny's *Panegyric*.

We return to the study of the academic orations in which the course of Muret's intellectual development is so clearly depicted. After the discourse on style, delivered in 1572 from a chair of rhetoric, there could be no turning back; he had reached the climax of a long development. But the process of change in his opinions had by no means ceased, and his services to the rising generation were to be even greater in the ten years of activity that remained to him than any that he had yet performed. If we are able to record them more briefly than the former steps in his career, this will only

---

[48] A single sentence will illustrate: "O Catherine, Queen-mother, most blessed of women, who, after she had by her admirable foresight and anxious care preserved for so many years his kingdom for her son, her son for his kingdom, at last beheld this son effectively a king." (O felicissimam mulierem Catharinam regis matrem, quae cum tot annos admirabili prudentia parique sollicitudine regnum filio, filium regno conservasset, tum demum secure regnatem filium adspexit.) [Croll cites the Teubner ed. I, 197, erroneously for this passage; it occurs in the Jacobus Thomasius ed. of the Orations (Venice, 1751), I, 160: Orat. xxii.] The sentence shows exactly the truth of the paradox that a style planned to express acuteness and subtlety of thought falls into a tumor and violence far worse than Ciceronian emptiness when it is used for the purposes of oratory. The vices of sermon style in the reign of Louis XIII and in seventeenth-century England are to be accounted for in this way. [Jacques Truchet makes an excellent survey of sacred eloquence, with bibliography, pp. 309-329 in "Aspects Divers des Questions Religieuses au XVIIe Siècle," a special issue (No. XXIX, Oct. 1955) of *XVIIe Siècle: Bulletin de la Société d'Étude du XVIIe Siècle*. See also Eugène Griselle, *Le Ton de la Prédication avant Bourdaloue* (Paris, 1906); Paul Jacquinet, *Des Prédicateurs du XVIIe Siècle avant Bossuet* (Paris, 1863); *Panegyrics of the Saints, from the French of Bossuet and Bourdaloue*, ed. D. O'Mahoney (London, 1924); works listed in *APS*, nn. 22, 58; *Lipse*, n.17.]

be because their significance is more easily understood in the light of what has already been said.

The defect of the Anti-Ciceronian movement before 1575 was its failure to offer a program of literary imitation in exchange for the one that it attacked. Erasmus himself had failed in this respect; and the reaction toward Ciceronianism noticeable in the third quarter of the century among men like Ascham and Melanchthon, who were the natural inheritors of Erasmus' ideas, was due to the feeling that he had led them out of Egypt into an educational wilderness—and left them there. Abstractly considered—if such questions ever could be abstractly considered—his reference of the choice of models to free individual taste and reason had everything in its favor; the time might even come when it would be a practical method of education. But actually, said Bembo and Ascham, it asked too much of men living in the sixteenth century. Whatever the theory of education might be, such men, they argued, must hold to the practice of imitation in their effort to learn the classical mode of thought; imitation, moreover, of prescribed models and by a defined method. And history has proved that they were right. For it was not until it had learned to suggest other models for imitation in place of Cicero and Isocrates, as it did in the last quarter of the sixteenth century, that the Anti-Ciceronian movement became a positive force and began its career of triumph.

What these models must be seems clear enough to the historian, who can look both before and after the event. For the range of choice was limited. Greek models of the classical period were out of the question because Greek education had so far proved impracticable for any but a small band of *savants,* and was declining rather than gathering power; and in Latin the poverty of the pre-Augustan ages in literary prose and the marks of approaching decay and medievalism in most of the literature produced after 200 A.D. were facts too evident to be overlooked. The only escape from the superstitious purism of Augustan imitation was in the literature of the first century of the empire, in the poetry of Lucan and Juvenal and Persius, and especially in the splendid prose of Seneca, Tacitus, and the younger Pliny, or in the Greek prose classics of the same period which had been made available by translation, Plutarch and Epictetus. Both philosophically and rhetorically, we can now see how admirably adapted this literature was to the needs of the seventeenth century; but the facts of a situation are never so clear to those who are involved in all its actual complexities as they are to the historian; and the duties of a prophet and leader were made more difficult in this case by the fact that the Latin writers of the first century were imputed dangerous to good Latinity, good morals, and good political philosophy. It required both the clearsightedness of a prophet and the courage of a warrior to proclaim a rehabilitation of the Silver Age in the third quarter of the sixteenth century.[49]

The honor of effecting, or at least initiating, such a program must be divided between Montaigne and Muret, who were arriving, at the same time, but by different processes, at the same conclusions. There was neither correspondence nor co-operation, however, between them;[50] and though Montaigne's ideas had vastly greater results in the course of time on the general opinion of the world, Muret's immediate influence upon the learned classes was greater, and the conspicuousness of the post in which he challenged and suffered attack may justify us in attributing to him a higher degree of courage. The gradual discovery and proclamation of this literary program was the work of his last decade. During this time he forgot his vow to jurisprudence; and indeed it is now clear that that stirring episode in his career, important as it was in the development of his ideas, was a following after false fires. He had long been seeking a formula to express his new intellectual needs, and the reformed study of law had for a time seemed to be the true center of all his desires. But it proved to be too special a theme for his peculiarly impatient mind; and it was not until he embraced the cause of Silver-Age literature that he found the single and significant word to express at the same time his political, his moral, and his literary philosophy.

It remains for us only to trace rapidly the course of this last development of his thought, by which he earns the title of the chief founder of the theory of Attic prose in the seventeenth century.

The first post-Augustan author to attract him was naturally the younger Seneca. But he could not proceed at once with the development of his true intellectual purposes after his declaration of opinion in 1572. The requirements of his new rhetorical post had

[49] For a fuller statement of the relations between seventeenth-century and first-century literature, see *APS*, VI.

[50] The fact that Muret was Montaigne's house tutor for a time, when Montaigne was a boy, probably has no especial relevance.

to be acknowledged. In 1573 he delivered a purely ceremonial oration for some important anniversary day of the University, on the theme—commanded, as he is careful to say, by the authorities—of the excellence of literary studies. Then he begins the reading of Plato's *Republic* during the winter term of 1573-1574, protesting against the opposition that is being made to his program, and renewing his praise of Aristotle's rhetorical principles. All this he continues in the spring term of 1574,[51] and his plan was to pursue the study of Plato in the following winter; but the authorities—whose reasons for their conduct it is not becoming in us, he says, to inquire into—have ordered him to devote the year to Cicero alone. His characteristic revenge is to renew his Anti-Ciceronian pledges and cite the authority of Cato beside that of Aristotle; and it is in the prelude oration of this course that we first detect the influence of Seneca clearly. For the first time the terms in which he describes the Anti-Ciceronian style are drawn from that author—though he does not mention his name—and his style betrays the influence of Seneca's brief antithetical sentences. *Vera et solida eloquentia,* he says, *non tantum in verbis posita est, sed in rebus.*[52] In the following year he gives a course in the *De Providentia,* preluded with a discourse in which he begs his auditors not to let their minds be poisoned by the reproaches they constantly hear directed against this author.

A word of explanation concerning these reproaches is necessary. Seneca was one of the ancients who needed least to be interpreted by the humanists of the Renaissance. His works had come down through the Middle Ages almost unimpaired and constantly studied; and in the fifteenth and sixteenth centuries the employment of them by teachers for the practical purpose of moral instruction continued without interruption. Probably it is in these facts that we are to find one of the reasons for his hard treatment by the rhetorical humanists. His long popularity had given him an air of medieval vulgarity; and his moral usefulness made the supposed defects of his Latinity peculiarly dangerous. It was a literary prejudice, therefore, that he had to overcome in order to take his place as the model and mentor of the new generation, and the chief significance of

---

[51] See the orations for these courses, 1629 ed., II, Orats. iv-v (not in *Scripta*).
[52] 1629 ed., II, Orat. vi, *Ingressurus Explanare M. T. Ciceronis Libros De Officiis.* [Montaigne paraphrases this statement in his essay "Considération sur Cicéron."]

147

Muret's oration about him is that it portrays him as a master of eloquence and wisdom alike, and an exemplar of that new style to which Muret was inviting his pupils—*ad graves et serias res bonis et lectis verbis explicandas.*[53]

In this oration Muret gives no hint of a purpose of rehabilitating the authors of the Silver Age, or even of a preference for any of them as such. But in the autumn of the same year this purpose has evidently taken definite form in his mind. He has elected to study the Thirteenth Satire of Juvenal, and in the first words of his discourse throws out a challenge to those who disapprove of the study of the authors of his age. He begins the discussion of this prejudice with a sketch of the history of culture since the beginning of the Renaissance—perhaps one of the earliest attempts to place the Renaissance in its historical relations.[54] The first effect, he shows, of the Renaissance was to create an indiscriminate classical erudition, in which the more obscure and difficult authors were even preferred, because of their novelty and the neglect of the Middle Ages. Then followed the generations of the Bembos and Sadoletos,[55] by whom the hands of the clock are set as far wrong in one direction as they had been before in the other. For now "no prose authors are allowed except Cicero and his contemporaries; all poets are dubbed barbarous save Virgil, Catullus, Lucretius, and three or four others"; and the whole effort of teachers is spent in proving that "silly orations may be made by using no words but Cicero's, bad verses of none but Virgil's." Writers of modern Latin, who have never heard a Roman speak, have become so infatuated that they prefer their own writings to the Latin of Silius Italicus, Lucan, and Seneca. They dare to despise Ovid, next to Virgil the best of Latin poets; and one of them has translated his works into the vernacular for his pupils' use, for fear their Latinity might suffer contamination

---

[53] 1629 ed., II, Orat. iii (misdated 1585).

[54] 1629 ed., II, Orat. xii; *Scripta*, I, Orat. xi. A similar sketch, possibly influenced by Muret's, will be found in Bacon's *Advancement* (ed. Wright, I.iv.2): this account of "the first distemper of learning, when men study words and not matter," is Bacon's sketch of the causes of Ciceronianism in the sixteenth century; he supplements it interestingly in *De Augmentis*, I, noting the rise of the Anti-Ciceronian movement and the imitation of Seneca and Tacitus since 1600 [for the text, see *Lipse*, n.40]. A similar and longer account occurs in John Barclay's *Satyricon* (Leyden, 1674), 90-95. Of course the late term "Renaissance" does not appear in Muret, Bacon, or Barclay.

[55] [Cardinal Jacopo Sadoleto.]

from his.[56] In fact, says Muret, in a fine frenzy raging, the cooks and mule-drivers of any of these ancients could write better Latin than a modern Latin rhetorician.

Muret, in short, has made another clear step forward in the formulation of his ideas. Though he may still choose the names of Ciceronians to point his scorn, the object of his attack is now the theory of Augustanism *in toto*—and that in a public oration. How much further he could go, how much franker he could be, when he was less hampered by conventional necessities, is shown by a long essay in one of the later series of his *Variae Lectiones*,[57] in which he reports a conversation with a young friend. Here Muret admits that he himself had once believed that only the Augustans should be imitated. But at a later time, when he had considered the matter more fully, he came to see how presumptuous it would be in him to pass judgment on the style of writers like Seneca, Valerius Maximus, Quintilian, Pliny, Tacitus, Vellius Paterculus, Firmianus Lactantius, and others of that kind who had lived so near to the time when Latin flourished at its best, and had been considered excellent writers at that time. Certainly, he says, none of the ancients ever accused them of writing faulty Latin. In this list he hardly extends his charity beyond the limits of the Silver Age (as it came to be called in the generation following Muret). But a little further on in the same essay he takes a flight which has caused his commentators and admirers the greatest concern. He describes the method of teaching and practicing style which was later to be taken up and much more fully developed by Lipsius in his treatise on style in letter writing.[58] His plan is, he says, to derive the general form of his style from Cicero, Caesar, Terence, and others of the best kind; but then also to imitate and adapt whatever beauties he can find that other writers have excelled in; and he will look for these beauties, he adds, not only in the authors of the Silver Age, but even in

[56] This association of Ovid with the writers of the Silver Age is interesting; in the seventeenth century Ovid and Sallust were generally recognized as the only Augustans who displayed the traits of style of the succeeding century and were therefore worthy to rank with Tacitus, Seneca, and Lucan as models of "Attic" style.

[57] xv.2; in *Scripta*, Ch. LVIII.

[58] *Epistolica Institutio*, esp. the concluding chapter [see n.66 below and *Lipse*, II, second paragraph following n.20]. Barclay (*Satyricon*, pp. 96-97) gives a similar method of teaching as his own. In fact, it may be considered the typical Anti-Ciceronian method.

Tertullian, Saint Jerome, Saint Augustine, or Saint Ambrose, and, yes, even in Apuleius, Sidonius Apollinaris, and Cassiodorus. There was nothing here to cause disturbance of mind to the Stoic or Libertine writers of the first half of the seventeenth century; for Tertullian at least became almost as great a favorite of a number of them as Seneca and Tacitus themselves. But commentators who were resolved at any cost to retain the authority of Muret on the side of orthodoxy were guilty of strange contortions in the attempt to rob these words of their sting. It was argued, for instance, that Muret put in this passage in order to have an excuse if he should by mistake have used any words or phrases that were not Ciceronian; and a comparatively recent commentator has been found to accept this explanation as correct.[59]

Another work of post-Augustan rehabilitation remained for him to perform, the most difficult and dangerous, but also the most congenial to his tastes and temperament. When he first contemplated the teaching of Tacitus, we cannot exactly determine; for he seems to have entered into a kind of truce with the orthodox party after his readings in Seneca and Juvenal, and the subjects of his courses during the next four years (1576-1579) were Aristotle, Virgil, and Sallust. But the fact that Lipsius applied himself to the editing of Tacitus immediately after his momentous visit to Muret in 1568 is not without significance; and a careful study of the orations of the period from 1576 to 1580 makes it clear that he was veiling with an appearance of conformity the preliminaries of a more startling offensive moment than any that he had yet attempted. His aim in all of these discourses is evidently to relate as closely as possible the several subjects he is now interested in: dialectic, history and politics (*prudentia*), and rhetoric, and to try to organize them into a definite program or curriculum of positivism. This purpose is apparent, for instance, in his Sallust discourse; and in the two orations of 1576, on the subject of Aristotle's *Rhetoric*, he has worked out much more fully than he did in 1572-1573 his conception of the uses of the *genus humile*, founded on the doctrines of that treatise. For the first time, too, he has here expressed or hinted the prophetic opinion that obscurity may be a virtue of style.

When he finally announced that his winter term subject for

---

[59] David Ruhnken, quoted in *Scripta*, II, 203, n.3. It was Gaspar Scioppius, in his *De Stilo Historico*, p. 64, who originally expressed the idea; see also his *De Rhetoricam Exercitationum Generibus* (1660).

1580-1581 would be the first book of the *Annals* of Tacitus, the storm he must have anticipated broke upon his head. The opposition from the authorities which he had met at every step in his progress from Ciceronianism to "Atticism" now became more acute. His overture-oration was a general and moderate defence of Tacitus; but it evidently roused his opponents to new energy, and there are hints that disorders in his classroom were fomented by their machinations. Muret was never diverted from his intellectual ends by persecution, though he was capable of Machiavellian policy in the pursuit of them; and on this occasion he returned to the defence of Tacitus in a second oration which is distinguished among all his productions by the originality of its thought and the energy of its style, and must be considered his most important contribution to the history of modern thought.[60]

Its abrupt beginning, "Those who have been attempting to debar me from the interpretation of Tacitus have brought five particular charges against him," was itself a challenge to the Ciceronian taste for copious and mellifluous exordiums; and he proceeds to consider the five objections in a discourse in which, for the first time probably in the Latin of a modern author, the pointed brevity, the studied asymmetry of Tacitus' own style are successfully imitated. It is unnecessary to follow his argument *seriatim*; but in answering the charges against his new hero he makes some observations so significant in the history of the ideas and the literary style of the succeeding century that they should be rescued from the obscurity in which they have been allowed to remain.

The most serious of all the scandals that attached themselves to the cult of Tacitus during the period from 1575 to 1650 was the alleged use of his writings as a manual of Machiavellian policy, especially by the supporters of the regime of absolutism in church

[60] This oration (ed. Leipzig, 1629, Orat. xiv) is dated November 4, 1580 (the day following his first Tacitus oration, II, xiii, in ed. Leipzig, 1629) in the early, and hence also in the modern editions; but for a number of reasons it seems to me likely that it was delivered in March, 1581, at the opening of a second term of reading in the *Annals*, probably in the Second Book. In November, 1581, he continued with the Third Book, thus completing a *triennium* in one author: his favorite method, as he had recorded. As regards the disorders in his classroom, Norden attributes them to Jesuit instigation; but Norden has falsely read the Jesuit literary doctrine as uniformly Augustan and Ciceronian; see above, pp. 6-7 [*sic*: Croll seems to refer to the pages of his original manuscripts, for no such pages occur in the 1924 publication. Presumably he has in mind pp. 130-131 and n.23, above.] At this time Muret's most intimate friends and some of his favorite former pupils were important members of the Order.

and state. The parallel that was constantly drawn during this period between the affairs of the Roman Empire as described by Tacitus and the contemporary affairs of European states[61] was as constantly (and justly) denounced by the lovers of liberty as an insidious corrupting influence in political thought. Well, Muret meets the charge with an astonishing frankness in a passage which must be quoted at length as an illustration of modes of thought that were to become extremely common in another generation.

In the first place [he says] it must be observed that there are very few republics to-day; there is almost no nation but hangs upon the beck and nod of one man, obeys one man, is ruled by one man: therefore in this respect at least the state of things in our time is more like that of Rome under the Emperors than when the people had the power. And the more like their history is to ours, the more things we may find to study in it that we can apply to our uses, and adapt to our own life and customs. Although by the blessing of God we have no Tiberiuses, Caligulas, and Neros, yet it is profitable for us to know how good and prudent men managed their lives under them, how and how far they tolerated and dissimulated their vices; how, on the one hand, by avoiding an unseasonable frankness they saved their own lives when they would have served no public end by bringing them into danger, and on the other hand showed that baseness was not pleasing to them by not praising things in the conduct of princes which a good man cannot praise, but which he can cover up or pass by in silence. Those who do not know how to connive at such things not only bring themselves into danger, but often make princes themselves worse. For many men, if they believe that their vices are concealed and unknown, gradually get out of them of their own accord, for fear they will be detected, and *become* good from thinking that they are *considered* good.[62] These same men, however, if they see that their baseness is recognized, their reputation fixed, will openly live up to what they know is openly said of them, and become indifferent to a bad reputation because they despair of a good one.[63] And again, a man

---

[61] E.g. in the essays of Bacon, Gracián, and Virgilio Malvezzi [1595?-1653?, author of discourses on Tacitus].

[62] An excellent Tacitean "point": *Dum se bonos haberi putant, boni fiunt.*

[63] Eidem si turpitudinem suam palam esse videant, jam famae securi, quae

(of the present time) will the better bear the fewer and lesser vices of his own princes, when he has observed how the good and brave men of a former day endured worse and more numerous ones.

This is a language quite familiar to students of Bacon, Malvezzi, Gracián, Naudé, and many other strong wits and Machiavellians of the seventeenth century.

In all of these authors, moreover, the love of Tacitus' singular wisdom is attended by a love of his significant darkness of utterance; for the *prince des tenèbres*, as they called him in the seventeenth century, was the chief model of the use of the conceit in prose. Muret deals as boldly and prophetically with this aspect of his author's reputation as with the other. On the subject of the "debased Latinity" of the Silver Age he had already made himself clear enough, and the only notable addition here is a statement to the effect that the lower limit of good Latinity is the reign of Hadrian. But in answering the charge of obscurity and harshness brought against Tacitus, he stirs the ground about the roots of seventeenth-century style; the peculiar merits and also some of the faults of the prose of Bacon, Donne, Greville, Browne, of Quevedo and Gracián, of Balzac and La Bruyère, and even of Pascal, are foretold in the novel and dangerous ideas he here expresses. After saying that the Greeks recognized his obscurity as one of the virtues of Thucydides, he goes on:—

> For although a bare and clear style gives pleasure, still in certain special kinds of writing *obscurity* will win praise sometimes. By diverting discourse from common and vulgar modes of expression, it wins a dignity and majesty even out of strangeness (*peregrinitas*) and grips the reader's attention.[64] It acts as a veil, to exclude the view of the vulgar. Thus those who enter the dark crypt of a temple feel a kind of awful solemnity sweep in upon their souls. *Asperity* of style, again, has almost

---

palam dici vident, palam quoque faciunt, et famam dum bonam desperant, malam negligunt.

[64] The idea of a style meant for readers, as contrasted with hearers, was new and anticipates Attic theory of the seventeenth century. See *APS*, n.19. [Williamson (*Senecan Amble*, pp. 122-123), notes how the passage here quoted by Croll "found its way into late seventeenth-century English from the work of La Mothe le Vayer."]

the same property as bitterness in wine: which is thought to be a sign that the wine will bear its age well.

In short, Muret has stated admirably in this oration all the chief causes of the popularity which Tacitus was now beginning to enjoy. He has left little to say; and in his third Tacitean discourse, in November 1581, he devotes himself to the praise of three other Post-Augustans: Plutarch, chiefly, and Seneca and Pliny, thus practically completing his task of the rehabilitation of the prose of the Silver Age.[65]

One other task, however, he had still to perform in the service of the new Attic prose: the discovery of the genre in which it best displays its peculiar merits. The discourse in which he introduced his students to a reading in Cicero's *Epistolae ad Atticum* is chiefly an argument to show that the only practical use that can now be made of rhetorical skill is in the writing of letters. He sketches again, as he had done once before, the history of culture in the Renaissance, and shows that though the Ciceronians had attained to excellent eloquence (though partial) there is no modern author "to whom simply and unexceptionably one can give the praise of *writing* Latin well." He commends, however, two writers of epistles, Giovanni Casa, and his friend Paulus Manutius [Paolo Manuzio], and then proceeds, after an invocation to his young hearers' love of dangerous truth, to show that the practical uses of oratory have ceased in the present state of society. For the decision of great affairs is no longer made in open senates or even in open law courts, but in the cabinets of single men (of course he means princes and their ministers). Of the three uses of oratory described by Aristotle, therefore, but one now remains, the epideictic: school disputations, sermons, panegyrics, and funeral orations. On the other hand, the writer who nowadays may hope to be admitted to the intimacy of princes and a part in the serious and great business of the world is one who has learned to write with charm and wisdom letters exactly adapted to the facts of the case, the character of the persons involved, and the actual state of society (*ad res, ad personas, ad tempora*).[66]

[65] On Bacon and Tacitus see my article: "Lipsius, Montaigne, Bacon" [i.e. *APL*, IV, (a)].

[66] *Scripta*, I, Orat. xvii; 1629 ed., II, Orat. xvi. See also his letter concerning the collection and publication of his own letters (1629 ed., I, Ep. I.i; *Scripta*, II, Ep. 1). Those who may wish to study the new literary significance of the letter at the

Muret's work was now complete. He had traveled all the way from sixteenth-century rhetorical culture to the naturalism of Montaigne, Lipsius, and Bacon; and in his latest discourses had illustrated a new art of prose, as somber in mood, as heightened in emphasis, as the new sculpture, painting, and architecture devised in his time to express the spirit of the Counter-Reformation. And now, in the last act of his career, his withdrawal from the public scene, he was to show once more how sensitively he felt the spirit of the changing age in which he lived. One of the most striking signs of the spiritual transformation of Europe in the period from 1575 to 1650 was the voluntary withdrawal of so many of its representative men from the affairs of the world, to seek unity of mind and moral self-dependence in a contemplative retirement, either philosophical or religious. The external activities of the Renaissance had lost the power to satisfy their minds; it was an inward weakness that demanded their attention. To the list of these students of wisdom must perhaps be added the name of Muret. In or about the year 1573 he had taken holy orders, and the latter years of his life were lived in complete sobriety and with an attention to the duties of Christian observance which—there is every reason to believe— reflected the true state of his mind. Finally in 1584 he requested and obtained his release from academic duties, refused a professorship urged upon him by Bologna, and spent the few remaining months of his life in domestic retirement with a nephew, the son of a brother

---

beginning of the seventeenth century will find interesting points in the following: Lipsius, *Institutio Epistolica* in his *Opera Omnia*, 4 vols. (Wesel, 1675), II, esp. 1083-86 [Croll refers to this work as *Epistolica Institutio* when he describes and quotes from it in *Lipse*, II, p. 23; it was written in 1590 and was appended to *Justi Lipsi Epistolarum Selectarum* (Antwerp, 1605); previous citations made by Croll were usually from *Opera Omnia* (Antwerp, 1637), II; cf. *Lipse*, nn. 24, 26, 27, 30]; Étienne Pasquier, "Lettres," I.1, citing Erasmus, Budé, and Politian as models, and x.12, citing Cyprian, Jerome, and (chiefly) Seneca, in *Œuvres* (Amsterdam, 1723), II; a very interesting letter by Donne in *Life and Letters of John Donne*, ed. Edmund Gosse (London, 1899), I, 122-123, and another extraordinary one, I, 168; Joseph Hall, *Epistles in Six Decads* (London, 1608), epistle dedicatory to Prince Henry; Bacon's intended dedication to Prince Henry of the 1612 ed. of his *Essays* (Bacon's *Letters and Life*, ed. Spedding, IV, 340). In all of these the novelty of the letter as a literary genre is insisted on or implied. As an intimate and "moral" form, like the essay, it was in fact new, and was associated in all minds with the "Attic" tendency. See a passage in Victor Fournel's *De Malherbe à Bossuet* (Paris, 1885), p. 54. [See also Dunn, "Lipsius and the Art of Letter Writing"; Jean Robertson, *The Art of Letter Writing* (Liverpool, 1942); Katherine Gee Hornbeak, *The Complete Letter-Writer in English, 1568-1800* (Smith College Studies in Modern Languages, xv, nos. 3-4); Trimpi, Ch. III, "The Epistolary Tradition"; Williamson, *Senecan Amble*, pp. 136ff.]

who had died some years before, and in so strict an intimacy with several Jesuit friends that an opinion—probably false—became current that he himself had joined their order.

One of his aims in seeking quiet and leisure was undoubtedly to contribute some lasting work of erudition to the cause for which he had spent so much active energy as a teacher. He in fact completed his Latin translation of the first two books of Aristotle's *Rhetoric*; but his commentary on all the works of Seneca was interrupted by his death in June 1585, and the glory of domesticating the Stoic philosopher in the seventeenth century remained to Lipsius, Muret's greatest disciple.

✧ IV ✧

Muret's Reputation

A number of leaders of European culture in the post-Renaissance period, the period, that is, from 1575 to 1660, have been restored of late years to the honors due to them: Lipsius, for instance, as the founder of Neo-Stoicism in thought and style; Donne as the voice of a new age in poetry; Donne, Quevedo, and Gracián as masters of a new art of prose style; El Greco and Bernini in the other arts. That Marc-Antoine Muret has not taken his proper place in the history of this period is partly due, no doubt, to the fact that he was primarily an oral teacher. He left no very substantial and extended works as monuments of his doctrines, and a great deal of his influence passed into the works of others without being expressly recorded as his. There are several other important reasons, however, for the confusion and misapprehension that early settled down upon Muret's reputation, and have finally left him in modern times the mere shadow of a name as a rhetorician and the champion of the cause of Augustan purism which he spent most of his life attacking! Without some attention to these special circumstances we can hardly have a clear conception of his career.

His position in the world was unfavorable, not indeed to the dissemination of his doctrines, but to the open recognition of his influence. In the century of the Reformation, when sectarian partisanship colored all intellectual opinion, in the part of this century, moreover, when the leadership in humanism was rapidly passing from the South to the North and both sections had become aware of this new condition, a professorship at Rome and the open patronage of Cardinal d'Este and Pope Gregory were not points of vantage for a disinterested teacher of new ideas. Muret, moreover, suffered in Protestant countries, and, especially, in France, the peculiar suspicion and dislike that fall to the lot of the renegade. There is some doubt, it is true, whether he was actually—as it was charged in the indictment that drove him out of France—a Huguenot; but he had been a house pupil of the elder Scaliger; his associates, it seems, had been chiefly of that sect; and it is clear that the malice of the younger Scaliger in some public utterances concerning him are due to the memory of these early experiences. Even Lipsius, who was professor at the Calvinistic University of Leyden when he visited Muret at Rome, and remained in that position for ten years afterwards, during all that time carefully veiled much of what he learned from Muret. Only in letters, did he reveal the full change of his opinions and the cause of it.

Muret was unquestionably a *literary* renegade, and the literary world has never yet recovered from the confusions and obstinate perversions of opinion concerning him into which it fell, even during his lifetime, as a result of the change of his ideas during the years from 1558 to 1568. A few men of his own age, a good many men twenty or thirty years younger than he, made the same change, some of them much more abruptly than he; but none had to execute the dangerous *volte-face* on so exposed an eminence or after so express a commitment; and the world could never quite learn that the successor of the tradition of Bembo had become an Anti-Ciceronian and the rehabilitator of Seneca and Tacitus. In Germany and the Netherlands, particularly, it appears that his rhetorical reputation kept growing after he had cut its taproot, partly because the "new learning" that he had espoused was slower to be understood there, partly through a deliberate unwillingness to renounce a model of pure style which had already found its way into the schools. There were amusing efforts to conceal or even to deny that Saul also was among the prophets of a new style. Joseph Juste Scaliger was no less than disingenuous in his admiration for Muret's early Ciceronian prose and his disregard of all the prose of his maturer years; for he at least must clearly have understood the significance of Muret's change of literary opinions.[67] And one hardly

[67] There is no way of explaining the younger Scaliger's various opinions about Muret except by assuming a constant interplay of malice and intelligent admiration in his mind. Thus he says that Muret could write excellent prose style (it is clear

knows what to make of the argument by which Gaspar Scioppius
(echoed by other Germans) attempted to find in his Anti-Augustan
tirades a subtle expression of Ciceronian orthodoxy.[68] Curious but
not unjust return of the extravagance of an ironist upon his own
head! In Germany and England, at all events, the youthful Muret
won the victory over the mature man, and his early Ciceronianisms
kept their place in the educational curriculum of many schools, it
is said, until the end of the eighteenth century—a fact exactly paralleled in the study of Cicero himself in the sixteenth century, when
the first two orations were regularly studied in England and Germany as the best models for imitation, though Cicero in his mature
years regretted their style as too Asian.[69]

Even in Anti-Ciceronian quarters Muret met the kind of ill-luck
that often attends the man who changes. It is frequently seen in
politics, science, and all kinds of affairs that the originators of
programs and policies lose the credit of their achievements merely
because men hate to associate themselves with a name blown upon
by violent controversy; the policy lives while its author is repudiated. Muret's radicalism in thought and letters was made the mark
of obloquy by the reactionary party at Rome, because the European
reputation he had won by his early Ciceronian style could so easily
be turned against him; the contest became confused with other than
literary kinds of partisanship; violent and irrelevant prejudices were
aroused; and on the whole men found it safer to avoid Muret's
name than to explain their indebtedness to him. An illustration of
how his reputation was obscured a generation after his death may
be seen in Boccalini's, *I Ragguagli di Parnaso*,[70] where Lipsius is
presented to Apollo for the honors of literary immortality by Velleius Paterculus and attended by "Seneca the moralist" and "Tacitus

that he means *Ciceronian* excellence), if only he had not chosen sometimes to
write in different modes; yet there are sayings in the *Scaligerana* that show how
well he understood Muret's later stylistic aims and how much he admired his later
style; e.g. in *Scaligerana* (The Hague, 1668), II, 235-236: *Muretus optime percepit
mentem Aristotelis in Rhetoricis*, and *Quid elegantius ejus oratione de Tacito aliis?*
[For other sayings see "Muret," in the alphabetized ed. (Cologne, 1695), where
the quoted passages occur on pp. 276-278. Cf. *Lipse*, n.35.]

[68] See above, n.59.

[69] Another interesting parallel in the criticism of Lipsius:—C. Nisard, himself
a Ciceronian of the old school, commends the style of Lipsius' first work, *Variae
Lectiones*, as the best he ever wrote (*Le Triumvirate Littéraire*, p. 7: see *Lipse*,
n.1). Having been converted by Muret soon after its publication, Lipsius always
looked on it as a youthful error.

[70] (Milan, 1614), I, 23. [See *APS*, n.57.]

the politician," one riding on either hand. Here the whole program of realistic studies and late Latin rehabilitation is transferred from the master to the disciple who learned it of him.

The most important cause, however, of the depression of Muret's reputation was the character of his opinions. In the rapid development of rationalistic thought that went on during the last quarter of the sixteenth century, two strains soon made themselves apparent: a general movement of scepticism, or, as it was more commonly called, libertinism, and a revival of the Stoic morality of the ancients. The former of these is probably to be regarded as the more important in the history of modern thought: it was in the form of libertinism that the rationalist movement first attained to full consciousness of itself in the last quarter of the sixteenth century; this was the form, too, in which it finally triumphed and produced the philosophic liberalism of the eighteenth century. But by the end of the sixteenth century it had already begun to be clear that libertinism was in advance of its age. Its anarchical, or centrifugal, tendencies had at that time to be corrected by the strengthening and unifying moral discipline of Stoicism; and the philosophers who best represent normal rationalism in the period from 1575 to 1660 are men, like Montaigne and Browne, who are both Sceptics and Stoics. Muret's opinions, on the other hand, were formed too early to include the Stoic element of the new intellectual amalgam; and he is to be looked upon chiefly as a precursor of libertine doctrines in thought and letters. It is true, of course, that he was not conscious of a dichotomy which had not yet revealed itself plainly; and how he would have been affected if he could have seen later developments of libertinism we cannot say. But his temperament constantly led him into extravagance of statement in his running fight against intellectual orthodoxy and commonplaceness, and some of his opinions, often exaggerated and distorted by oral tradition, made him too much a favorite of the "strong wits" of a later generation.

Illustrations of this phase of his reputation are numerous. We have already seen that the praise of St. Bartholomew's became a favorite paradox of radicals like Naudé and La Mothe le Vayer in the middle of the seventeenth century, and there is reason to believe that Muret's notorious oration of 1572 suggested this method of startling "plebeian intelligences." How little the praise of persecution had to do with sectarian partisanship or religious prejudice is shown by the fact that Muret was also spoken of sometimes (quite unjustly) as an "atheist." He was regarded, says Imperiali, in his *Musée Historique*, as one of those Italians, like Paolo Giovio and Della Casa, who never opened their breviaries and were therefore attacked by those "little minds that love to hang a quarrel on the point of a needle";[71] and this opinion at last gained such currency that he was one of the many writers to whom was attributed late in the seventeenth century the authorship of the mysterious work, *De Tribus Impostoribus* (that is to say, Moses, Jesus, and Mahomet): one of the highest honors that libertinism could bestow.[72] The most valuable evidence, however, concerning the libertine tendency in Muret's opinions, recognized by men who were familiar with them, is to be found in the fact that his portrait was among those gathered by Guy Patin to adorn the interesting room in his Paris house in which a company of strong wits sometimes held their convivial synods.[73] Other sixteenth-century worthies honored in this carefully chosen collection were Erasmus, Montaigne, Charron, Justus Lipsius, and "enfin François Rabelais." It is a kind of genealogy of positivism from 1500 to 1600.

In his temperament as well as in his doctrines Muret showed his kinship with the philosophers of the libertine tendency; and with some consideration of this point we may fitly close the present consideration of his career.—Certain traits of character and temper are common to sceptical rationalists of all periods. Curiosity about new ideas, for example, and readiness to adopt new opinions, an individual turn of wit and a constant tendency toward satire—these are traits just as conspicuous in scholars like Petrarch, Politian, and Erasmus as they are in their successors, the libertines of the later Renaissance. In the latter, however, they are attended by others peculiar to their own age. For reasons that need not be specified, these later rationalists felt themselves even more hostile to the accepted commonplaces of their time than it is the usual lot of the radical intellectualist to be; and their sense of estrangement betrayed itself frequently in excess, or even violence, of statement; sometimes in pride, sometimes in exasperation, they allowed themselves to abound, even extravagantly, in their own peculiar sense. Many *libres penseurs*, like Naudé, were secretly delighted with the

[71] Quoted by Charbonnel, p. 102.

[72] Erasmus, Rabelais, Aretino, Machiavelli, Bruno, Hobbes were among others similarly honored (Charbonnel, p. 696).

[73] See Guy Patin's letter to Falconet, Dec. 2, 1650. [Presumably Croll had in mind Patin's *Lettres*, ed. J. H. Reveillé-Parise, 3 vols., Paris, 1846.]

name of atheists, when it was thrown at them by horrified weaklings; and even a meditative philosopher like Browne allowed his doctrines of tolerance to cover a multitude of startling paradoxes. Some hardy adventurers, like Donne and Gracián, guarded their speculations from the apprehension of vulgar wits behind a veil of obscurity; while many others, like Estienne and Burton, expressed their protest against convention by an affectation of eccentricity. In fact, for every classical virtue of the Renaissance the strong wits of the seventeenth century discovered a counter-virtue of romantic individualism and violence.

Muret was temperamentally of the new school and was among the first who displayed its virtues and vices in their conduct. To speak more exactly, he gradually discovered the temper appropriate to the new positivism as he gradually discovered its program. Enough has already been said of his eulogy of absolutism and persecution. It may be—it doubtless is—true that the famous orations on these subjects were prompted by a sudden and sincere conversion to the doctrine of authoritarianism. But the excess with which he charged his guns on this occasion was none the less symptomatic of a new violence of intellectual temper. And this was but one of many occasions on which he invited danger. Challenged to defend his championship of later Latin authors, he encouraged his pupils to study Tertullian, Apuleius, and Cassiodorus. The opposition to his teaching of Tacitus in 1580 struck from his mind— like flint on steel—a sketch of the rapid decline of freedom and public counsel in the politics of the sixteenth century. When he was charged with corrupting the purity of Latin style, he retorted with an all-but-public acknowledgement of the doom that hung over the modern use of the ancient tongue.

A display of extravagance and violence of opinion may doubtless be accounted for in various ways. It may be the expression, for instance, of normal joy in the noise of combat; it may be the vehicle of a healthy sense of humor; it may be a somewhat provincial way of showing confidence and ardor in one's cause. And in one or another of these ways we can usually explain the excesses and oddities of the earlier humanists of all parties, of men like Rabelais, Erasmus, Budé, and the elder Scaliger, for instance. Their exuberance of wit may be regarded, on the whole, as a sign of mental well-being. But their successors in the last period of the Renaissance were not conscious of mental well-being, but of the contrary, and their extravagances are the signs of an inward exasperation, an inward dis-ease, seeking an opportunity to vent itself upon some external object. To appease their own sense of maladjustment they wreak their pain upon dull intelligences that know nothing of the agues that shake the mind. The Rabelaisian humors of Henri Estienne and Robert Burton are not an overflow of high spirits, but the symptoms of an unappeasable restlessness of soul; the raillery of Lipsius and the paradoxes of Donne are the guiled shore to a most dangerous sea of melancholy. Melancholy, in fact, was the root of the bitter wisdom of the seventeenth century; and Muret showed himself to be of the spiritual company of Montaigne, Donne, Browne, and Balzac (not to say of Pascal himself) when he voluntarily withdrew to a contemplative retreat in the midst of an active career.[74] His death within a year after he had taken this step of course suggests that his physical condition may have been the cause of it. But even though this may be true, the earlier moves by which he had gradually submitted his mind to the spiritual direction of his Jesuit friends show that he was aware of the same inward weakness that drove so many of his intellectual kindred into solitude and philosophy. The sense of strength and unity of mind which men of the high Renaissance had been able to enjoy without effort, by mere conformity with the world, or in unreflective industry, had now to be studied in the quietness of thought and a rigorous discipline of self-examination.

[74] Observe the interesting characterization of him by Bernays (*Lipse*, n.3), quoted by Dejob, p. 400n.: "Muret was a complete virtuoso in the art of smiling; his patronizing compliments, his contempt, his frivolity, and, in his later years, his melancholy also, express themselves in the smile, and conceal themselves behind it; but just because he is always smiling, he never laughs. [On the theme of retirement see Maren-Sofie Røstvig, *The Happy Man: Studies in the Metamorphoses of a Classical Ideal, 1600-1700* (Oslo and Oxford, 1954).]

Foreword to Essay Four

"Attic Prose: Lipsius, Montaigne, Bacon" marks a stage in the development of Professor Croll's ideas about prose styles in the sixteenth and seventeenth centuries. In this article he clarified, summarized, and furthered the theories presented in earlier essays, advancing his concept that a style both reflects and in part conditions its age, and making more precise his history and definition of the Anti-Ciceronian or "Attic" movement, especially its philosophic base in a Neo-Stoicism which he preferred to call libertinism. In his judgment, the revolt against the prescriptive and proscriptive emphases of the so-called Ciceronians began with Montaigne but did not become a force until Muret's conversion to Atticism and Lipsius' development and spread of its practice and principles.

It is well to remember that Cicero was master of varied styles used for different purposes and that the "Ciceronianism" of the late Middle Ages and Renaissance deviated from its alleged model; similarly, the "Aristotelianism" that Bacon and Milton attacked distorted Aristotle's own teachings.

It is also wise to remember that although Croll refers to Anti-Ciceronian or "Attic" style, he meant not one but at least two styles, one loose and informal, the other terse. Both were reactions against the artificialities and rigidities of sixteenth-century emphases on words and forms; their common goal was maximal expressivity; in each, content and the mind in the process of thinking took precedence over conventional form and the rigidities of genre and tradition.

One respect in which this article marked a stage in the development of Croll's ideas is that in the penultimate paragraph he remarks upon "a tendency which . . . manifests itself everywhere as the peculiar mark of the genius of the seventeenth century," a tendency for which "there is unfortunately no convenient name in English." He rejects "metaphysical" as being even less happy as a term to describe the kinds of prose in which this tendency appears than it is as a description of the related kinds of poetry. Having granted that "It may be known as the 'prose of imaginative conceit' in order that we may keep in line with the terms of current criticism," he admitted a temptation "to make the bold innovation of calling it 'the baroque style' in prose, for no other term will so exactly describe its characteristic qualities." According to Professor René Wellek, it was he who first, in a Princeton seminar, suggested that Croll use "Baroque" instead of "Attic" for this style in prose. It was, of course, neither of these two scholars who invented the idea of transferring the terminology of art to literature. As early as the eighteenth century that game was being played—by critics of Spenser, for example; and in the twentieth century Spengler filled his *Decline of the West* with such phrases as the "Titian style of the madrigal." Nor was Croll the first to apply *baroque* to literature. Certainly Oskar Walzel preceded him with the general usage in his article "Shakespeares Dramatische Baukunst," *Jahrbuch der Shakespearegesellschaft*, LII (1916), 3-35. Walzel was adopting the criteria of Heinrich Wölfflin (*Kunstgeschichte Grundbegriffe*, Munich, 1915) to literary matters, and René Wellek in "The Concept of Baroque in Literary Scholarship," originally published in *JAAC*, v (1946), 77-109, and reprinted, with updating, in his *Concepts of Criticism* (New Haven, 1963), seems ready to credit Walzel with having introduced the term with respect to an English writer, though he adds that, as far as he knows, Friedrich Brie's *Englische Rokokoepik* (1927) was the first attempt of this sort. But Valdemar Vedel's pioneer article, "Den Digteriscke Barokstil om Kring aar 1600," *Edda* (Christiana), II (1914), 17-40, should not be overlooked. Parallel to the style of painters like Rubens, Vedel perceives a poetic baroque style in English and French literature between 1550 and 1650. However, credit for the peculiar application of the word *baroque* to Attic style belongs to Croll's adoption of Wellek's suggestion. Whether or not it is a satisfactory term has been debated, but it has had wide currency and will probably persist, though it is now being partially replaced by *mannerist*. (See the fuller discussion in Croll's "The Baroque Style in Prose," in the foreword and notes to that essay, and in *Muret*, n.22.)

Too much emphasis should not be placed on mere terminology.

What deserve attention are the main theses of this article: for example, that the central idea of Anti-Ciceronianism was the adaptation of style to the differences of men and times, and that the "new" style not only paralleled but also imitated the Anti-Ciceronianism of the first century A.D., both in its character and in its relation to the oratorical prose which preceded it.

J. MAX PATRICK AND ROBERT O. EVANS

Attic Prose: Lipsius, Montaigne, Bacon*

EDITED BY J. MAX PATRICK AND ROBERT O. EVANS

✧ I ✧

THE decade beginning just before 1570 is clearly indicated as the time at which the Anti-Ciceronian, or "Attic," movement first arrived at a program and became conscious of its connection with a general change of intellectual interests that was coming over the world. It was the beginning of a century in which, in spite of many oppositions, at first from a dying generation, and later from a generation just coming to birth, it was to dictate the prevailing form of prose style in all the countries of Europe. In the career of Muret, for instance, we are able to mark with definiteness the late sixties and the early seventies as the time when he first arrived at a complete sense of his own meaning and mission; the succeeding years of his life were spent in working out the philosophical implications of the Anti-Ciceronian rhetoric in moral and political science.[1]

It was not only Muret's conversion, however, that made this the decisive moment in the history of the movement. Muret was then too old to make the world clearly aware of his changed intentions: his record was confusing. Moreover, other men of his generation, almost equally authoritative, had taken the opposite direction to his. In the North particularly, whence it seemed that new impulses must come, in the great Protestant countries of Germany and England, the leading humanists, Ascham and Car, Sturm, Melanchthon, and Camerarius were all Ciceronian, mildly and moderately so, it is true, since Erasmus had spoken, but still definitely in the tradition of rhetorical education and eminently puristic in their theory of style. The situation was not clear, and the world

---

* Originally published in *Schelling Anniversary Papers by his Former Students*. New York: The Century Co., 1923, pp. 117-150.

[1] The present essay is meant to follow one with the title "Marc-Antoine Muret and Attic Prose," which appears in a current number (1923) of *PMLA*. [The title was changed; the text was apparently revised, and publication was deferred to 1924.] In that essay I have tried to show the relations of the Anti-Ciceronian movement to the thought of the sixteenth and seventeenth centuries. As regards the relations between this movement and its models in antiquity, see *APS*, above.

might be going in either direction for all one could tell. It depended on what the *young* men would say, what formulas they would adopt, what challenges they would respond to; and it is chiefly because of what was thought and said by two men who were both comparatively young at that time that we are able to date the beginning of the Anti-Ciceronian period at approximately 1570.

These two men were Joest Lips (better known as Justus Lipsius) and Montaigne. In 1567 Montaigne was thirty-four years old but not yet an author or a philosopher; Lipsius was twenty years old and had already published. We will consider the latter first.

✧ II ✧

JUSTUS LIPSIUS

His Discovery of the Stoic Model

There is no scholar of the Renaissance concerning whom the opinion of scholars has undergone so radical a change in recent years as Justus Lipsius, of Leyden and Louvain. His association, from 1586 onward, with the Jesuits of Louvain won him the hatred and abuse of Protestant partisans in the Northern countries; on the other hand, the more orthodox of his own party regarded him with constant suspicion and refrained from acknowledging their real intellectual indebtedness to him because it was believed that he had imbibed from his Stoic masters in antiquity doctrines dangerous to the faith of a Christian; and, finally, the shadow of academic disapproval always rested upon his literary doctrines, even during the period when they were enjoying almost unrivaled success in the actual practice of the world. For these and other reasons his name appears much oftener in the seventeenth century in hostile than in friendly allusion, though it was recognized that he deserved his place beside Scaliger and Casaubon in the intellectual triumvirate of his time; and modern scholars were content until a few years ago to accept the judgment of his contemporary foes at their face value. It was sometimes recalled, with facile humor, that there was a Lepidus in the Roman triumvirate; and it was the custom to hold him up to scorn as a typical linguistic pedant insensible to the philosophy and literature of the ancient authors whom he edited. These were strange judgments to be passed on the philosopher who has now come to be known as "the founder of seventeenth-century

Neo-Stoicism" and the writer who must finally take an almost equal place with Montaigne and Bacon among the founders of the prose style of the seventeenth century.[2]

The stages in Lipsius' development as a philosopher can be clearly discerned. His history properly began, when he was twenty-one years old, with his visit to Muret at Rome in 1568, though at that time he had already won considerable reputation as a linguist and rhetorician. The first result of this encounter was his quick—if we may believe him, his *instantaneous*—conversion from a purely literary and rhetorical learning to a realistic—or, as we should say, a positivistic—study of politics. He began at once the intense and rapid labors which bore fruit, after only seven years, in his famous edition of Tacitus (1575), and a little later in the important compilation known as *Six Books of Politics*.[3] These works won him a reputation as a "politician," or student of *prudentia*, which was never equalled or corrected, at least in Italy, by the fame of his later work. The *Politics* unfortunately won him also the hatred of most scholars of the North by its advocacy of the policy of "fire and sword" in dealing with heresy, though a careful student of his mind will be convinced that his ruthlessness, like the orthodoxy of Montaigne and Browne, was founded in scepticism and not in bigotry.

These first works do not, however, represent his matured interests. They reflect directly the influence of Muret, just as we may discover in all the first part of his career the mobility of mind, the physical restlessness, the extravagance of wit veiling an inward dissatisfaction, which are observable in his master. The time of his full self discovery may be fixed with some certainty at the point of his career when he severed his connection with the Protestant University at Leyden and deliberately chose a life of quiet and retirement as teacher in his own Louvain college. There was an interval in which he was received as an honored guest at several German courts and universities and was offered more than one brilliant and conspicuous position of public activity. He deliberately chose to

---

[2] I have used again, in this section, some of the materials more fully elaborated in *Lipse*. An excellent and full study of Lipsius' philosophical doctrine and its influence will be found in Zanta, *La Renaissance du Stoïcisme au XVIe Siècle*. See also Strowski, *Histoire du Sentiment Religieux . . . Pascal et son Temps*, I, [and the works cited in *Lipse*, n.2 and *APS*, n.36].

[3] [*Politicorum, sive Civilis Doctrinae Libri Sex*, begun as early as 1583, published 1589; trans. into French by Simon Goulart as *Les Politiques* (Geneva, 1613). See Saunders, p. 27.]

retire to the house on a quiet side street of Louvain not far from the college, where he spent the rest of his life in the placid orderliness that he describes in his letters, teaching a small number of chosen students, walking in the country with his Scotch dog Mops, and cultivating his tulips.

In the *De Constantia*, his first work of Stoic philosophy, he attributes his choice of retirement and his study of "apathy" to the trouble of his time and the varied spectacle of human suffering that he has witnessed in the devastated towns and country regions of the Netherlands. But the roots of seventeenth-century Stoicism lie much deeper than the events of a generation. Once started by Muret in the way of a naturalistic study of public and private morality, Lipsius could never have rested until he had attained the formula of spiritual recollection and cure which his age required. Having found this, he had found himself at last, and the rest of his life was devoted to Seneca and the doctrines of Stoic *sapientia*.[4]

The progress of his literary ideas was like that of his philosophy and seems always to have kept a step in advance of it. Like Muret, he blundered into the wrong track at the beginning of his career—the back-track of Ciceronianism. In 1569, having scarcely finished his studies at Louvain, he published a volume of precocious learning containing three books of *Variae Lectiones*.[5] It is dedicated to the mighty Cardinal Granvelle—so high does he dare to aspire already—in copious Ciceronian periods, indistinguishable from many other examples of the same style produced by the rhetorical humanists of the sixteenth century. But his conversion was early, instantaneous, and thorough. Muret had gradually divined the new program of studies, had worked out their relations one to another, had discovered their appropriate rhetorical medium; Lipsius' task was merely to understand the meaning of his message, to develop the implications in it which Muret himself had not dared to reveal, and to devote the energy and fire of his youth to its propagation. It was in 1568, only a year after his Ciceronian debut, that he met

[4] Of course his *Manuductionis ad Stoicam Philosophicam* (1604), written as a preparation for his ed. of Seneca (1605), had a greater influence upon the better instructed part of the public, but the *De Constantia* (1584), reached a *larger* audience everywhere. [On the former, see Saunders, Ch. III; on the latter, *Lipse*, n.4.]

[5] [The date erroneously given by Croll, "1567," has been rectified. Cf. *Lipse*, n.10a.]

Muret in Cardinal Hippolito d'Este's palace at Tivoli, and a few days later wrote to him as a disciple to a master. Muret has found the true way of study: nothing more *Attic* has ever met Lipsius' eyes than the letter he has just received from him. A year later Muret wrote, admitting him, as it were, to the mysteries. At Tivoli, he said, it is true that we live in all the delights of the senses—a truly Phaeacian life—but there are none who delight in the same studies that you and I enjoy. There is something of the strange secrecy and sense of danger in this correspondence that is often to be noted as characteristic of the Anti-Ciceronian movement; and it is not unlikely that Muret's description of the sensual life of Tivoli alludes in a veiled style to the rhetorical, purely literary tastes of the patrons whom he was serving, contrasting them with his own enthusiasm for the virile and "modern" studies which he did not dare to profess openly.[6]

Lipsius' resolve is taken at once. Political and moral science, not rhetoric; Attic style, not Ciceronian, shall be the objects of his effort. And he begins to work on an edition of Tacitus. But how shall he make the transition decently from the opinions that the public still thinks he holds to those he has actually espoused? It was an embarrassing situation for a young man who had already attained reputation as a stylist; and we can follow—not without enlightenment—the steps of his cautious preparation. First he publishes nothing of any import for eight years after the date of his first work; and then he comes out, in a new preface, in 1577, with the astonishing statement that Plautus' old style has more savor for him than Cicero's.[7] The quaint and ancient words, the piquant realism of this author made him a favorite of Anti-Ciceronians from Cujas to Guy Patin; he was tonic to minds suffering from the lassitude of a long season of purism. But Lipsius is careful to give the air of a whimsical and ingenuous weakness to his preference, and in the same tone he continues to speak of the style he uses in this new work, the *Quaestiones Epistolicae*. While he professes that his sub-

[6] See an account of this correspondence, with references, in "M.-A. Muret and Attic Prose," *PMLA*, as above. [Apparently this account was deleted before the article was published under its revised title.]

[7] [Errors in the original of this sentence ("seven years" and "1574") have been corrected. Eight years after the appearance of *Variae Lectiones* in 1569, *Quaestiones Epistolicae* was published (Antwerp, 1577). The passage mentioned is quoted in *Lipse*, n.11.]

ject compels him here to employ a style more pointed and significant than he has heretofore employed, he seeks a justification for his new manner in the *Letters* of Cicero.

The disingenuousness of all this is apparent when we consider that his Tacitus had already been printed[8] when these words were written. The true account of the style he employs in the *Quaestiones* is contained in a letter to a friend, and the words are worth quoting as one of the best descriptions of the new Attic. "I am afraid," he says, "of what you will think of this work [the *Quaestiones*]. For this is a different kind of writing from my earlier style, without showiness, without luxuriance, without the Tullian concinnities; condensed everywhere, and I know not whether of too studied a brevity. But this is what captivates me now. They celebrate Timanthes the painter because there was always something more to be understood in his works than was actually painted. I should like this in my style."[9] Both the terms of criticism in this passage and the style in which it is written come from Seneca.

Of course the air of mystery could not long be maintained after the appearance of his Tacitus in 1575. It is true that he continued to write to his literary intimates, even to Montaigne, as if he and they had been initiated into an esoteric cult, a secret order of taste and ideas, which involved them in opinions contrary to those they were bound to profess in public and odious to vulgar and orthodox intelligences.[10] But this curious attitude continued to be characteristic of certain phases of the Anti-Ciceronian movement during at least two generations. The world soon became aware, through his voluminous and international correspondence, that Lipsius was a man with a philosophical and literary mission. Almost immediately after the appearance of the Tacitus he let it be known that he would

8 [Corrected from Croll's original, "Tacitus must already have been in the press." In 1575, when his ed. of Tacitus was published, Lipsius also wrote commentaries on Plautus' comedies, *Antiquae Lectiones*. In them (vii.8) he cautiously grants that Tacitus is better than ordinary writers (*Tacitus scriptor haud paullo melior quam vulgus*) and that he will not deny his liking for the elegant wit and urbanity of Plautus (ii,1: *Negare nolo: amo Plauti elegantes et urbanos sales*). Cf. Saunders, p. 15.]

9 [See *Lipse*, n.11.]

10 *Epp. Misc.*, II.87. [We have not identified the edition referred to: numbering varies. A letter beginning *Scripsi ad te ante menses*, addressed to Montaigne and dated 1588, and containing a reference to the work on Tacitus occurs as II.45 in *Justi Lipsi Epistolarum Centuriae Duae* (Paris, 1601), along with two other letters to Montaigne expressive of intellectual sympathy (II.59 and 96). In *Eppistolarum Selectarum Centuria Miscellanea* (Antwerp, 1611-1614), these letters are numbered II.41, 55, and 92.]

devote the rest of his life to preparing an edition of Seneca.[11] This resolve he faithfully carried out, and the great work did not appear until 1605, the year before his death. It was then already world-famous, however, and almost immediately attained a currency such as few works of learning have enjoyed. It was the chief instrument of the extraordinary diffusion of Seneca's influence throughout the seventeenth century and was so closely identified with the study of the Stoic philosopher that people sometimes spoke of "Lipsius" when they meant the works of Seneca. There seems to have been doubt during the years following his death whether his influence was to be of more use to the imitators of Tacitus or to the imitators of Seneca. But there can be none in the mind of a modern student who studies the works of the many writers who derive from him. He and Montaigne are the chief sources of the Senecan literary mode, and his own style is obviously formed by a slight exaggeration of Seneca's point and brevity, and unfortunately a great exaggeration of his play upon words.

In the course of twenty-five years of preparation for his Seneca, Lipsius' program of studies gradually enlarged and at the same time defined itself. He found himself involved, like Muret, in the enterprise of rehabilitating the Latin masters of the Silver Age, but with the difference that his interests were almost wholly limited to prose writers—he is like Bacon, Browne, Balzac, Pascal, and many other literary masters of the seventeenth century in this respect—and that he was much clearer in his literary purposes than Muret. What these purposes were is described in a passage from a Latin eulogy composed by a Mechlin judge, a literary disciple of Lipsius, immediately after his death. The reader will perhaps be rewarded for his patience in enduring Rivius' style for a few sentences—somewhat mitigated in translation, it is true—for the sake of the information he conveys, and also because the passage will show that a certain kind of Asianism arises, as Cicero observed, from an exaggeration of the very qualities called Attic. Gaugericus Rivius is

---

[11] [*L. Annaei Seneca Philosophi Opera, Quae Exstant Omnia . . . Emendata et Scholiis Illustrata* (1605); trans. Thomas Lodge, *Workes of Seneca* (1614; rev. 1620); used as a basis for Roger L'Estrange, *Seneca's Morals* (1678), especially "Of Seneca's Writings" (extracted from Lipsius), appended to the preface. The source of Lipsius' announced intention to edit Seneca is not given by Croll, but among his lecture notes preserved in Princeton Library, he states concerning Lipsius (again without source), "In a letter to a Spanish humanist he wrote *Dederam Tacitum, prudentiae (tuo quoque judicio) patrem; debui certe volui, et Senecam, sapientiae fontem.*"]

plainly one of those disciples of Lipsius, often mentioned in contemporary criticism, who imitated only the faults of his master.

> Declaring, Rivius says, that he existed for the good of the State, not the State for *his* good, he [Lipsius] decided at the beginning to save the lives of his own kind by his labors, to recover health to the sick by his ministrations, to restore their original possessions to those who had been unjustly despoiled, and to liberate them from their chains. It was for this purpose that he visited all the prisons and took note of Seneca, the tragic poet, Velleius Paterculus, the famous Pliny, that once-celebrated panegyrist of Trajan, and many others besides, wearing the chains and the dress of prisoners, living there in mud and ordure, branded with the red-hot iron, shaven, half-dead. In the same wretched gang he saw also Valerius Maximus, so unlike himself, so unlike his name.
>
> . . . And two prisoners were particularly noteworthy as having been unjustly condemned—L. A. Seneca and G. Cornelius Tacitus. These men, who had held consular rank, he beheld crawling out of I know not what *barathrum*, what cave of Polyphemus, or rather what cavern peopled with tigers and panthers. . . . To Lipsius, who took pity on them and demanded to know why men who had served the public good as citizens had been thrown into chains, why they were bound who had attached all humanity in bonds to themselves by their services, and ought to be held in the hands and in the hearts of princes; why they lay darkened in filth who had cast a light beyond the limits of the world, beyond nature—the dazzling light of *prudentia* and *sapientia*; to Lipsius, inquiring thus. . . . [The period continues to much greater length.][12]

Rivius' words are valuable as indicating the full scope and deliberateness of Lipsius' innovations. They help us to understand, for instance, why several minor contemporaries of Tacitus and Seneca enjoyed so much more favor in the seventeenth century than they have done since: why Valerius Maximus is so often quoted by Montaigne, Jonson, and Browne, Velleius Paterculus by the concettisti in prose, and the younger Pliny by panegyrists and students of "point." But they also reveal the fact that Lipsius limited his

---

[12] Rivius' discourse appeared in a volume issued by Moretus in 1607, the year after Lipsius' death. [See *Lipse*, n.16.]

charity to authors of this school and century. Though his classicism is deliberately not Augustan, it is a true classicism, and he carefully avoids the dangerous mistake which Muret did not sufficiently guard his followers against, and which the "libertine" prosaists of the seventeenth century were frequently to make, of frolicking anew in the semi-barbarism of the "low Latin" style.

His Place in Seventeenth-Century Culture

Of course Lipsius was not the sole founder of the Stoical philosophy of the seventeenth century or even of the Senecan imitation which accompanied it in prose literature. Du Vair, Montaigne, and Charron had all discovered the path of renunciation and self-dependent morals before him or without his aid. But the clearness and exclusiveness of his program, his international authority as a humanist, and his use of the new prose model in the authoritative Latin language gave the impetus to the Stoic philosophy and style which carried them into every part of Europe and almost every lettered circle of society. He soon had many followers among professed scholars at the universities who dared to brave the imputation of heterodoxy. But the greatest success of his program (though he himself always wrote in the ancient tongue) was won in the more open fields of the vernacular languages and the popular philosophy of laymen. Most conspicuous among his professed disciples was Francisco Quevedo, the young Spanish nobleman who had already won a brilliant reputation in burlesque fiction. There was a correspondence between the two men during Lipsius' last years in which Quevedo hailed Lipsius as the hierophant of a new mystery in terms that recall the letter that Lipsius had written to Muret forty years before. To Lipsius he owes the discovery of the way that he will henceforth follow throughout his life.[13] His writings soon showed what he meant; for he became the consistent and enthusiastic exponent of Christian Stoicism in many works of philosophy in Spanish and Latin, in which Job, Socrates, Cato, and Seneca appear as the saints and heroes of one dispensation. When one reads the bold and extravagant pages in which he equalizes pagan and Hebraic models of morality, one easily understands why Lipsius himself narrowly escaped the Index, and why he felt it necessary to destroy his dissertation called *Thraseas* in defence of the right of suicide, which had won, even though unpublished, a

---

[13] See *Lipse*, pp. 42-43.

dangerous notoriety. Quevedo's discipleship was complete, for he adopted not only Lipsius' philosophy but also his literary style and his devotion to the masters of Silver-Age Latinity. "Mi Seneca, mi Lucano, mi Juvenali," he exclaims, in a kind of rapture. It was a literary program which gained peculiar plausibility in Spain from the fact that Seneca and Lucan had been natives of that country. The somber dignity of the Spanish character was believed to be as friendly to Stoic ideals of conduct as the Spanish love of "emphasis" was to the significant rhetoric of the first century.

The impression made by Lipsius upon England was almost as great, however. His dialogue *Of Constancy* was translated and published in 1593 by Sir John Stradling, a minor author who had a part also in disseminating the taste for Martial and the epigram in this decade.[14] Jonson studied the political, the rhetorical, and the Stoic writings of Lipsius and may have learned from them some of the admiration for the two Senecas which is displayed in his prose and poetry alike, and some of the Stoic philosophy which he expounds—or translates—so admirably in many a passage of his verse.[15] A Senecanism more obsequious to Jacobean defects of taste is revealed in Bishop Hall's *Epistles* and *Meditations*. It is hard to believe that these works have not been directly influenced by the Belgian scholar, who Hall met in person, encountered in sectarian controversy, and mentioned frequently in his writings. Lipsius' influence at least appears far and wide in many other English moral writings of the century, and it is recorded that his letters were sometimes used as Latin texts in English schools.

These are remarkable instances of Lipsius' authority; yet the knowledge of its range and power must chiefly be won, for reasons that have been explained, from the vigorous opposition it aroused. The attacks made by his opponents during his lifetime are of little value to the historian, because of the religious prejudices that

[14] *Lipse*, n.4.
[15] The facts are recorded in the eds. of *Discoveries* by Schelling and Castelain. [See *Lipse*, n.24 for subsequent scholarship that shows that Jonson received Lipsian ideas through Hoskyns.] See a series of articles, in various periodicals, by Professor Briggs on Jonson's classical adaptations. [William D. Briggs, "Note on the Sources of Ben Jonson's *Discoveries*," *MLN*, XXIII (Feb. 1908), 43-46; "Studies in Ben Jonson," *Anglia*, XXXVII (1913), 463-493; XXXVIII (1914), 101-120; XXXIX (1916), 16-44, 209-251, 303-318; "Source-Material for Jonson's *Epigrams Forest*," *CP*, XI, 2 (April 1916); and "Source-Material for Jonson's *Underwoods* and Miscellaneous Poems," *MP*, XV (1917). See also J. E. Spingarn, "The Sources of Jonson's *Discoveries*," *MP*, II (1905); and Trimpi, esp. pp. 60-75.]

mingle with and obscure their literary purposes. Henri Estienne, who was himself an Anti-Ciceronian—though more nearly akin to Montaigne than to Lipsius—published in his old age a long and fantastic book *De Lipsii Latinitate*.[16] But he has so entangled the literary doctrines of Lipsius with the intrigues of Spain and the Ligue and the supposed alliance of the Catholic powers with the Turk that no modern reader can hope or care to discover his exact meanings. Scaliger is a better critic and has left the first intelligent description of the new Senecan style by an opponent.[17] But he was the official voice of Protestant literary orthodoxy, and his appointment to the chair of rhetoric at Leyden vacated by Lipsius was probably meant to have both sectarian and rhetorical significance.

Two decades later the cause of correct classicism in style rests in different hands, the hands of the Jesuit rhetoricians who have taken charge of the literary education of the French court and society. To rally the taste of their time to pure Augustanism is the task of Father Caussin and Father Vavasseur, and the tendencies they are hopelessly struggling against are chiefly those that were set going by Lipsius and his school.[18] It is still so in the middle of the century, when Balzac is the arbiter of taste; Montaigne and Lipsius are the protagonists of the tradition from which he seeks—in vain—to disengage himself. And even a generation later, Bouhours attributes both good and bad elements in the prevailing modes of style to Lipsius' teaching.[19] It is remarkable that a model set in Latin writing by a philologist should have had so much power in determining the form of prose style in several of the living languages. But the explanation is clear: Lipsius provided the model of a Stoic style.

[16] [See *Lipse*, n.34.]
[17] In *Poemata Omnia* and in *Scaligerana*, under "Lipsius," the brief dictum, *male scribit*; see *Lipse*, n.35.
[18] See *Lipse*, pp. 34-35, for more on Caussin; cf. *APS*, n.44 and *Muret*, n.25. Vavasseur's third oration (cited in *APS*, n.59) was in favor of the old style and opposed the new. This *novum genus* was the Anti-Ciceronian, the post-Augustan, which had become almost universal in his time.
[19] Bouhours, *La Manière* (Paris, 1687), passim; see the copious index. [In *Lipse*, n.25 and *APS*, nn.39, 61, Croll cites the Amsterdam, 1688 ed.; cf. *Muret*, n.26.] There is some discussion of Bouhours' criticism in my essay "Attic Prose" [i.e. pp. 71-72, 98; cf. *Muret*, p. 98].

✦ III ✦

MONTAIGNE

The Founder of Libertine Style

There is a striking similarity between the moral experience of Montaigne at the time of his retirement and that through which Lipsius passed more gradually in arriving at the ultimate form of his thought. He too was touched with the melancholy of the late Renaissance. His confessed aim in his retirement was to study it and come to terms with it, and the method of his study in the first phase of his philosophical development was purely Stoic. The essays which we can prove to have been written during the first five or six years after his retirement are as like in tone and spirit to the Stoical treatises of Lipsius as the writings of two authors working independently are ever likely to be. The essay on *Solitude*, for instance, is a kind of companion piece or complement to Lipsius' dialogue on *Constancy*.

Rhetorically, too, Montaigne effected his escape from humanistic orthodoxy through the Stoic doorway; and he asserted his freedom with more boldness and promptitude, perhaps actually became conscious of it at an earlier date, than Lipsius. He is in no doubt, even in the earliest of his Essays, about his distaste for Cicero's style, and indeed is the only Anti-Ciceronian who dares to express his independence with perfect frankness. "Fie upon that eloquence," he says, when speaking of Cicero, "that makes us in love with itself, and not with the thing."[20] The very beauty of Cicero's language, the faultlessness of his oratorical rhythm, is the defect he finds in him, just as Erasmus had found him too perfect. "He will sometimes," he admits, "confound his numbers; but it is seldom." "As for me, I like a cadence that falleth shorter, cut like Iambics." He may make his opposition more particular and varied in his later writings; he cannot make it more clear and positive than it is in the period between 1572 and 1576.

But he has not yet attained the characteristic independence of his matured opinions. Like Lipsius', his opposition to Cicero's sole authority is that of a school. The terms of his polemic are all Stoic

---

[20] "A Consideration upon Cicero," *Essays*, I.xxxix (xl in most modern eds.). [The main comments of Montaigne on Cicero occur in I.xxxix and II.x; on rhetoric otherwise, in I.xxv and li. The other quotations in this paragraph appear to be Croll's own translations, based on I.xxxix. Cf. *APS*, nn.2, 45; *Muret*, n.10.]

terms; the books that he reads, he says, in words that are almost
identical with a later phrase of Lipsius, are only those that will
make him "more *wise* and *sufficient*, not more worthy or eloquent";[21] and the authors who have won away his admiration from
"the master of those who speak" are also those in whom he has
studied the Stoic philosophy which meets his moral need at this
time: Seneca and, in a less degree, Lucan. The "soldatesque" style
of Caesar, it is true, also commands his special admiration; for
what is it but the language of a great Stoic in action; but he is after
all a writer, that is to say, a rhetorician, and as a model for his own
imitation Seneca alone could serve his turn. Upon this model, in
fact, his style was formed in his early writing, and the general
character it took at that time was never radically changed, as he
himself observed, even though his theory of style and his tastes
passed through more than one phase of development in succeeding
years. Étienne Pasquier described him as *un autre Sénèque de notre
langue*, Père François Garasse as *un Sénèque en désordre*, and the
careful analysis of his style by many modern critics has but confirmed these judgments of an earlier day. His style, says Sainte-
Beuve, is "a tissue of metaphors," and, as regards the other conspicuous trait of a Senecan style, Pasquier has truly said of his book
that it is "un vrai séminaire de belles et notables sentences."[22]

If Montaigne had advanced no further in the development of
his moral and rhetorical theory than the stage he had reached in
1576, he would not have become the pioneer in a new phase of
modern thought. His talent, his inimitable skill would of course
have made his writings more familiar to the world than those of
Muret and Lipsius, but he would still have occupied a place similar
to theirs and about equal to it in the history of the rationalist
movement of the age.

Doubtless his freedom from the obligations of a professional con-

[21] *Essays*, I.xxxix.
[22] [Croll failed to document the sources of these quotations. In *The Happy
Beast in French Thought of the Seventeenth Century* (Baltimore, 1933), George
Boas gives an account of the attack on Montaigne and Montaigne's follower,
Pasquier, by Garasse and others. See also Pierre Villey, *Montaigne devant la
Postérité* (Paris, 1935), and Alan M. Boase, *The Fortunes of Montaigne: A History of the Essays in France, 1580-1669* (London, 1935) and its excellent bibliography. In *The Influence of Montaigne* (New York, 1908), Grace Norton gathers
comments on Montaigne and allusions to him in French and English. See also
Floyd Gray, *Le Style de Montaigne* (Paris, 1958) and the excellent dissertation
by Camilla Hill Hays, *Montaigne, Lecteur et Imitateur de Sénèque* (Poitiers,
1938).]

sistency was a cause that his influence was not bounded by these limitations; some would prefer to say that it was merely an effect of the native superiority of genius to any circumstances whatever, and perhaps the truest statement of all would be that his preference of an unrelated freedom to the embarrassments of a defined career was in and of itself the decisive manifestation of his genius, including all the rest as its natural consequence. At all events, he passed beyond the limits of the "new kind of learning," even at the time when Muret and Lipsius were still seeking its exact academic formulae and definitions. By the time his first volume appeared, in 1580, he had already renounced systematic stoicism—though he never moved out of the zone of intellectual and literary interests into which his stoic study had introduced him—and had found his way to the main highway of modern thought, which leads directly from Petrarch and Erasmus to the liberal scepticism of the eighteenth century. He had discovered that the progress of rationalism meant much more than a change of orthodoxies, meant nothing less in fact than the full exercise of curiosity and the free play of individual differences.[23]

A change of literary tastes kept pace with this philosophic development. Students of Montaigne's *Essais* have discovered that the publication of Amyot's translations of Plutarch's works, and particularly of *Les Œuvres Morales et Meslées* in 1572, had a decisive effect in this respect upon all his later work.[24] The full meaning of the extraordinary delight he always took thenceforth in the reading of this work cannot be discussed here: we need only observe that it was quite as much an effect as a cause of the progress that was going on in his literary opinions. In an addition to his last volume, in the edition of 1588, he said that of all the authors he knew Plutarch was the one who "best mingled art with nature,"[25] and

[23] The change of Montaigne from Stoicism to Libertinism is well treated in Fortunat Strowski, *Montaigne* (Paris, 1906; rev. 1931) and also in his *Histoire du Sentiment Religieux . . . Pascal et son Temps*, I, 28-58. Villey's *Les Sources* provides the exact details necessary. [See also Victor Giraud, *Maîtres d'Autrefois et d'Aujourd'hui* (Paris, 1912), pp. 1-54 (discusses Villey); the criticisms of Villey and Strowski in Arthur Armaingaud, "Montaigne, Socrate et Épicure," *Nouvelle Revue*, 4th S., XLII (1919), 97-104, 215-224, 309-318; Busson, *Sources*, pp. 434-459; and the works listed in *APS*, n.36 and *Muret*, n.6.]

[24] [Joseph de Zangroniz, *Montaigne, Amyot and Saliat: Étude sur les Sources des Essais* (Paris, 1906); Pierre Villey, "Amyot et Montaigne," *Revue d'Histoire Littéraire de la France*, XIV (1907), 713-727; Grace Norton, *Le Plutarque de Montaigne* (New York, 1906).]

[25] III.vi, "Des Coches," near the beginning. [In "Des Livres," (II.x), Montaigne

the phrase exactly describes the literary ideal toward which he was tending throughout his career. He was always in quest of the natural man in himself, the free individual self who should be the ultimate judge of the opinions of all the sects and schools; and as the natural complement of this philosophic enquiry he was always feeling his way at the same time toward a theory of style which should allow the greatest possible scope to the expression of differences of individual character, or, in other words, the greatest possible naturalness of style that is consistent with the artificial limits necessarily imposed upon all literary composition. We can observe through all the stages of his development a steady approximation to such a theory, but in the latest editions of his *Essais* he has worked out its formulae with surprising definiteness and has become, both as teacher and model, the initiator of a particular tendency within the general bounds of the Anti-Ciceronian movement which is destined to have even greater consequences in literary history than the Stoic model of style described by Lipsius. To this tendency we are justified in giving the name "Libertine"—though the term is new in *literary* criticism—because it not only indicates the connection between the kind of prose style which it produces and the philosophy to which it is related but also exactly describes the character of this prose style itself.

The freedom of Montaigne's literary opinions was partly due, as we have already observed, to his deliberate choice of a career free from official responsibilities: he became a "man writing for men." But it was also due in large measure to the fact that he was the first of the Anti-Ciceronian leaders to use a vernacular language in his writings, and this is so great a point of difference that it cannot be passed over in a discussion of seventeenth-century prose style.

Latin and the Vernacular Tongues 1575-1625

The last quarter of the sixteenth century was the period when the literary claims and pretensions of Latin and the modern languages were almost evenly balanced, when it was easiest to pass from one to the other without a change of subject matter or style. Before that

---

groups Plutarch with Seneca and Pliny as advocating that each writer follow his own bent, not otherwise prescribing a *Hoc Age*; in his essay in Defence of Seneca and Plutarch (II.xxxii) he states that his book "is merely framed of their spoils"; in "Des Livres," he says that they served him to "range his opinions and dress their conditions." "Their instruction is the prime and cream of philosophy, and presented in a plain, unaffected, and pertinent fashion."]

time there had been a fairly clear, though by no means a deliberate, differentiation of their uses. The chief artistic use of the vernacular in the sixteenth century had been to express the surviving medievalism of the culture of that age. It was the language, for instance, of what had been perhaps the most general medium of medieval literary expression, the sermon; it was the language of a multitude of romantically retold tales of both antiquities, in which the fading ideals and customs of chivalry were adapted to an age of courtiers; it was the language of courtly ceremonial and show; it was the medium in which the medieval book of etiquette and universal instruction enjoyed a brief revival. It reflected, in brief, the customs of a courtly life which had not been modified in its essential features by the intellectual effort of the Renaissance. On the other hand, whatever was really new and forward looking in the Renaissance found its prose expression in the ancient tongue. Some humanists, it is true, foresaw the modern uses of their mother languages: Bembo, DuBellay, Ascham, for instance. Yet their writings are not representative of the usual vernacular prose of their time; and there is little distortion in the statement that in 1550 all serious, modern thought was expressed in Latin; all that was traditional, or merely popular, in its character tended to find its way into vernacular prose.

One hundred years after that date the progress of modernism had reversed these relations in most respects. The usual language of serious criticism, and even of philosophy, had become English, French, or Italian; and, what is more important, the *subject* of literary criticism had become chiefly the vernacular languages and their usages; Latin was already the language of a dead literature, whose chief value was to enrich the native styles with romantic allusion, heroic images, and far-echoing rhythms.

In these observations there is of course nothing new, and the purpose of reviving them here is to call attention to a fact which scholarship has not yet clearly enough taken account of, that between the two *termini* that have just been mentioned there was a most interesting period in which the two languages, or the two kinds of languages, the ancient and the vernacular, were present in the minds of most well-educated people in relations of almost exact balance and equality, and there were no real differences whatever between the uses of the one and the other. This period, which extended over about two generations, one before the turn of the century, one after, was the hinge on which the great change turned, a quiet revolution, effected unconsciously in the main, it would seem, and participated in by many who would have regretted it if they had known what they were doing, but of vastly more importance than most of the changes which have been the subject of literary controversy. This period should be more carefully studied by literary historians with reference to the history of the modern languages than it has yet been, and there are two comments on it which are directly suggested by the study of "Attic" prose.[26]

The first has to do with the effect of the equalization of the languages upon the vernacular literatures and is to the effect that out of this passing state of equilibrium emerged a standard form of literary prose in every modern language, upon which all later forms are founded and out of which they have developed without radical or revolutionary change.

Italian, English, and French prose of the preceding periods has various merits which antiquarians love to point out for the reproof or exhortation of writers of the present day. But none of it is quite *standard* prose. Some of it is too popular and crude and violent. Some of it is too highly wrought and fantastically mannered. And a third kind, the smallest class, though pure and correct, is too poverty-stricken, thin, and limited in its expressive resources. The explanation of this fact of course is that, as we have just observed, men of ideas reserved all the serious, progressive, and modern uses of their intellects for expression in Latin; they felt that the spoken languages had not been sufficiently conventionalized to carry the definite meanings and logical processes of continued exposition. It was good for *concrete* uses alone. And as long as this sort of differentiation continued in force there could not be a standard prose style in either Latin or the various vernaculars, for a standard form of prose is determined by the *general* thought of the age which it expresses, its collective wisdom and experience; it is neither remotely and professionally intellectual, on the one hand, nor a simple record of facts and sensations, on the other; its function is rather to relate the varied phenomena of the external life of each period to its dominant ideas and the general philosophic trend of its mind. It is clear that no such style could make its appearance in an age when the intellect spoke one language, the senses another.

[26] Many interesting points concerning the relation of the vernacular languages and Latin in the sixteenth century are brought out by Clément in *Henri Estienne et son Œuvre Française* (Paris, 1888), pp. 197-304 and elsewhere.

On the other hand, when these two languages had become virtually interchangeable in the minds of a great many writers, as they were, for example, in the minds of Montaigne and Bacon, when one and the other came with equal ease and idiomatic freedom from their pens, it made little difference in fact which one they used, for each would have some of the characteristic quality of the other. A writer in Latin would show the colloquial and concrete qualities of his speech in his own language; a writer in French or English would derive from his Latin the rhetorical firmness, the exact use of abstraction, the logical process which the learned language imposes.

This is the phenomenon that we observe in fact in the period of Montaigne and Bacon. These are the first writers in the vernacular languages who employ a style which renders the process of thought and portrays the picturesque actuality of life with equal effect and constantly relates the one to the other, and it is in this sense that we may justify the statement that the Anti-Ciceronian leaders—Montaigne, Charron, Pasquier in France, Bacon, Hall, Jonson, Wotton in England—are the actual founders of modern prose style in their respective languages. In the works of these authors, and in none of those that precede them, we can find a style in the popular language which is at once firm, uniform, and level enough to be called a style and also adaptable enough to adjust itself to the changing life of the modern world—a style which may grow and change in later generations without losing its recognizable features.

The second comment to be made in this connection is that the character of the Anti-Ciceronian movement in prose style—whether we consider its fundamental principles or the models it proposed for imitation—was eminently favorable to the process of leveling and approximation, the virtual blending, in fact, of Latin and vernacular style that was going on during this period. Ciceronian purism had tended to keep the two kinds of speech apart from one another. Not that the Ciceronians had been unfavorable to the study of prose style in the vernacular. Bembo and Ascham, on the contrary, had studied the subject carefully. But their purism in Latin style begot a corresponding temper in their treatment of the native languages, and they mistakenly attempted to shut up Italian, French, and English within the inadequate limits of the literary vocabulary which they had acquired at the beginning of the sixteenth century. Misled by the lack of a proper historical sense which was characteristic of their school, they pretended that the vernacular tongues had already attained their full maturity and were ready to be standardized in grammars, dictionaries, and rhetorics. The central idea of the Anti-Ciceronian movement, on the other hand, was that style should be adapted to the differences of men and times. The great modern principle of unending change and development was implicit in its rhetorical theory, and many of its leaders expressed their new-found joy in freedom by indulging in strange caprices of vocabulary. English and French are suddenly deformed by a riot of freakish Latinisms, on the one hand, and expanded at the same time by new and piquant discoveries in the expressiveness of colloquial speech. The Latin of humanist and scholar of course loses its remoteness by the same process and begins to bristle with strange words picked up from Plautus, or Greek, or medieval Latin, or the living languages.

To discuss the interesting results in the style of seventeenth-century prose that followed this general prevalence of the hedge-breaking custom would require a separate essay, perhaps a volume. We must proceed here merely to point out that there was a more specific way in which Anti-Ciceronianism aided the process of leveling and the transference of the qualities of Latin prose to the various vernaculars, namely, through the character of its preferred Latin models. The Ciceronian style cannot be reproduced in English, or indeed in any modern language. The ligatures of its comprehensive period are not found in the syntax of an uninflected tongue, and the artifices necessary to supply their function must produce either fantastic distortion or insufferable bombast. This is true after all the experiments of four centuries in quest of formal beauty. Certainly in the sixteenth century no modern speech had developed an art of prose adequate to the imitation of so difficult a model, and the best that any of them could do was to reproduce the oratorical style of medieval Latin, in which only the ornaments and the simpler elements of the form of the Ciceronian pattern are employed for the purpose of formal beauty. That these could indeed be transferred with some success into vernacular forms and style had been proved in Spain and England, and even in Italy and France; but it was evident that none of the varieties of *estilo culto* developed by this process was adequate to serve as a vehicle for the advancing thought of the new age or to portray the actualities of any real world. No oratorical prose, indeed, whether based on the pure Ciceronian, or on the derived medieval, pattern, could serve for this purpose. As long as these were the preferred models a normal form of French or English prose could not appear.

But Seneca is easy. There is nothing in his syntax that could prove a bar to the expression of the ideas of a keen-minded critic of the end of the sixteenth century concerning the moral experience of his times or himself; on the contrary, the brevity of his constructions, the resolved and analytic character of his sentences, would provide such a writer with a mold exactly adapted to the character of his mind and the state of his language. Tacitus, of course, is harder reading; but the kind of difficulty that he offers would prove to be no more than a welcome stimulus and challenge to the trained wits of rationalists like Lipsius, Bacon, Malvezzi, Gracián, and Balzac. In brief, ancient Anti-Ciceronianism worked in a *resolved* style, and the perfect success with which its manner was transferred to French, Italian, Spanish, and English style during the early seventeenth century is proof of its fitness to serve as the model on which a standard modern prose could be formed.

Finally, it is to be observed that the equilibrium between the languages determines the sources from which the student of the Anti-Ciceronian movement must draw his knowledge of contemporary opinion. He must learn to disregard linguistic boundary lines. He must use the Latin discussions of contemporary and ancient Latin style, discussions in Latin of contemporary vernacular style (and these are frequent until the middle of the seventeenth century), and of course more and more as time goes on, discussions of vernacular tendencies in the vernacular; and he must learn that all of these are of equal value. It has already been seen that the beginnings of the movement were in humanistic Latin prose, in the works of Erasmus, Muret, Lipsius; and naturally the theory and criticism of it are found in the same place. But it is somewhat surprising to discover that, a whole generation after the balances have tipped in favor of the literary use of the vernacular, criticism of the vernacular tendencies in prose style continues to appear in Latin. Descartes, for instance, writes to Balzac in Latin an illuminating letter concerning the French style of the time, and Bacon was certainly thinking of English, French, and Italian style in the paragraph concerning recent prose which he added to his Latin translation of the *Advancement of Learning* in 1622.[27] The student

27 See *Lipse*, IV (p. 38 and n.).

must learn, in short, that as far as style is concerned there was no difference in the mind of this period between Latin prose, on the one hand, and English, French, Italian, or Spanish, on the other: Lipsius writes to Montaigne of his style, after reading his first volume of *Essais*, in similar terms to those he had used in writing at an earlier date to Muret of his new manner of writing.[28]

Nor are these facts valuable only as indicating a method of study. They are of first-rate importance in the history of the movement itself as showing that in the minds of most of its leaders it was in the classical and not in the popular tradition. On this point there can be no question. Even when the custom of writing prose in the native languages had become very common, as it did during the decades 1590-1610, most of those who fell in with the new tendency felt that they were following in the train of Politian, Erasmus, and Muret, and ultimately of Seneca and Tacitus. They thought of their vernacular style as having come over to them from the Latin of the humanists or as directly derived from the Latin style of antiquity; and they seem usually to have been unaware of any relation, either of opposition or evolution, with the vernacular prose of the preceding age.[29]

The only very important exception to this general rule is to be found in the critical utterances of Montaigne and of certain writers, like Étienne Pasquier, for instance, who were directly influenced by him. Montaigne was well read in the vernacular literature of the sixteenth century and even of an earlier period, and he was too humane a critic of life to pass by the true mirrors of his age without studying his own features in them too, even though his grand enthusiasms are all for certain of the ancients. His criticisms, it is

---

[28] Lipsius to Montaigne, 1588, *Ep. Misc.*, II.41, in *Opera Omnia* (Antwerp, 1637), II. 86. [For a translation of what Lipsius wrote to Montaigne, see p. 66.] See also the correspondence between Mlle. de Gournay and Lipsius in which the lady writes in French, the savant in Latin; yet the style is of the same mold. Concerning this correspondence see Paul Bonnefon, *Montaigne et ses Amis* (Paris, 1898), II, 334-352.

[29] [E.g. Ascham in a Latin epistle sent to Bishop Stephen Gardiner with a copy of *Toxophilus* (1545) says that in contrast with the artistic license prevalent in vernacular prose, he has "taken pains to depart far and differ from almost the entire rout of English authors. . . . For indeed they have a sufficiency of neither dialectic for reasoning nor rhetoric for the embellishment of style; and thus in our vulgar tongue they strive to be, not familiar and appropriate, but rather outlandish and strange" (Ascham, *Works*, ed. Giles, I, 79; cf. Ryan, *Ascham*, p. 60). It should be remembered that Cicero was neither unknown nor uninfluential in the Middle Ages and, on the other hand, that relatively little sixteenth-century English prose is truly Ciceronian.]

THE ANTI-CICERONIAN MOVEMENT

true, are too few and inexplicit to be satisfying, but they tend to
show that he regarded the ornate prose and poetry of the past age
with something of the same contempt that he felt for Bembo and
other Ciceronianizing Latinists. We wish that he had been more
definite in telling us why he scorned Guevara's famous *Golden
Book*,[30] but we may be reasonably certain that the poverty of their
content and the richness of their stylistic ornament were equal
causes of his distaste. We should like to be certain too that he is
thinking of the Spanish prosaists and the style of Guevara and
Mexia[31] when he speaks of "l'affectation et la recherche des fan-
tastiques élévations espagnoles et petrarchistes,"[32] for the association
of Petrarchanism in verse and the *estilo culto* of Guevara and Lyly
in prose as two similar manifestations of the medieval love of
rhetoric would be exactly what we should expect in an Anti-Ciceronian and rationalist like Montaigne. But the passage as a whole
does not permit us to say with *certainty* that he was thinking of
Spanish *prose*, and we must be content to know that he did actually
dislike both these kinds of vernacular writing. The *franche naïveté*
of Froissart was, on the other hand, wholly to his taste, and if he
seems not to understand the real importance of Rabelais he at least
enjoyed him.[33]

✧ IV ✧

BACON

(a) Bacon and Tacitus

There is only one other author of nearly equal importance with
Lipsius and Montaigne in the history of the establishment of the
Attic tradition—Francis Bacon. He was not quite the first professed
Anti-Ciceronian in England. Thomas Nashe and Gabriel Harvey

---

[30] "Des Destries." [Croll refers to Antonio de Guevara's *Libro Aureo* as adapted
by John Bouchier, Baron Berners, from the French version of René Bertaut and
entitled *The Golden Boke of Marcus Aurelius* (1534; ed. J. M. G. Olivares, Berlin,
1916); for Guevara's possible influence on Montaigne, see Louis Clément, "Antoine de Guevara, ses Lecteurs et ses Imitateurs Français au XVIe Siècle," *RHL*,
VII (1900), 590-602 and VIII (1901), 214-233.]
[31] [Pedro Mexia or Mejía whose *Silva* influenced Montaigne. See G. L. Michaut,
"The Spanish Sources of Certain Sixteenth Century Writers," *MLN*, XLIII (1928),
157-163, and Janet Girvan (Scott) Espiner, "Quelques Érudits Français du XVIe
Siècle et l'Espagne," *RLC*, XX (1940-1946), 203-209, for the influence of both
Guevara and Mexia.]
[32] II.x, "Des Livres."
[33] See Villey, *Sources*, I, 204.

188

undertook a vigorous attack during the nineties against both Ciceronian Latin and the ornate vernacular style of Lyly and his school,
each of them seeking an escape from formalism through the
method of extravagance and licentious freedom of style, and there
are interesting similarities between their efforts and those of some
Continental "libertines" of the same period. But neither of these
writers had philosophy or authority enough to lead his age, and their
attack on tradition was soon lost sight of in the great success of
Bacon's more imposing offensive movement.

As a historian, Bacon offers useful aid to the student of prose
style. In a passage in the *Advancement of Learning* (most of which
was probably written some years before its publication in 1605),
he has sketched the history of the Ciceronian cult and described
the causes that produced it. He is perhaps following a faulty sketch
in one of Muret's orations (delivered at Rome in 1575, in introducing a course in Juvenal), but his account is so much more
complete and correct that it may be considered the first attempt to
place the Renaissance in historical perspective.[34] (Should we add
that his success is a sign that the Renaissance has already passed or
is passing? Perhaps so.) Ciceronianism is his illustration of that
distemper of learning "when words are valued more than matter";
its origin, he finds, was in the excessive zeal of the scholars of the
sixteenth century for an exact knowledge of the words of antiquity,
and he attributes this in turn—acutely enough but not altogether
correctly—to the controversial needs created by the Reformation,
and the search for authority among the Fathers of the Church. He
quotes a joke from Erasmus' *Ciceronianus*, names as leading
Ciceronians since Erasmus' time Ascham and Car, the Protestant
German humanist Sturm, and the "Portugal bishop Osorius" (the
latest exemplar of the pure cult), describes their style with his usual
analytic skill, and closes with the striking statement, which perhaps
is due to hints in Erasmus' dialogue, that if he should have to
choose between the "weight" of the scholastic philosophers and the
"copie" of the rhetorical humanists he would take the former.

The words of this passage are probably familiar to most literary
scholars, but this is not true of the supplement to it which Bacon
added when his work was translated into Latin and published as
De Augmentis Scientiarum in 1622. The new passage provides a

[34] [*Advancement*, ed. Wright, i.iv.2; *Lipse*, n.40; Croll discusses Muret's oration
in *Muret*, iii (pp. 148-149).]

fairly exact measure of the amount of water that has run under the bridge in three or four decades of literary history, and has an additional interest as an illustration of a new kind of curiosity, in the men of this generation, which enables them to turn upon themselves and recognize their own changes of taste and temper. Their perception of historical perspectives has made them more observant of change and progress in their own world; a new intelligence is emerging from the methods of sceptical inquiry taught by Petrarch, Erasmus, and Montaigne. In translation, Bacon's words are as follows:

> Somewhat sounder is another form of style,—yet neither is it innocent of some vain shows,—which is likely to follow in time upon this copious and luxuriant oratorical manner. It consists wholly in this: that the words be sharp and pointed; sentences concised; a style in short that may be called "turned" rather than fused. Whence it happens that everything dealt with by this kind of art seems rather ingenious than lofty. *Such a style is found in Seneca very freely used, in Tacitus and the younger Pliny more moderately; and it is beginning to suit the ears of our age as never before.* And indeed it is pleasant to subtle and low-ranging minds (for by means of it they conciliate the honor due to letters); however better-trained judgments disapprove it; and it may be looked upon as a distemper of learning, in as far as it is accompanied by a taste for mere words and their concinnity.[35]

This passage tells admirably what the Anti-Ciceronian movement is and how it arose. It describes the form of the new style and provides a motive for its rapid diffusion at the beginning of the seventeenth century. Not only this, however; it also establishes the parallel between this contemporary Anti-Ciceronianism and that of the first century, both in the character of its style and in its relation to the oratorical prose of the preceding century. The only point we miss is that Bacon does not clearly say that the new tendency is due to actual imitation of the ancients; and this defect is easily accounted for by Bacon's unwillingness to admit the effective survival of the principle of imitation and authority either in himself or his age; it is of a piece with the unfortunate, and sometimes mean,

[35] [*De Aug.* I, *Works* (1868), I, 452; see *Lipse*, n.40 for Wats' strikingly different translation of this passage.]

reticence he displays concerning his own great obligations to intellectual masters of the ancient and modern worlds.

And in fact, notwithstanding the apparent cool detachment of his criticism, Bacon knows very well that he is here describing his own style. He has left sufficient evidence in his own utterances of the truth of his secretary's statement that Tacitus, Caesar, and Seneca were his favorite authors, and that the order of his preference was that in which these three names are here mentioned. Nor have the critics required the aid of such statements; the resemblance of Bacon's style to that of his masters has often been observed by them. The praise he bestows on Seneca's style, says one of them, *ad ipsum Verulamium haud immerito detorqueri possit*. He was attracted to Seneca and Tacitus, this writer continues, by kinship of talent; and it was in the assiduous reading of these authors that he cultivated his taste for a style of acute and condensed brevity, ornamented, at the same time, with the riches of rhetoric and an almost poetic splendor of words.[36]

How are we to account then for the derogatory, or at least balancing, tone of the passage we have just quoted? Properly interpreted, it may serve as an aid to a more exact description of Bacon's tastes and the character of his literary influence than has yet been attempted, or to a correction of some misconceptions concerning them. It has been the custom to place Seneca first among Bacon's models and favorites, but this is an error. When his words are carefully examined, it is apparent that what he says in discommendation of the style "freely used" by Seneca is all directed toward "vain shows" and verbal ornament, the same fault of undue love of concinnity, in short, which was a cause of the revolt against Cicero's form of rhetoric. This is somewhat puzzling, especially in view of the fact that Seneca himself had made current among Anti-Ciceronian critics the phrases they habitually used to express their contempt for the sensuous beauty of the balanced Ciceronian phrase: *non ornamentum virile concinnitas*, and so forth. But the reader of Seneca can reconcile the contradiction. For that very literary and rhetorical essayist customarily framed his *antitheses* and *argutiae* in a balanced form, different indeed from that of the copious oratorical style, but yet capable of becoming almost as transparently artificial. At its best an excellent literary form for the insinuation of subtle

[36] See Paul Jacquinet, *Francisci Baconi de Re Litteraria Judicia* (Paris, 1863), pp. 98ff.

shades of thought and fine distinctions, at its worst it is indeed no more than "mere words and their concinnity." And it must be added that Bacon has in mind the imitators of Seneca more than Seneca himself: almost certainly Lipsius' Latinity; probably the English style of Bishop Hall's *Epistles* and other moral writings; perhaps also the Senecan manner of a number of English essayists who had written since his own first volume of 1597. All these writers had shown how easily the imitation of Seneca could descend to verbal ingenuity or mere pun on occasions when the idea was not worthy of the artifice bestowed upon it.

The faults of Tacitus and his imitators were clear enough to seventeenth-century critics, but they did not run in this direction. Obscurity, enigma, contortion are not qualities of style that comport with concinnity and the study of the abstract charm of words. Evidently Bacon is drawing a vertical line of distinction down through the area of Anti-Ciceronianism in addition to the other transverse line that divides it as a whole from the Ciceronian types of prose; and when this is observed and confirmed by a reference to the qualities of his own style, his literary comments and judgments throughout his works become more consistent. It becomes clear that he has not expressed anywhere a positive approval of Seneca's subject matter or style, though he refers to his letters as a model for the new essay form and cites his father as skilful in antitheses.[37] But on the contrary he has praised Tacitus in a private letter to Sir Fulke Greville, as the first of historians, and again, in the *Temporis Partus Masculus*, with the characteristic emphasis of his laconic style: "Many like the moral doctrines of Aristotle and Plato; but of Tacitus it may be said that he utters the very morals of life itself."[38] The former of these passages is worthy of a careful consideration. He says that history is of most use for those who wish to know only humanity, and continues: "For poets, I can commend none, being resolved to be ever a stranger to them. Of orators, if I must choose any, it shall be Demosthenes, both for the

[37] ["as a model"—in the cancelled dedication to Prince Henry intended for the 2nd ed. of the Essays. The citation of the "father" (more probably, uncle), Lucius Annaeus Seneca is in *De Aug.* VI.iii just before the examples of antitheses (*Works*, I, 688).]

[38] *Aristotelis et Platonis moralis plerique mirantur; sed Tacitus magis vivas morum observationes spirat* (*Works*, III, 538). [Croll's misquotation, *admirant* instead of *mirantur*, has been corrected.]

argument he handles, and for that his eloquence is more proper for a statesman than Cicero's. Of all stories, I think Tacitus simply the best; Livy very good; Thucydides above any of the writers of Greek matters."[39] In every respect this is a characteristic Anti-Ciceronian utterance: in its rejection of poetry from useful studies, in its preference of Tacitus to Livy (along with which goes a liking for Thucydides), and in its contemptuous treatment of oratory, partly veiled by the exaltation of Demosthenes above Cicero. Finally, it is to be noted that the extraordinary enthusiasm of the writer for history—which virtually means politics when connected with the influence of Tacitus—associates him with a particular phase of the Anti-Ciceronian complex which had already declared itself in the programs of Muret and Lipsius. It is true that at about the same time that Bacon was writing these words he must also have been writing the passage in an early section of the *Advancement of Learning* in which he speaks without qualification of Cicero as the first, or second, of orators, Livy as the first of historians, Virgil and Varro as first in their kinds of all those known to men.[40] But the apparent conflict only gives us the opportunity to note a fact that every student of one subject must take account of: that the Anti-Ciceronian critics, even the boldest of them, always keep an Augustan and Ciceronian orthodoxy in reserve; and even Montaigne will admit that if an abstract literary excellence, independent of the practical and moral uses of the works in which it is displayed, be the basis of one's judgment, the Augustan Age and the ages that resemble it are on a higher plane than any others. It is sometimes necessary to surprise them in the more confidential tone of letters and casual notes in order to discover the full range of their heterodoxy.

In Bacon's case, the frequency of his quotation from Tacitus may be accepted as evidence of his preference of that author to all others, for an acquaintance with Tacitus was not in that age to be taken for granted, nor was the citation of his difficult phrases a literary convention, as was that of the Senecan "sentences." On

---

[39] I accept the attribution of this letter to the hand of Bacon suggested by James Spedding, *The Letters and the Life of Francis Bacon* (London, 1861-1874), II, 2-6 [the quoted passage is in II, 25], though it was sent in the name of Essex. It seems to me impossible that Essex should have been so familiar with the new trend of thought and studies in the nineties as the writer shows himself to be.

[40] *Advancement*, ed. Wright, I.ii.8.

the contrary, it was the mark of an individual taste or a peculiar initiation.[41] Bacon's influence, like his own prose style, can best be explained in terms of his admiration and imitation of Tacitus, and the point has had to be elaborated at some length for the reason that it has a special bearing upon the development of seventeenth-century English style. The other models of Anti-Ciceronian prose were already known to Englishmen: Hall and the letter writers were familiarizing them with the Senecan manner of Lipsius, and the intimate whimsical vein of Montaigne was beginning to be domesticated in their own prose. From these sources they could learn most of what Anti-Ciceronianism had to teach concerning the expression of acute wit by ingenious rhetoric. But the desire for wit and ingenuity was only one phase of seventeenth-century taste. Combined with it was a desire for ceremonious dignity, an ideal of deliberate and grave demeanor, which was partly, no doubt, an inheritance from the courtly past but was modified and indeed largely created by the profound moral experience which the new age was undergoing. A prose style that should adequately express this age must contrive, therefore, to mingle elements that in any other period would appear oddly contrasted. It must be at once ingenious and lofty, intense yet also profound, acute, realistic, revealing, but at the same time somewhat grave and mysterious. It must have in short that curious sublimity which is felt in the painting of El Greco, in the sermons and letters of Donne, and in certain sculptures of Bernini.

Seneca—its favorite author—might *suggest* the ideal manner;

[41] [The conventional view is expressed by Henry Savile whose final note to the *Life of Agricola* in his translation of Tacitus, *The Ende of Nero and Beginning of Galba. Fower Bookes of the Histories of Cornelius Tacitus* (Oxford, 1591) refers to "that Heresie of Style begun by *Seneca, Quintillian*, the *Plinies*, and *Tacitus.*" It is noteworthy that Savile links Seneca and Tacitus, for Williamson, partly in criticism of Croll, argues that Tacitus' style "offers more likeness than difference when compared with 'Seneca's own style—disconnected, pointed, antithetic, metaphorical and piquant' " (*Senecan Amble*, p. 187, quoting J. W. Duff, *A Literary History of Rome in the Silver Age* [London, 1927], p. 108). Cf. Williamson, pp. 82-83, 113-115, 127, 187-190, and passim for refinements on Croll's ideas, especially those about Bacon, Seneca, and Tacitus.

Croll's remarks should not obscure the fact that Tacitus was popular in the first half of the seventeenth century (cf. Williamson, p. 191), because of his mastery of statecraft and court wisdom, his poignant significance of utterance, his moral sententiousness, and his individualism. Tacitus' popularity was a European phenomenon which began about 1575 with Lipsius' ed. of his works and Diego Hurtado de Mendoza's account of the War of Granada, which imitated the historian's style and method.]

but he was too superficial, too familiar, to furnish a complete model of it. Lucan's nodosity and rhetorical pomp served better as a guide to the poets; and Tacitus, if he had not been too difficult (and indeed too novel, for he had not been widely read in the sixteenth century) would have been the usual exemplar of English prose style. Bacon's great service to English prose was that he naturalized a style in which ingenious obscurity and acute significance are the appropriate garb of the mysteries of empire, and by means of his example the Tacitean strain became familiar to many English writers who were not sufficiently trained in Tacitus himself to imitate his style directly.[42]

(b) *Science and Seventeenth-Century Prose*

Besides domesticating the style of Tacitus in English prose, Bacon aided in various technical ways which cannot be described here in the formulation of a new rhetorical program.[43] But of course his greatest service to the prose movement of his time was not directly and expressly a literary one. It is to be found in his contributions to the great intellectual movement of which Anti-Ciceronianism is but the rhetorical and literary expression.

The progress of rationalism during the sixteenth century had been rapid, and it had been increasingly so as the century drew to an end. But the complete triumph which it was to obtain was still adjourned by a partial lack of co-operation among its leaders in the various fields of intellectual endeavor. Many of them were specialists, of course, who failed to understand as clearly as the defenders of orthodoxy in the universities and courts did how closely their various subjects were related to one another in the general interests of progress. Cujas and Alciati, for instance, were jurists; Ramus' studies ranged widely, but he impressed himself on his age

[42] On the sublimity of Tacitus, see an interesting passage in François de La Mothe le Vayer, *Jugemens sur les Anciens et Principaux Historiens Grecs et Latins* in his *Œuvres* (1685), III, 208: "Son genre d'écrire grave (etc.)." [Cf. *Muret*, III (pp. 153-154 and n.64).]

[43] To avoid repetition I have omitted several points concerning Bacon's rhetorical theory which are more or less developed in *Muret* [II, par. 5 and the second paragraph following n.9; III, par. 7; nn. 33, 43, 47, 54, 61, 65, 66 and, by implication, *passim*]. Most important of these perhaps is Bacon's constant dependence upon Aristotle's *Rhetoric*—often a peculiar sign of Anti-Ciceronian intention. There is need of a thorough and complete study of Bacon's rhetorical writings [the need is largely satisfied by Wallace, Crane, and Howell, cited in *APS*, n.38 and *Lipse*, n.9. The account of the progress of rationalism which follows in the present essay is paralleled in *Muret*, II; for relevant bibliography, see *Muret*, n.6].

as a logician; Montaigne was a moralist pure and simple; and though Muret and Lipsius were both fully aware of the revolutionary implications in their methods of study, they were daunted by the formidable front of orthodoxy. Intellectually free, they were involved in practical relations with the powers of conservatism which compelled them to protect themselves by disingenuous compromises and a shocking Machiavellianism. Of course their hesitations and concealments were only the usual marks of all movements of radicalism and innovation; a forward tendency never presents as solid a front as the established system that it is bound to conflict with, because its aims are partly concealed in the future and no one can tell how the various elements that co-operate in it will relate and adjust themselves in the final settlement. But reformers had more than the usual reasons for fear and vacillation in the sixteenth century because the orthodoxies of all kinds, religious, political, intellectual, and literary, were more than usually aware at that time of the community of their interests and more effectively united in self-defense. What was needed at the end of the century was such an appraisement of the situation as would give an equal consciousness of their common aims, and equal clearness of purpose, to the champions of the more progressive and positive modes of thought.

This was the most important part of the task undertaken by Bacon in the *Advancement of Learning* and the *Novum Organum*. It is now generally recognized that the materials of which these works were made were most of them old and familiar; many of them had even been worked up by his predecessors into almost the form in which Bacon used them. Aristotelianism, medieval scholasticism, Barthollism, Platonism, Ciceronianism, Euphuism, and whatever other shadowy phantoms of reality had haunted the Renaissance, had already been severally exposed to the criticism of reason. But Bacon gathered them all together within the limits of a single survey and covered them all over with one narrow *hic jacet*. After that they were as pallid and ridiculous as ghosts astray in the open daylight; they could no longer frighten anyone.

But that was not all that he did for the new rationalism. He put the vigorous new natural sciences of his age at the center of all his projects for the progress of knowledge. The program of education announced by Muret and elaborated by Lipsius included only the two branches of moral philosophy (the *sapientia*, or private morality, of the ancient Stoics and Peripatetics, and the *prudentia*, or worldly wisdom, which they studied in Tacitus, Machiavelli, and other ancient and modern politicians), with the rhetoric appropriate to them. The effect of Bacon's writings was to put natural science in a definite place in this program—not the first place, it is true, because the century that began with Montaigne and ended with La Bruyère and Halifax was above all else the century of moral philosophy—but yet in a recognized position of authority, from which it could exercise a constant influence upon the moral researches of the age by clarifying, illustrating, defining their method of procedure. This modification had such important literary effects that it must not be passed over here with a mere mention.

The method introduced by Lipsius and Montaigne in the study of the moral situation of their time was in fact the method of science. It does not appear that these philosophers thought of it in that way or were in any profound way affected by the scientific studies that preceded Bacon's work: their intellectual houses were without windows, or had very narrow ones. But they were compelled by the impulse of their positivistic purposes to adopt the same method of experiment and induction in their own subjects that has since produced such astounding results in natural science. These philosophers were in revolt, not only against the medieval forms of thought, as they are often said to have been, but also against the aims of the Renaissance itself as they had chiefly displayed themselves hitherto. For the effort of their own century had been devoted, exactly like that of the more remote past, chiefly to the rearing of conspicuous philosophic constructions which had no foundations in immediate observation or experience. "Men have despised," said Bacon, "to be conversant in ordinary and common matters . . . ; but contrariwise they have compounded sciences chiefly of a certain resplendent or lustrous matter, chosen to give glory either to the subtility of disputations or to the eloquence of discourses."[44] They themselves took the humbler task of searching these glorious Houses of Pride to their sandy foundations. Nor did they pretend to raise other constructions in their stead, except only such modest shelters as would serve their immediate moral needs. To be conversant in ordinary and common matters was their only boast. To distinguish the facts of moral experience with critical and

---

[44] *Advancement of Learning*, in *Works* (1868), III, 418 [ed. Wright, II.xx.2. Croll's misquotation, "either to give glory to the subtlety" has been corrected].

inquiring eyes, to record their observations with the acuteness and exactness of the new literary style they had devised for this purpose, this was an intellectual exercise well adapted to their subtle wits; and it was a task moreover that afforded them the thrill of novel adventure. In short, the intellectual program of the seventeenth century was the scientific work of moral observation and delineation, and Montaigne's avowal of his purpose to portray for the first time exactly what the thing is that goes by the name of a man is echoed at the other end of the century with only a slight difference of tone, in La Bruyère's truly scientific program, "the *description* of man."

Bacon therefore did not have to teach the method of science to the moralists of his age, for they had already learned it. But the new studies in natural history which Bacon helped to make popular were of great aid to them in their own work, because it trained them, and of course their audiences too, in the habit of exact observation, sharp definition, and clear classification which were necessary for their purpose. Bacon himself provides an excellent illustration of scientific method in the realm of moral observation; for the aphorisms, *Antitheta*, "topics," "colours of good and evil," etc., from which, as from a spinner's bottom,[45] he says, he unwound the thread of his essays, are pieces of scientific apparatus used in a moralist's workshop. They are the notes he has taken at the moment when the experiment was on and observation was keenest and then allocated, by a rough and ready scheme of classification, among certain headings and subheadings which will make them available for future reference. To enumerate the works of seventeenth-century morality that were composed by this method would be tedious: Descartes' *Meditations*, Wotton's *Aphorisms of Education*, and countless other works display the method even in their form; and it is but slightly veiled by a more elaborate manner in Browne's *Religio Medici*; Pascal, La Bruyère, Temple, and Halifax all employed it.

To distinguish rhetorical from intellectual process in the writings of professed naturalists is to divide between the bark and the tree; whatever the motions of their minds, they will betray themselves in their style. But some of the results of the addition of science to the intellectual program may be traced most clearly in the history of prose style. They are chiefly of two opposite kinds, which finally

---

[45] [bobbin.]

came into open conflict in the second half of the century. At first the natural sciences tended to give greater imaginative range and freedom to the new Attic prose. We may observe this phenomenon most clearly in the writings of certain professed men of science who became literary men and stylists through an interesting blending in their thought of the ideas of Bacon and Montaigne, students of medicine especially, like Sir Thomas Browne and Robert Burton or the Parisian doctor Guy Patin, who bring into new and curious relations the results of their physical explorations of man's nature and the moral speculations of their time. Essentially moralists, as all men of their age were, they were able to add to the common stock of ideas and images a wealth of curious detail derived from their professional pursuits and their knowledge of unfamiliar facts. The courageous scepticism of the new kind of morality and the rhetorical audacity that accompanied it appealed equally to their tastes, and they contributed in their turn out of their mastery of physiological research to the effects of curiosity and novelty on which so much of the success of the new prose depended. In two writers in whom we may fairly describe the union of scientific and moral interest as perfect and equal, in Sir Thomas Browne and Pascal, we may observe at their highest development the powers of intellectual imagination which might be born of this union.

As the century advanced, however, it became apparent that science was not to remain on the side of poetry and the imagination; on the contrary, it allied itself more and more closely with the movement for clarity and common sense which was gathering strength from so many different sources. A well-known pronunciamento of the Royal Society in England expressly dissociated the literary aims of that scientific body from the rhetoric of Bacon and aligned them with the new taste for a plain and clear style. At the same time, in France, the influence of Descartes was gradually making itself felt even among those who were not at all willing to accept his philosophy: *imagination* began to be a word of derision; Malebranche taught an almost geometrical use of reason as a corrective of its evil influence; the teachers of Port Royal found in logic the way to a Christian plainness and purity of style; and the quality that distinguishes the style of La Bruyère, and even the nobler language of Pascal, is a strictly scientific precision rather than those occasional, and as it were accidental, triumphs of revelation which are effected by an ambitious imagination or a roving fancy.

✧ V ✧

Conclusion

Muret, Lipsius, Montaigne, and Bacon, though the period of their collective activity covers three quarters of a century, belong to a single generation in the development of Renaissance culture, the generation in which modern rationalism definitely declared itself as the doctrine of the future, and the new, the Anti-Ciceronian, form of prose style assumed its place in the world of letters. But Muret belongs at the beginning of this generation; he is partly the pioneer, partly the founder of its intellectual program. The three philosophers we have considered in the preceding pages lived in the full flower of its career, when its conflict with the forces of the past was virtually over. Rationalism had now won its victory, and displayed that tendency to divide into various schools or phases which always appears when a general idea mingles with the several elements of a varied intellectual life and takes different color from each of them.

In this phase of its history Attic prose divides into three main forms, or perhaps we should call them merely tendencies toward distinct forms, which displayed themselves more conspicuously in the generation that followed, and even can be distinguished, though less clearly, in the "classical" prose which developed in a succeeding generation out of seventeenth-century Attic. Lipsius, Montaigne, and Bacon each represents one of these three forms or tendencies, and the discussion of their ideas has perhaps made clear what they are. A specific statement will serve, however, to make more definite what has already been said of them.

First in order of importance is a tendency due to the prevalence of Stoic philosophy. The prose in which this tendency is manifest can best be known as prose of the Stoic model. "Senecan prose" would be more definite, but it would sometimes include too much, and on the other hand it would fail to indicate the full scope of Stoic imitation. Lipsius is as clearly the founder of this style as he is of the Neo-Stoic philosophy which usually accompanied it in the first half of the century.

To the student of events beyond the limits of the seventeenth

200

century, a tendency in style associated with the sceptical or "liber-tine" thought of that century and especially with the influence of Montaigne, would seem worthy of the first place in order of impor-tance. This we can only call "libertine" prose, whether we consider its philosophical implications or its rhetorical theories and form. The groundwork of this style is the Senecan pattern, which is so much more apparent in the Stoic model; but it aims at freedom, and chooses several other writers, ancient and modern, as the models by which it seeks, through the method of imitation, to escape from the method of imitation. Rabelais is the chief of these. Montaigne adds the taste for Plutarch's essays; and the form of Montaigne's own style, from 1600 onward, mingles with that of Rabelais' in almost equal proportions in the prevailing forms of libertine style in the seventeenth century.

Next to these in the favor of the age was the prose of "politicians" and students of "prudential wisdom": Bacon, Malvezzi, Gracián, Grotius, and a host of others, who get their rhetorical and often their political ideas chiefly from Tacitus.

To these three major forms must be added a tendency which cannot be separated from any of them but manifests itself every-where as the peculiar mark of the genius of the seventeenth century, a tendency observable in writers as normal as Bacon, Browne, and Balzac, but apparent in its full efflorescence in the letters of Donne, the essays of Gracián and Malvezzi and many of their fellow countrymen, the histories of Pierre Mathieu, and many similar works. For this tendency there is unfortunately no convenient name in English. "Metaphysical" is even a less happy term to describe the kinds of prose in which it appears than the related kinds of poetry, and there seems to be no possibility of making a practicable adjective or noun in English from the continental terms *concet-tismo*, etc. It may be known as the "prose of imaginative conceit" in order that we may keep in line with the terms of current criticism. But I am tempted to make the bold innovation of calling it "the baroque style" in prose, for no other term will so exactly describe its characteristic qualities.

In the three forms enumerated above (with due regard to the *concettistic* tendency in each of them) may be ranged all the Attic prose of the century from 1575 to 1675, and that is to say all its characteristic prose, except the writings of one or two great indi-vidualists who escape the influence of their time; and it is upon the lines laid down in this classification that the further study of seventeenth-century prose style must be conducted. What is now necessary is a thorough survey of Stoic prose, libertine prose, and Tacitean prose separately, each treated with reference to its philosophical theory, its preferred models in antiquity and modern times, its relation to the culture of the age, and its rhetorical forms. Only the outlines of such a survey can be suggested, of course, in the study of individual authors—even of such representative and influential leaders as Muret, Lipsius, Montaigne, and Bacon.

Foreword to Essay Five

Croll's abandonment of his earlier term "Attic," with its associations of simplicity and plain brevity, for the controversial title "baroque" indicates an even greater commitment than before to the idea of the "self-conscious modernism" of the Renaissance.[1] After the previous essays, there is some disingenuousness in using a word connected with the greatest decorative period Europe has known to describe a movement which professed to be antirhetorical. "Baroque," however, contains for Croll exactly the suggestions he wanted of

[1] René Wellek, "The Concept of Baroque in Literary Scholarship," cited in the Foreword to *APL*, should be consulted for a basic bibliography of works on the baroque. See also W. Stechow, "The Baroque: A Critical Summary," *JAAC*, xiv (1955), 171-174, and "Definitions of the Baroque in the Visual Arts," *JAAC*, v (1946), 109-115; William Halewood, "The Uses of the Term 'Baroque' in Modern English Literary Criticism," Diss. Univ. Minnesota, *DA*, xx (1959), 2290; Bernard C. Heyl, "Meanings of Baroque," *JAAC*, xix (1961), 275-287. General studies of the problem, all having a bibliographical value, may be found in the first chapter of Giuliano Pellegrini, *Barocco Inglese* (Florence, 1953), and the ever-increasing number of works by Helmut A. Hatzfeld: "A Critical Survey of Recent Baroque Theories," *Boletín del Instituto Caro y Cuervo*, v (1948), 1-33; "A Clarification of the Baroque Problem in the Romance Literatures," *CL*, i (1949), 113-139; *Literature through Art* (New York, 1952); "The Baroque from the Viewpoint of the Literary Historian," *JAAC*, xiv (1955), 156-164; "Italia, Spagna e Francia nello Sviluppo della Letteratura Barocca," *Lettere Italiane*, ix (1957), i-29; *Der Gegenwärtige Stand der Romanistischen Barockforschung*, Bayerische Akademie der Wissenschaften, Philosophische-historische Klasse: Sitzungberichte, iv (Munich, 1961); also R. A. Sayce, "The Use of the Term Baroque in French Literary History," *CL*, x (1958), 246-253; Roy Daniells, "Baroque Form in English Literature," *UTQ*, xiv (1944-45), 393-408, and *Milton, Mannerism and Baroque* (Toronto, 1963); Gustav R. Hocke, *Manierismus in der Literatur* (Hamburg, 1959); Paul Meissner, *Die Geisteswissenschaftlichen Grundlagen des Englischen Literaturbarocks* (Munich, 1934); Part iii of James V. Mirollo, *The Poet of the Marvelous, Giambattista Marino* (New York, 1963); Lowry Nelson, Jr., *Baroque Lyric Poetry* (New Haven, 1961); Harold M. Priest, *Renaissance and Baroque Lyrics* (Evanston, 1962); Frank J. Warnke, *European Metaphysical Poetry* (New Haven, 1961); also the Baroque issue of *Cahiers du Sud*, xlii (1955); *La Critica Stilistica e il Barocco Letterario: Atti del Secondo Congresso Internazionale di Studi Italiani* (Florence, 1958); and *Rettoria e Barocco: Atti del III Congresso Internazionale di Studi Umanistica*, ed. Enrico Castello (Rome, 1955). From among the applications of the term to prose, the following may be mentioned: R. A. Sayce, "Baroque Elements in Montaigne," *French Studies*, viii (1954), 1-16; Imbrie Buffum, *Studies in the Baroque from Montaigne to Rotrou* (New Haven, 1957); Helmut A. Hatzfeld, "Per una Definizione dello Stile di Montaigne," *Convivium*, n.s. i (1964), 284-290; Sister Julie Maggioni, *The Pensées of Pascal: A Study in Baroque Style*, Catholic University Studies in Romance Languages and Literatures, Vol. xxxix (Washington, D.C., 1950). "Baroque" as a literary term is so involved in defining itself and so committed to metaphorical descriptions of literary qualities and analogies between the arts that its value is highly questionable.

the human mind struggling bravely with resistant masses of thought, and producing in the effort masterpieces of asymmetric design. It has proved impossible to write about the curt and the loose styles without employing Croll's distinctions, but Williamson has found the "desire for speed of communication, for returns on one's time" sufficiently explains much Senecan brevity, without invoking the craving for expressiveness which Croll sees everywhere in baroque style.

With twice the space available it would be difficult to do justice to Williamson's revisions of Croll's work. Fundamentally, they consist in making more complicated the overlapping of styles which Croll described firmly as Euphuistic, Senecan, Tacitean, libertine, and so on. Croll's own division of styles was basically twofold: on the one hand were the styles which specialized in patterns of sound (*schemata verborum*), and which were distinguished by rigid parallelism, paromoion, and jingles of every kind—even Cicero must be included in this group, as well as Isocrates, Lyly, and many patristic writers; on the other hand were the new expressive writers whose schemes were the figures of thought or wit, and whose styles as a whole were marked by deliberate asymmetry. Williamson returned to the three ancient categories of style, which he defined structurally as the circular (Ciceronian), the antithetic (Euphuistic), and the loose (Senecan), and he has shown conclusively that all these styles share different qualities with each other: that Gorgian patterns are common in Seneca, that Bacon's prose is often Euphuistic, that terse Asian and Stoic styles are hard to tell from all but the plainest Attic, and that antithetic constructions can be used to display either thought or sound. The use to which the schemes are put, not their mere presence or absence, is to Williamson of primary importance. Croll's division of the Anti-Ciceronian style into its curt, loose, and obscure forms Williamson alters so as to make curt the norm, from which writers moved either towards a Tacitean truncatedness (and Lipsius belongs here), or towards the loose, which is not essentially a brief style at all. These realignments have resulted in a demonstration that Croll, especially in this essay, overemphasized asymmetry as the mark of Senecanism (though it would be true of Tacitean imitation), and have revealed many cases of disguised symmetry which Croll overlooked. One may still accept Croll's description of a curt period as "a series of imaginative moments occurring in a logical pause or suspension," but one has to relinquish the notion of the unpremeditated nature of Senecan style, even in its looser form, although the latter generally aimed at effects which appear unpremeditated.

If Williamson has noted, however, that Croll's analyses of style are more subtle than those the seventeenth century often recognized, the same comment can be made of Williamson's. His book remains indispensable to serious students, less so to readers who want only the ground rules. For these Croll is still an excellent cicerone to the first half of the century, but an untrustworthy guide to the second half, when the "natural" style was one which increasingly buttressed its spontaneity with logic, in which second thoughts were always preferable to first thoughts, and Sprat's style could be praised for being "as polite and as fast as marble." For the earlier period, Croll's "baroque" has been triumphantly vindicated by Jonas Barish's *Ben Jonson and the Language of Prose Comedy*, which is the most important study of Jacobean prose style to appear since Williamson's; the second chapter in particular needs to be read in conjunction with Croll's essay. Not only has Barish added "baroque" techniques to Croll's list—such as the disturbing of logical word order, separating grammatically-related words, coupling incongruous elements in parallel forms—but he has shown with many examples how these techniques were used dramatically to portray states of mind like anger, distraction, simple-mindedness, indignation, and ceremonial foppishness. The roughness of Jonson's style, Barish suggests, was painstakingly achieved, and served not to express the doubts and introspections of Jonson himself (who would have denied he had them), but as a means of representing the follies of the world in its language. An objective use of the baroque Croll did not envisage. By successfully proving the use of baroque style as linguistic satire, and by documenting its devices so thoroughly, Barish has freed the baroque from some of Croll's moorings, while justifying, in one important case, Croll's insistence on the asymmetry of its design.

Barish's study of the witty use of baroque style, in a writer famous for the strength of his judgment, is a reminder that concepts of wit and decorum now enter all discussions of seventeenth-century literature. Croll himself was the first to point out how carefully the Anti-Ciceronians veiled their heterodoxy, and he regarded Royal Society prose as a plainer variety of Senecanism dictated solely by decorum. Wit, on the contrary, was always a means of amplification which delighted in ingenious comparisons and antitheses, and was extremely compatible therefore with the hidden symmetries and bold asymmetry of baroque style. If Croll may be said to have underplayed the controlling power of these artistic canons, in the interests of his thesis concerning the humane importance of the Anti-Ciceronian movement, he did expose with a new clarity the prevalence of Stoic and libertine tendencies in the seventeenth century. When he explained how the Renaissance could be classical and modern at the same time, prose from Muret to the Royal Society acquired a sharper outline and a more rational history.

JOHN M. WALLACE

THE JOHNS HOPKINS UNIVERSITY

The Baroque Style in Prose*

EDITED BY JOHN M. WALLACE

✧ I ✧

Introduction

IN THE latter years of the sixteenth century a change declared itself in the purposes and forms of the arts of Western Europe for which it is hard to find a satisfactory name. One would like to describe it, because of some interesting parallels with a later movement, as the first modern manifestation of the Romantic Spirit; and it did, in fact, arise out of a revolt against the classicism of the high Renaissance. But the terms "romantic" and "classical" are both perplexing and unphilosophical; and their use should not be extended. It would be much clearer and more exact to describe the change in question as a radical effort to adapt traditional modes and forms of expression to the uses of a self-conscious modernism; and the style that it produced was actually called in several of the arts—notably in architecture and prose-writing—the "modern" or "new" style. But the term that most conveniently describes it is "baroque." This term, which was at first used only in architecture, has lately been extended to cover the facts that present themselves at the same time in sculpture and in painting; and it may now properly be used to describe, or at least to name, the characteristic modes of expression in all the arts during a certain period—the period, that is, between the high Renaissance and the eighteenth century; a period that begins in the last quarter of the sixteenth century, reaches a culmination at about 1630, and thenceforward gradually modifies its character under new influences.

Expressiveness rather than formal beauty was the pretension of the new movement, as it is of every movement that calls itself modern. It disdained complacency, suavity, copiousness, emptiness, ease, and in avoiding these qualities sometimes obtained effects of

* From *Studies in English Philology: A Miscellany in Honor of Frederick Klaeber*, ed. Kemp Malone and Martin B. Ruud (Minneapolis: University of Minnesota Press, copyright 1929; renewed 1957 by Kemp Malone).

contortion or obscurity, which it was not always willing to regard as faults. It preferred the forms that express the energy and labor of minds seeking the truth, not without dust and heat, to the forms that express a contented sense of the enjoyment and possession of it. In a single word, the motions of souls, not their states of rest, had become the themes of art.

The meaning of these antitheses may be easily illustrated in the history of Venetian painting, which passes, in a period not longer than one generation, from the self-contained and relatively symmetrical designs of Titian, through the swirls of Tintoretto, to the contorted and aspiring lines that make the paintings of El Greco so restless and exciting. Poetry moves in the same way at about the same time; and we could metaphorically apply the terms by which we distinguish El Greco from Titian to the contrast between the rhythms of Spenser and the Petrarchans, on one hand, and the rhythms of Donne, on the other, between the style of Ariosto and the style of Tasso. In the sculptures of Bernini (in his portrait busts as well as in his more famous and theatrical compositions) we may again observe how ideas of motion take the place of ideas of rest; and the operation of this principle is constantly to be observed also in the school of architecture associated with the same artist's name. In the façade of a Baroque church, says Geoffrey Scott, "a movement, which in the midst of a Bramantesque design would be destructive and repugnant, is turned to account and made the basis of a more dramatic, but not less satisfying treatment, the motive of which is not peace, but energy."[1]

And finally the change that takes place in the prose style of the same period—the change, that is, from Ciceronian to Anti-Ciceronian forms and ideas—is exactly parallel with those that were occurring in the other arts, and is perhaps more useful to the student of the baroque impulse than any of the others, because it was more self-conscious, more definitely theorized by its leaders, and more clearly described by its friends and foes. In some previous studies I have considered the triumph of the Anti-Ciceronian movement at considerable length; but I have been concerned chiefly with the theory of the new style; and my critics have complained, justly, that I have been too difficult, or even abstract. In the present study I hope to correct this defect. Its purpose is to describe the *form* of Anti-Ciceronian, or baroque, prose.

[1] *The Architecture of Humanism* (London, 1914), p. 225.

There are of course several elements of prose technique: diction, or the choice of words; the choice of figures; the principle of balance or rhythm; the form of the period, or sentence; and in a full description of baroque prose all of these elements would have to be considered. The last-mentioned of them—the form of the period—is, however, the most important and the determinant of the others; and this alone is to be the subject of discussion in the following pages.

The Anti-Ciceronian period was sometimes described in the seventeenth century as an "exploded" period; and this metaphor is very apt if it is taken as describing solely its outward appearance, the mere fact of its form. For example, here is a period from Sir Henry Wotton, a typical expression of the political craft of the age:

> Men must beware of running down steep hills with weighty bodies; they once in motion, *suo feruntur pondere*; steps are not then voluntary.[2]

The members of this period stand farther apart one from another than they would in a Ciceronian sentence; there are no syntactic connectives between them whatever; and semicolons or colons are necessary to its proper punctuation. In fact, it has the appearance of having been disrupted by an explosion within.

The metaphor would be false, however, if it should be taken as describing the manner in which this form has been arrived at. For it would mean that the writer first shaped a round and complete oratorical period in his mind and then partly undid his work. And this, of course, does not happen. Wotton gave this passage its form, not by demolishing a Ciceronian period, but by omitting several of the steps by which roundness and smoothness of composition might have been attained. He has deliberately avoided the processes of mental revision in order to express his idea when it is nearer the point of its origin in his mind.

We must stop for a moment on the word *deliberately*. The negligence of the Anti-Ciceronian masters, their disdain of revision, their dependence upon casual and emergent devices of construction, might sometimes be mistaken for mere indifference to art or contempt of form; and it is, in fact, true that Montaigne and Burton, even Pascal and Browne, are sometimes led by a dislike of formality

---

[2] "Table Talk," in *Life and Letters*, ed. Logan Pearsall Smith (Oxford, 1907), II, 500.

into too licentious a freedom. Yet even their extravagances are purposive, and express a creed that is at the same time philosophical and artistic. Their purpose was to portray, not a thought, but a mind thinking, or, in Pascal's words, *la peinture de la pensée*. They knew that an idea separated from the act of experiencing it is not the idea that was experienced. The ardor of its conception in the mind is a necessary part of its truth; and unless it can be conveyed to another mind in something of the form of its occurrence, either it has changed into some other idea or it has ceased to be an idea, to have any existence whatever except a verbal one. It was the latter fate that happened to it, they believed, in the Ciceronian periods of sixteenth-century Latin rhetoricians. The successive processes of revision to which these periods had been submitted had removed them from reality by just so many steps. For themselves, they preferred to present the truth of experience in a less concocted form, and deliberately chose as the moment of expression that in which the idea first clearly objectifies itself in the mind, in which, therefore, each of its parts still preserves its own peculiar emphasis and an independent vigor of its own—in brief, the moment in which truth is still *imagined*.

The form of a prose period conceived in such a theory of style will differ in every feature from that of the conventional period of an oratorical, or Ciceronian, style; but its most conspicuous difference will appear in the way it connects its members or clauses one with another. In the period quoted above from Wotton the members are syntactically wholly free; there are no ligatures whatever between one and another. But there is another type of Anti-Ciceronian period, in which the ordinary marks of logical succession—conjunctions, pronouns, etc.—are usually present, but are of such a kind or are used in such a way as to bind the members together in a characteristically loose and casual manner. The difference between the two types thus described may seem somewhat unimportant; and it is true that they run into each other and cannot always be sharply distinguished. The most representative Anti-Ciceronians, like Montaigne and Browne, use them both and intermingle them. But at their extremes they are not only distinguishable; they serve to distinguish different types, or schools, of seventeenth-century style. They derive from different models, belong to different traditions, and sometimes define the philosophical affiliations of the authors who prefer them.

They will be considered here separately; the first we will call, by a well-known seventeenth-century name, the *période coupée*, or, in an English equivalent, the "curt period" (so also the *stile coupé*, or the "curt style"); the other by the name of the "loose period" (and the "loose style"); though several other appropriate titles suggest themselves in each case.[3]

✧ II ✧

Stile Coupé

(a)

One example of the *période coupée* has already been given. Here are others:

> Pour moy, qui ne demande qu'à devenir plus sage, non plus sçavant ou eloquent, ces ordonnances logiciennes et aristoteliques ne sont pas à propos; je veulx qu'on commence par le dernier poinct: i'entends assez que c'est que Mort et Volupté; qu'on ne s'amuse pas à les anatomizer. (Montaigne)

> 'Tis not worth the reading, I yield it, I desire thee not to lose time in perusing so vain a subject, I should be peradventure loth myself to read him or thee so writing, 'tis not *operae pretium*. (Burton)

> No armor can *defend* a fearful heart. It will kill itself, within. (Felltham)

> Oui; mais il faut parier; cela n'est pas volontaire, vous êtes embarqués. (Pascal)

> L'éloquence continue ennuie.

> Les princes et les rois jouent quelquefois; ils ne sont pas toujours sur leurs trônes, ils s'y ennuient: la grandeur a besoin d'être quittée pour être sentie. (Pascal)

> The world that I regard is myself; it is the microcosm of my own frame that I cast mine eye on: for the other, I use it but like my globe, and turn it round sometimes for my recreation. (Browne)

---

[3] For example, the *stile coupé* was sometimes called *stile serré* ("serried style"), and Francis Thompson has used this term in describing a kind of period common in Browne. For synonyms of "loose style" see section III of this paper.

Il y a des hommes qui attendent à être dévots et religieux que tout le monde se déclare impie et libertin: ce sera alors le parti du vulgaire, ils sauront s'en dégager. (La Bruyère)[4]

In all of these passages, as in the period quoted from Wotton, there are no two main members that are syntactically connected. But it is apparent also that the characteristic style that they have in common contains several other features besides this.

In the first place, each member is as short as the most alert intelligence would have it. The period consists, as some of its admirers were wont to say, of the nerves and muscles of speech alone; it is as hard-bitten, as free of soft or superfluous flesh, as "one of Caesar's soldiers."[5]

Second, there is a characteristic order, or mode of progression, in a curt period that may be regarded either as a necessary consequence of its omission of connectives or as the causes and explanation of this. We may describe it best by observing that the first member is likely to be a self-contained and complete statement of the whole idea of the period. It is so because writers in this style like to avoid prearrangements and preparations; they begin, as Montaigne puts it, at *le dernier poinct*, the point aimed at. The first member therefore exhausts the mere fact of the idea; logically there is nothing more to say. But it does not exhaust its imaginative truth or the energy of its conception. It is followed, therefore, by other members, each with a new tone or emphasis, each expressing a new apprehension of the truth expressed in the first. We may describe the progress of a curt period, therefore, as a series of imaginative moments occurring in a logical pause or suspension. Or—to be less obscure—we may compare it with successive flashes of a jewel or prism as it is turned about on its axis and takes the light in different ways.

[4] References are as follows: Montaigne, "Des Livres," *Essais* II.x, ed. J.-V. Le Clerc (Paris, 1865), II, 122; Robert Burton, "To the Reader," *The Anatomy of Melancholy*, ed. A. R. Shilleto (London, 1893), p. 24; Owen Felltham, "Of Fear and Cowardice," *Resolves* I.71 (London, 1677), p. 110; Pascal, *Pensées*, ed. Léon Brunschvicg (Paris, 1904), II, 146 (section VII in 1670 Port-Royal ed.); *Pensées*, II, 269 (section XXI in Port-Royal ed.); Sir Thomas Browne, *Religio Medici*, Part II, section 11, in *Works*, ed. Simon Wilkin (London, 1846), II, 110; La Bruvère, "Des Esprits Forts," *Œuvres*, ed. G. Servois (Paris, 1865), II, 239. These editions have been used for subsequent quotations from the authors' works.

[5] The phrase comes from a midseventeenth-century work on prose style, and is there applied to *il dir moderno*: Daniello Bartoli, "Dello Stile," *Dell' Uomo di Lettere*, in *Opere* (Venice, 1716), III, 101.

It is true, of course, that in a series of propositions there will always be some logical process; the truth stated will undergo some development or change. For example, in the sentence from Montaigne at the beginning of this section, the later members add something to the idea; and in the quotation from Pascal's *Pensées sur l'Éloquence*, given below it, the thought suddenly enlarges in the final member. Yet the method of advance is not logical; the form does not express it. Each member, in its main intention, is a separate act of imaginative realization.

In the third place, one of the characteristics of the curt style is deliberate asymmetry of the members of a period; and it is this trait that especially betrays the modernistic character of the style. The chief mark of a conventional, or "classical," art, like that of the sixteenth century, is an approximation to evenness in the size and form of the balanced parts of a design; the mark of a modernistic art, like that of the seventeenth, and the nineteenth and twentieth, centuries, is the desire to achieve an effect of balance or rhythm among parts that are obviously not alike—the love of "some strangeness in the proportions."

In a prose style asymmetry may be produced by varying the length of the members within a period. For example, part of the effect of a sentence from Bishop Hall is due to a variation in this respect among members which nevertheless produce the effect of balance or rhythmic design.

What if they [crosses and adversities] be unpleasant? They are physic: it is enough, if they be wholesome.[6]

But the desired effect is more characteristically produced by conspicuous differences of form, either with or without differences of length. For instance, a characteristic method of the seventeenth century was to begin a succession of members with different kinds of subject words. In the sentence quoted from Wotton the first two members have personal subjects, the third the impersonal "steps"; in the quotation from Pascal the opposite change is made.

Mais il faut parier; cela n'est pas volontaire, vous êtes embarqués.

[6] Joseph Hall, *Heaven upon Earth*, XIII, in *Works* (Oxford, 1837), VI, 20. Note how exactly this reproduces a movement characteristic of Seneca: *Quid tua, uter* [Caesar or Pompey] *vincat? Potest melior vincere: non potest pejor esse qui vicerit.*

In both of these periods, moreover, each of the three members has a distinct and individual turn of phrase, meant to be different from the others. Again, in the period of La Bruyère quoted at the beginning of this section, each new member involves a shift of the mind to a new subject. (Observe also the asymmetry of the members in point of length.)

Sometimes, again, asymmetry is produced by a change from literal to metaphoric statement, or by the reverse, or by a change from one metaphor to another, as in the last example quoted from Pascal, where the metaphor of one embarked upon a ship abruptly takes the place of that of a man engaged in a bet. Or there may be a leap from the concrete to the abstract form; and this is an eminently characteristic feature of the *stile coupé* because this style is always tending toward the aphorism, or *pensée*, as its ideal form. The second passage quoted from Pascal illustrates this in a striking way. It is evident that in the first three members—all concrete, about kings and princes—the author's mind is turning toward a general truth, which emerges complete and abstract in the last member: *la grandeur a besoin d'être quittée pour être sentie.*

The curt style, then, is not characterized only by the trait from which it takes its name, its omission of connectives. It has the four marks that have been described: first, studied brevity of members; second, the hovering, imaginative order; third, asymmetry; and fourth, the omission of the ordinary syntactic ligatures. None of these should, of course, be thought of separately from the others. Each of them is related to the rest and more or less involves them; and when they are all taken together they constitute a definite rhetoric, which was employed during the period from 1575 to 1675 with as clear a knowledge of its tradition and its proper models as the sixteenth-century Ciceronians had of the history of the rhetoric that they preferred.

In brief, it is a Senecan style; and, although the imitation of Seneca never quite shook off the imputation of literary heresy that had been put upon it by the Augustan purism of the preceding age, and certain amusing cautions and reservations were therefore felt to be necessary, yet nearly all of the theorists of the new style succeeded in expressing their devotion to their real master in one way or another. Moreover, they were well aware that the characteristic traits of Seneca's style were not his alone, but had been elaborated before him in the Stoic schools of the Hellenistic period; and all the earlier practitioners of the *stile coupé*, Montaigne (in his first phase), Lipsius, Hall, Charron, etc., write not only as literary Senecans, but rather more as philosophical Stoics.

Senecanism and Stoicism are, then, the primary implications of *stile coupé*. It must be observed, however, that a style once established in general use may cast away the associations in which it originated; and this is what happened in the history of the curt style. Montaigne, for instance, confessed that he had so thoroughly learned Seneca's way of writing that he could not wholly change it even when his ideas and tastes had changed and he had come to prefer other masters. And the same thing is to be observed in many writers of the latter part of the century: St. Évremond, Halifax, and La Bruyère, for instance. Though these writers are all definitely anti-Stoic and anti-Senecan, all of them show that they had learned the curt style too well ever to unlearn it or to avoid its characteristic forms; and there was no great exaggeration in Shaftesbury's complaint, at the very end of the century, that no other movement of style than Seneca's—what he calls the "Senecan amble"—had been heard in prose for a hundred years past.

(b)

The curt or serried style depends for its full effect upon the union of the several formal traits that have been described in the preceding section. We have assumed hitherto that these traits are as rigorous and unalterable as if they were prescribed by a rule; and in the examples cited there have been no significant departures from any of them. But of course slight variations are common even in passages that produce the effect of *stile coupé*; and some searching is necessary to discover examples as pure as those that have been cited. This is so evidently true that it would need no illustration except for the fact that certain kinds of period eminently characteristic of seventeenth-century prose arise from a partial violation of the "rules" laid down. Two of these may be briefly described.

(A) In a number of writers (Browne, Felltham, and South, for example) we often find a period of two members connected by *and*, *or*, or *nor*, which evidently has the character of *stile coupé* because the conjunction has no logical *plus* force whatever. It merely connects two efforts of the imagination to realize the same idea; two as-it-were synchronous statements of it. The following from Browne will be recognized as characteristic of him:

'Tis true, there is an edge in all firm belief, and with an easy metaphor we may say, the sword of faith.

Again:

Therefore I perceive a man may be twice a child, before the days of dotage; and stand in need of Æson's bath before three-score.[7]

Often, too, in a period consisting of a larger number of members the last two are connected by an *and* or the like. But this case can be illustrated in connection with the one that immediately follows.

(B) The rule that the successive members of a *période coupée* are of different and often opposed forms, are asymmetrical instead of symmetrical, is sometimes partly violated inasmuch as these members begin with the same word or form of words, for example, with the same pronoun subject, symmetry, parallelism, and some regularity of rhythm thus introducing themselves into a style that is designed primarily and chiefly to express a dislike of these frivolities. It is to be observed, however, that the members that begin with this suggestion of oratorical pattern usually break it in the words that follow. Except for their beginnings they are as asymmetrical as we expect them to be, and reveal that constant novelty and unexpectedness that is so characteristic of the "baroque" in all the arts.

One illustration is to be found in the style of the "character" writings that enjoyed so great a popularity in the seventeenth century. The frequent recurrence of the same subject word, usually *he* or *they*, is the mannerism of this style, and is sometimes carried over into other kinds of prose in the latter part of the century, as, for instance, in writings of La Bruyère that are not included within the limits of the "character" genre,[8] and in passages of Dryden. It is indeed so conspicuous a mannerism that it may serve to conceal what is after all the more significant feature of the "character" style, namely, the constant variation and contrast of form in members that begin in this formulistic manner.

The style of the "character," however, is that of a highly specialized genre; and the form of the period with reiterated introductory formula can be shown in its more typical character in other kinds of

[7] *Religio Medici*, I.10 and I.42, in *Works*, II, 14, 61.
[8] For instance, in the famous passage "De l'Homme," 128, in *Œuvres*, II, 61, describing the beast-like life of the peasants of France.

prose, as, for example, in a passage from Browne describing the Christian Stoicism of his age:

> Let not the twelve but the two tables be thy law: let Pythagoras be thy remembrancer, not thy textuary and final instructer: and learn the vanity of the world, rather from Solomon than Phocylides.[9]

Browne touches lightly on these repetitions, and uses them not too frequently. Balzac uses them characteristically and significantly. A paragraph from his *Entretiens* may be quoted both in illustration of this fact and for the interest of its subject matter:

> Nous demeurasmes d'accord que l'Autheur qui veut imiter Seneque commence par tout et finit par tout. Son Discours n'est pas un corps entier: c'est un corps en pieces; ce sont des membres couppez; et quoy que les parties soient proches les unes des autres, elles ne laissent pas d'estre separées. Non seulement il n'y a point de nerfs qui les joignent; il n'y a pas mesme de cordes ou d'aiguillettes qui les attachent ensemble: tant cet Autheur est ennemy de toutes sortes de liaisons, soit de la Nature, soit de l'Art: tant il s'esloigne de ces bons exemples que vous imitez si parfaitement.[10]

The passage illustrates exactly Balzac's position in the prose development of the seventeenth century. Montaigne is indeed—in spite of his strictures upon him—his master. He aims, like Montaigne, at the philosophic ease and naturalness of the *genus humile*; he has his taste for aphorism, his taste for metaphor; he is full of "points," and loves to make them show; in short, he is "baroque." But by several means, and chiefly by the kinds of repetition illustrated in this passage (*c'est . . . ce sont; il n'y a point . . . il n'y a pas mesme; tant . . . tant*), he succeeds in introducing that effect of art, of form, of rhythm, for which Descartes and so many other of his contemporaries admired him. He combines in short the "wit" of the seventeenth century with at least the appearance of being "a regular writer," which came, in the forties and fifties, to be regarded in France as highly desirable. In his political writings, and especially in

---

[9] *Christian Morals*, section XXI, *Works*, IV, 107. The period occurs in the midst of a paragraph in which each main member of each period begins with a verb in the imperative mood.

[10] No. XVIII, "De Montaigne et de ses Escrits," in *Œuvres*, ed. L. Moreau (Paris, 1854), II, 402-403.

Le Prince, his iterated opening formula becomes too evident a mannerism, and on page after page one reads periods of the same form: two or three members beginning alike and a final member much longer and more elaborate than the preceding that may or may not begin in the same way. The effect is extremely rhetorical.

(c)

Finally, we have to observe that the typical *période coupée* need not be so short as the examples of it cited at the beginning of the present section. On the contrary, it may continue, without connectives and with all its highly accentuated peculiarities of form, to the length of five or six members. Seneca offered many models for this protracted aphoristic manner, as in the following passage from the *Naturales Quaestiones* (vii.31):

> There are mysteries that are not unveiled the first day: Eleusis keepeth back something for those who come again to ask her. Nature telleth not all her secrets at once. We think we have been initiated: we are still waiting in her vestibule. Those secret treasures do not lie open promiscuously to every one: they are kept close and reserved in an inner shrine.

Similar in form is this six-member period from Browne's *Religio Medici*:

> To see ourselves again, we need not look for Plato's year: every man is not only himself; there have been many Diogeneses, and as many Timons, though but few of that name; men are lived over again; the world is now as it was in ages past; there was none then, but there hath been some one since, that parallels him, and is, as it were, his revived self.[11]

What has been said in a previous section of the characteristic mode of progression in *stile coupé* is strikingly illustrated in such passages as these. Logically they do not move. At the end they are saying exactly what they were at the beginning. Their advance is wholly in the direction of a more vivid imaginative realization; a metaphor revolves, as it were, displaying its different facets; a series of metaphors flash their lights; or a chain of "points" and

---

[11] I.6, in *Works*, II, 11. Feltham uses this manner with too much self-consciousness. See, for instance, a passage on the terse style (*Resolves*, I.20) beginning "They that speak to *children*, assume a pretty lisping."

paradoxes reveals the energy of a single apprehension in the writer's mind. In the latter part of the seventeenth century a number of critics satirize this peculiarity of the Senecan form. Father Bouhours, for instance, observed that with all its pretensions to brevity and significance this style makes less progress in five or six successive statements than a Ciceronian period will often make in one long and comprehensive construction. The criticism is, of course, sound if the only mode of progression is the logical one; but in fact there is a progress of imaginative apprehension, a revolving and upward motion of the mind as it rises in energy, and views the same point from new levels; and this spiral movement is characteristic of baroque prose.

✧ III ✧

The Loose Style

(a)

In the preceding pages we have been illustrating a kind of period in which the members are in most cases syntactically disjunct, and we have seen that in this style the members are characteristically short. It is necessary now to illustrate the other type of Anti-Ciceronian style spoken of at the beginning, in which the members are usually connected by syntactic ligatures, and in which, therefore, both the members and the period as a whole may be, and in fact usually are, as long as in the Ciceronian style, or even longer.

It is more difficult to find an appropriate name for this kind of style than for the other. The "trailing" or "linked" style would describe a relation between the members of the period that is frequent and indeed characteristic, but is perhaps too specific a name. "Libertine" indicates exactly both the form of the style and the philosophical associations that it often implies; but it is wiser to avoid these implications in a purely descriptive treatment. There is but one term that is exact and covers the ground: the term "loose period" or "loose style"; and it is this that we will usually employ. In applying this term, however, the reader must be on his guard against a use of it that slipped into many rhetorical treatises of the nineteenth century. In these works the "loose sentence" was defined as one that has its main clause near the beginning; and an antithetical term "periodic sentence"—an improper one—was devised to name the opposite arrangement. "Loose period" is used here without reference to this confusing distinction.

In order to show its meaning we must proceed by means of examples; and we will take first a sentence—if, indeed, we can call it a sentence—in which Bacon contrasts the "Magistral" method of writing works of learning with the method of "Probation" appropriate to "induced knowledge," "the later whereof [he says] seemeth to be via deserta et interclusa."

> For as knowledges are now delivered, there is a kind of contract of error between the deliverer and the receiver: for he that delivereth knowledge desireth to deliver it in such form as may be best believed, and not as may be best examined; and he that receiveth knowledge desireth rather present satisfaction than expectant inquiry; and so rather not to doubt than not to err: glory making the author not to lay open his weakness, and sloth making the disciple not to know his strength.[12]

The passage is fortunate because it states the philosophy in which Anti-Ciceronian prose has its origin and motive. But our present business is with its form; and in order to illustrate this we will place beside it another passage from another author.

> Elle [l'Imagination] ne peut rendre sages les fous; mais elle les rend heureux, à l'envi de la raison qui ne peut rendre ses amis que misérables, l'une les couvrant de gloire, l'autre de honte.[13]

There is a striking similarity in the way these two periods proceed. In each case an antithesis is stated in the opening members; then the member in which the second part of the antithesis is stated puts out a dependent member. The symmetrical development announced at the beginning is thus interrupted and cannot be resumed. The period must find a way out, a syntactic way of carrying on and completing the idea it carries. In both cases the situation is met in the same way, by a concluding member having the form of an absolute-participle construction, in which the antithetical idea of the whole is sharply, aphoristically resumed.

[12] Of the Advancement of Learning, Bk. II, in Works, ed. Spedding, Ellis, and Heath (London, 1868), III, 403-404; ed. Wright, XVII.3.
[13] Pascal, Pensées, II, 3 (section XXV in 1670 Port-Royal ed.). There should, rhetorically speaking, be semicolons after raison and misérables.

The two passages, in short, are written as if they were meant to illustrate in style what Bacon calls "the method of induced knowledge"; either they have no predetermined plan or they violate it at will; their progression adapts itself to the movements of a mind discovering truth as it goes, thinking while it writes. At the same time, and for the same reason, they illustrate the character of the style that we call "baroque." See, for instance, how symmetry is first made and then broken, as it is in so many baroque designs in painting and architecture; how there is constant swift adaptation of form to the emergencies that arise in an energetic and unpremeditated forward movement; and observe, further, that these signs of spontaneity and improvisation occur in passages loaded with as heavy a content as rhetoric ever has to carry. That is to say, they combine the effect of great mass with the effect of rapid motion; and there is no better formula than this to describe the ideal of the baroque design in all the arts.

But these generalizations are beyond our present purpose. We are to study the loose period first, as we did the curt period, by observing the character of its syntactic links. In the two sentences quoted there are, with a single exception, but two modes of connection employed. The first is by co-ordinating conjunctions, the conjunctions, that is, that allow the mind to move straight on from the point it has reached. They do not necessarily refer back to any particular point in the preceding member; nor do they commit the following member to a predetermined form. In other words, they are the loose conjunctions, and disjoin the members they join as widely as possible. *And*, *but*, and *for* are the ones employed in the two sentences; and these are of course the necessary and universal ones. Other favorites of the loose style are *whereas*, *nor* (= *and not*), and the correlatives *though . . . yet*, *as . . . so*. Second, each of the two periods contains a member with an absolute-participle construction. In the loose style many members have this form, and not only (as in the two periods quoted) at the ends of periods, but elsewhere. Sir Thomas Browne often has them early in a period, as some passages to be cited in another connection will show. This is a phenomenon easily explained. For the absolute construction is the one that commits itself least and lends itself best to the solution of difficulties that arise in the course of a spontaneous and unpremeditated progress. It may state either a cause, or a consequence, or a mere attendant circumstance; it may be concessive or justificatory;

it may be a summary of the preceding or a supplement to it; it may express an idea related to the whole of the period in which it occurs, or one related only to the last preceding member.

The co-ordinating conjunctions and the absolute-participle construction indicate, then, the character of the loose period. Like the *stile coupé*, it is meant to portray the natural, or thinking, order; and it expresses even better than the curt period the Anti-Ciceronian prejudice against formality of procedure and the rhetoric of the schools. For the omission of connectives in the *stile coupé* implies, as we have seen, a very definite kind of rhetorical form, which was practiced in direct imitation of classical models, and usually retained the associations that it had won in the Stoic schools of antiquity. The associations of the loose style, on the other hand, are all with the more skeptical phases of seventeenth-century thought—with what was then usually called "Libertinism"; and it appears characteristically in writers who are professed opponents of determined and rigorous philosophic attitudes. It is the style of Bacon and of Montaigne (after he has found himself), of La Mothe le Vayer, and of Sir Thomas Browne. It appears always in the letters of Donne; it appears in Pascal's *Pensées*; and, in the latter part of the century, when Libertinism had positively won the favor of the world away from Stoicism, it enjoyed a self-conscious revival, under the influence of Montaigne, in the writings of St. Évremond, Halifax, and Temple. Indeed, it is evident that, although the Senecan *stile coupé* attracted more critical attention throughout the century, its greatest achievements in prose were rather in the loose or Libertine manner. But it must also be said that most of the sceptics of the century had undergone a strong Senecan influence; and the styles of Montaigne, Browne, Pascal, and Halifax, for instance, can only be described as displaying in varying ways a mingling of Stoic and Libertine traits.

(b)

Besides the two syntactic forms that have been mentioned—the co-ordinating conjunctions and the absolute construction—there are no others that lend themselves by their nature to the loose style, except the parenthesis, which we need not illustrate here. But it must not be supposed that it tends to exclude other modes of connection. On the contrary, it obtains its characteristic effects from the syntactic forms that are logically more strict and binding, such as the relative pronouns and the subordinating conjunctions, by using them in a way peculiar to itself. That is to say, it uses them as the necessary logical means of advancing the idea, but relaxes at will the tight construction which they seem to impose; so that they have exactly the same effect as the loose connections previously described and must be punctuated in the same way. In other words, the parts that they connect are no more closely knit together than it chooses they shall be; and the reader of the most characteristic seventeenth-century prose soon learns to give a greater independence and autonomy to subordinate members than he would dare to do in reading any other.

The method may be shown by a single long sentence from Sir Thomas Browne:

> I could never perceive any rational consequence from those many texts which prohibit the children of Israel to pollute themselves with the temples of the heathens; we being all Christians, and not divided by such detested impieties *as* might profane our prayers, or the place wherein we make them; *or that* a resolved conscience may not adore her Creator any where, *especially* in places devoted to his service; *where*, if their devotions offend him, mine may please him; if theirs profane it, mine may hallow it.[14]

The period begins with a statement complete in itself, which does not syntactically imply anything to follow it; an absolute participle carries on, in the second member. Thereafter the connectives are chiefly subordinating conjunctions. Observe particularly the use of *as, or that*, and *where*: how slight these ligatures are in view of the length and mass of the members they must carry. They are frail and small hinges for the weights that turn on them; and the period abounds and expands in nonchalant disregard of their tight, frail logic.

This example displays the principle; but of course a single passage can illustrate only a few grammatical forms. Some of those used with a characteristic looseness in English prose of the seventeenth century are: relative clauses beginning with *which*, or with *whereto, wherein*, etc.; participial constructions of the kind scornfully called "dangling" by the grammarians; words in a merely ap-

---

[14] *Religio Medici*, I.3, in *Works*, II, 4. Italics are mine.

positional relation with some noun or pronoun preceding, yet constituting a semi-independent member of a period; and of course such subordinating conjunctions as are illustrated above. It is unnecessary to illustrate these various cases.

(c)

The connections of a period cannot be considered separately from the order of the connected members; and, in fact, it is the desired order of development that determines the character of the connections rather than the reverse. In the oratorical period the arrangement of the members is "round" or "circular," in the sense that they are all so placed with reference to a central or climactic member that they point forward or back to it and give it its appropriate emphasis. This order is what is meant by the names *periodos, circuitus,* and "round composition," by which the oratorical period has been variously called; and it is the chief object of the many revisions to which its form is submitted.

The loose period does not try for this form, but rather seeks to avoid it. Its purpose is to express, as far as may be, the order in which an idea presents itself when it is first experienced. It begins, therefore, without premeditation, stating its idea in the first form that occurs; the second member is determined by the situation in which the mind finds itself after the first has been spoken; and so on throughout the period, each member being an emergency of the situation. The period—in theory, at least—is not made; it becomes. It completes itself and takes on form in the course of the motion of mind which it expresses. Montaigne, in short, exactly described the theory of the loose style when he said: "J'ecris volontiers sans project; le premier trait produit le second."

The figure of a circle, therefore, is not a possible description of the form of a loose period; it requires rather the metaphor of a chain, whose links join end to end. The "linked" or "trailing" period is, in fact, as we have observed, an appropriate name for it. But there is a special case for which this term might better be reserved, unless we should choose to invent a more specific one, such as "end-linking," or "terminal linking," to describe it. It is when a member depends, not upon the general idea, or the main word, of the preceding member, but upon its final word or phrase alone. And this is, in fact, a frequent, even a characteristic, kind of linking in certain authors, notably Sir Thomas Browne and his imitators. The

sentence last quoted offers two or three illustrations of it: the
connective words *as, especially,* and *where* all refer to the immediately preceding words or phrases; and in another period by the
same author there is one very conspicuous and characteristic
instance.

As there were many reformers, so likewise many reforma-
tions; every country proceeding in a particular way and
method, according as their national interest, together with
their constitution and clime, inclined them: some angrily and
with extremity; others calmly and with mediocrity, not rend-
ing, but easily dividing, the community, and leaving an honest
possibility of a reconciliation;—*which,* though peaceable spirits
do desire, and may conceive that revolution of time and the
mercies of God may effect, yet that judgment that shall consider the present antipathies between the two extremes,—their
contrarieties in condition, affection, and opinion,—may with
the same hopes, expect a union in the poles of heaven.[15]

Here the word *which* introduces a new development of the idea,
running to as much as five lines of print; yet syntactically it refers
only to the last preceding word *reconciliation.* The whole long passage has been quoted, however, not for this reason alone, but
because it illustrates so perfectly all that has been said of the order
and connection of the loose period. It begins, characteristically,
with a sharply formulated complete statement, implying nothing of
what is to follow. Its next move is achieved by means of an absolute-
participle construction.[16] This buds off a couple of appositional
members; one of these budding again two new members by means
of dangling participles. Then a *which* picks up the trail, and at once
the sentence becomes involved in the complex, and apparently tight,
organization of a *though . . . yet* construction. Nevertheless it still
moves freely, digressing as it will, extricates itself from the complex
form by a kind of anacoluthon (in the *yet* clause), broadening its
scope, and gathering new confluents, till it ends, like a river, in an
opening view.

The period, that is, moves straight onward everywhere from the
point it has reached; and its construction shows ideally what we

---

[15] *Religio Medici,* I.4, in *Works,* II, 5.
[16] Observe that the period from Browne quoted on p. 223 begins with movements of the same kind.

mean by the linked or trailing order. It is Browne's peculiar mastery of this construction that gives his writing constantly the effect of being, not the result of a meditation, but an actual meditation in process. He writes like a philosophical scientist making notes of his observation as it occurs. We see his pen move and stop as he thinks. To write thus, and at the same time to create beauty of cadence in the phrases and rhythm in the design—and so Browne constantly does—is to achieve a triumph in what Montaigne called "the art of being natural"; it is the eloquence, described by Pascal, that mocks at formal eloquence.

(d)

The period just quoted serves to introduce a final point concerning the form of the loose period. We have already observed that the second half of this period, beginning with *which*, has a complex suspended syntax apparently like that of the typical oratorical sentence. The Anti-Ciceronian writer usually avoids such forms, it is true; most of his sentences are punctuated by colons and semi-colons. But, of course, he will often find himself involved in a suspended construction from which he cannot escape. It remains to show that even in these cases he still proceeds in the Anti-Ciceronian manner, and succeeds in following, in spite of the syntactic formalities to which he commits himself, his own emergent and experimental order. Indeed, it is to be observed that the characteristic quality of the loose style may appear more clearly in such difficult forms than in others. For baroque art always displays itself best when it works in heavy masses and resistant materials; and out of the struggle between a fixed pattern and an energetic forward movement often arrives at those strong and expressive disproportions in which it delights.

We shall return to Browne in a moment in illustration of the point, but we shall take up a simpler case first. In a well-known sentence, Pascal, bringing out the force of imagination, draws a picture of a venerable magistrate seated in church, ready to listen to a worthy sermon. *Le voilà prêt à l'ouïr avec un respect exemplaire.*

Que le prédicateur vienne à paraître, que la nature lui ait donné une voix enrouée et un tour de visage bizarre, que son barbier l'ait mal rasé, si le hasard l'a encore barbouillé de surcroît, quelque grandes vérités qu'il annonce, je parie la perte de la gravité de notre sénateur.[17]

Unquestionably a faulty sentence by all the school-rules! It begins without foreseeing its end, and has to shift the reader's glance from the preacher to the magistrate in the midst of its progress by whatever means it can. Observe the abruptness of the form of the member *quelque grandes vérités*. Observe the sudden appearance of the first person in the last member. Yet the critic who would condemn its rhetorical form would have also to declare that there is no art in those vivid dramatic narratives that so often appear in the conversation of animated talkers; for this period moves in an order very common in such conversation.[18]

In this passage the free and Anti-Ciceronian character of the movement is chiefly due to its dramatic vividness and speed. It follows the order of life. Sometimes, however, we can see plainly that it is the mystical speculation of the seventeenth century that changes the regular form of the period and shapes it to its own ends. Sir Thomas Browne provides many interesting illustrations, as, for instance, in the period quoted in the preceding section, and in the following:

I would gladly know how Moses, with an actual fire, calcined or burnt the golden calf into powder: for that mystical metal of gold, whose solary and celestial nature I admire, exposed unto the violence of fire, grows only hot, and liquefies, but consumeth not; so when the consumable and volatile pieces of our bodies shall be refined into a more impregnable and fixed temper, like gold, though they suffer from the action of flames, they shall never perish, but lie immortal in the arms of fire.[19]

With the first half of this long construction we are not now concerned. In its second half, however, beginning with *so when*, we see one of those complex movements that have led some critics to speak of Browne as—of all things!—a Ciceronian. It is in fact

---

[17] *Pensées*, II, 4-5 (section xxv in Port-Royal ed.).

[18] It may be said that Pascal's *Pensées* should not be cited in illustration of prose form because they were written without revision and without thought of publication. But a good deal of characteristic prose of the time was so written, and the effect at which Bacon, Burton, Browne, and many others aimed was of prose written in that way.

[19] *Religio Medici*, I.50, in *Works*, II, 73.

THE ANTI-CICERONIAN MOVEMENT

the opposite of that. A Ciceronian period closes in at the end; it reaches its height of expansion and emphasis at the middle or just beyond, and ends composedly. Browne's sentence, on the contrary, opens constantly outward; its motions become more animated and vigorous as it proceeds; and it ends, as his sentences are likely to do, in a vision of vast space or time, losing itself in an *altitudo*, a hint of infinity. As, in a previously quoted period, everything led up to the phrase, "a union in the poles of heaven," so in this everything leads up to the concluding phrase, "but lie immortal in the arms of fire." And as we study the form of the structure we can even observe where this ending revealed itself, or, at least, how it was prepared. The phrase "like gold" is the key to the form of the whole. After a slow expository member, this phrase, so strikingly wrenched from its logical position, breaks the established and expected rhythm, and is a signal of more agitated movement, of an ascending effort of imaginative realization that continues to the end. In a different medium, the period closely parallels the technique of an El Greco composition, where broken and tortuous lines in the body of the design prepare the eye for curves that leap upward beyond the limits of the canvas.

The forms that the loose period may assume are infinite, and it would be merely pedantic to attempt a classification of them. In one of the passages quoted we have seen the dramatic sense of reality triumphing over rhetorical formalism; in another, the form of a mystical exaltation. For the purpose of description—not classification—it will be convenient to observe still a third way in which a loose period may escape from the formal commitments of elaborate syntax. It is illustrated in a passage in Montaigne's essay "Des Livres," praising the simple and uncritical kind of history that he likes so much. In the course of the period he mentions *le bon Froissard* as an example, and proceeds so far (six lines of print) in a description of his method that he cannot get back to his general idea by means of his original syntactic form, or at least cannot do so without very artificial devices. He completes the sentence where it is; but completes his idea in a pair of curt (*coupés*) sentences separated by a colon from the preceding: "c'est la matiere de l'histoire nue et informe; chascun en peult faire son proufit autant qu'il a d'entendement."[20] This is a method often used by Anti-Cicero-

[20] *Essais*, ii.x, ed. Le Clerc, ii, 127.

nians to extricate themselves from the coils of a situation in which they have become involved by following the "natural" order. A better example of it is to be seen in a passage from Pascal's essay on "Imagination," from which another passage has already been cited.

> Le plus grand philosophe du monde, sur une planche plus large qu'il ne faut, s'il y a au-dessous un précipice, quoique sa raison le convainque de sa sûreté, son imagination prévaudra. Plusieurs n'en sauraient soutenir la pensée sans pâlir et suer.[21]

Nothing could better illustrate the "order of nature"; writing, that is, in the exact order in which the matter presents itself. It begins by naming the subject, *le plus grand philosophe*, without foreseeing the syntax by which it is to continue. Then it throws in the elements of the situation, using any syntax that suggests itself at the moment, proceeding with perfect dramatic sequence, but wholly without logical sequence, until at last the sentence has lost touch with its stated subject. Accordingly, this subject is merely left hanging, and a new one, *son imagination*, takes its place. It is a violent, or rather a nonchalant, anacoluthon. The sentence has then, after a fashion, completed itself. But there is an uneasy feeling in the mind. After all, *le plus grand philosophe* has done nothing; both form and idea are incomplete. Pascal adds another member (for, whatever the punctuation, the *plusieurs* sentence is a member of the period), which completely meets the situation, though a grammatical purist may well object that the antecedent of *plusieurs* was in the singular number.

Pascal is usually spoken of as a "classical" writer; but the term means nothing as applied to him except that he is a writer of tried artistic soundness. He is, in fact, as modernistic, as bold a breaker of the rules and forms of rhetoric, as his master Montaigne, though he is also a much more careful artist. *La vraie éloquence*, he said, *se moque de l'éloquence.*

(e)

Two kinds of style have been analyzed in the preceding pages: the concise, serried, abrupt *stile coupé*, and the informal, meditative, and "natural" loose style. It is necessary to repeat—once more —that in the best writers these two styles do not appear separately

---

[21] *Pensées*, II, 5.

in passages of any length, and that in most of them they intermingle in relations far too complex for description. They represent two sides of the seventeenth-century mind: its sententiousness, its penetrating wit, its Stoic intensity, on the one hand, and its dislike of formalism, its roving and self-exploring curiosity, in brief, its sceptical tendency, on the other. And these two habits of mind are generally not separated one from the other; nor are they even always exactly distinguishable. Indeed, as they begin to separate or to be opposed to each other in the second half of the century we are aware of the approach of a new age and a new spirit. The seventeenth century, as we are here considering it, is equally and at once Stoic and Libertine; and the prose that is most characteristic of it expresses these two sides of its mind in easy and natural relations one with the other.

✧ IV ✧

The Punctuation of the Seventeenth-Century Period

The "long sentence" of the Anti-Ciceronian age has received a remarkable amount of attention ever since it began to be corrected and go out of use; and there have been two conflicting views concerning it. The older doctrine—not yet quite extinct—was that the long sentences of Montaigne, Bacon, Browne, and Taylor were sentences of the same kind as those of Cicero and his sixteenth-century imitators; only they were badly and crudely made, monstrosities due to some wave of ignorance that submerged the syntactic area of the seventeenth-century mind. Their true character, it was thought, would be shown by substituting commas for their semicolons and colons; for then we should see that they are quaint failures in the attempt to achieve sentence unity.

The other view is the opposite of this, namely, that we should put periods in the place of many of its semicolons and colons. We should then see that what look like long sentences are really brief and aphoristic ones. The contemporary punctuation of our authors is again to be corrected, but now in a different sense. This is the view urged by Faguet in writing of Montaigne, and by Sir Edmund Gosse concerning the prose of Browne and Taylor.

This later view is useful in correcting some of the errors of the earlier one. But, in fact, one of them is just as false as the other; and both of them illustrate the difficulties experienced by minds trained solely in the logical and grammatical aspects of language in interpreting the forms of style that prevailed before the eighteenth century. In order to understand the punctuation of the seventeenth century we have to consider the relation between the grammatical term *sentence* and the rhetorical term *period*.

The things named by these terms are identical. *Period* names the rhetorical, or oral, aspect of the same thing that is called in grammar a *sentence* and in theory the same act of composition that produces a perfectly logical grammatical unit would produce at the same time a perfectly rhythmical pattern of sound. But, in fact, no utterance ever fulfils both of these functions perfectly, and either one or the other of them is always foremost in a writer's mind. One or the other is foremost also in every theory of literary education; and the historian may sometimes distinguish literary periods by the relative emphasis they put upon grammatical and rhetorical considerations. In general we may say, though there may be exceptions, that before the eighteenth century rhetoric occupied much more attention than grammar in the minds of teachers and their pupils. It was so, for instance, in the Middle Ages, as is clear from their manuals of study and the curricula of their schools. It was still true in the sixteenth century; and the most striking characteristic of the literary prose of that century, both in Latin and in the vernacular tongues, was its devotion to the conventional and formal patterns of school-rhetoric.

The laws of grammatical form, it is true, were not at all disturbed or strained at this time by the predominance of rhetorical motives. There was no difficulty whatever in saying what these rhetoricians had to say in perfect accordance with logical syntax because they had, in fact, so little to say that only the most elementary syntax was necessary for its purposes. Furthermore, the rhetorical forms they liked were so symmetrical, so obvious, that they almost imposed a regular syntax by their own form.

But a new situation arose when the leaders of seventeenth-century rationalism—Lipsius, Montaigne, Bacon—became the teachers of style. The ambition of these writers was to conduct an experimental investigation of the moral realities of their time, and to achieve a style appropriate to the expression of their discoveries and of the mental effort by which they were conducted. The content of style became, as it were, suddenly greater and more difficult; and the stylistic formalities of the preceding age were unable to bear the burden. An immense rhetorical complexity and license took the place of the simplicity and purism of the sixteenth century; and, since the age had not yet learned to think much about grammatical propriety, the rules of syntax were made to bear the expenses of the new freedom. In the examples of seventeenth-century prose that have been discussed in the preceding pages some of the results are apparent. The syntactic connections of a sentence become loose and casual; great strains are imposed upon tenuous, frail links; parentheses are abused; digression become licentious; anacoluthon is frequent and passes unnoticed; even the limits of sentences are not clearly marked, and it is sometimes difficult to say where one begins and another ends.

Evidently the process of disintegration could not go on forever. A stylistic reform was inevitable, and it must take the direction of a new formalism or "correctness." The direction that it actually took was determined by the Cartesian philosophy, or at least by the same time spirit in which the Cartesian philosophy had its origin. The intellect, that is to say, became the arbiter of form, the dictator of artistic practice as of philosophical inquiry. The sources of error, in the view of the Cartesians, are imagination and dependence upon sense impressions. Its correctives are found in what they call "reason" (which here means "intellect"), and an exact distinction of categories.

To this mode of thought we are to trace almost all the features of modern literary education and criticism, or at least of what we should have called modern a generation ago: the study of the precise meaning of words; the reference to dictionaries as literary authorities; the study of the sentence as a logical unit alone; the careful circumscription of its limits and the gradual reduction of its length; the disappearance of semicolons and colons; the attempt to reduce grammar to an exact science; the idea that forms of speech are always either correct or incorrect; the complete subjection of the laws of motion and expression in style to the laws of logic and standardization—in short, the triumph, during two centuries, of grammatical over rhetorical ideas.

This is not the place to consider what we have gained or lost by this literary philosophy, or whether the precision we have aimed at has compensated us for the powers of expression and the flexibility of motion that we have lost; we have only to say that we must not apply the ideas we have learned from it to the explanation of seventeenth-century style. In brief, we must not measure the customs of the age of semicolons and colons by the customs of the age of commas and periods. The only possible punctuation of seventeenth-century prose is that which it used itself. We might sometimes reveal its grammar more clearly by repunctuating it with commas or periods, but we should certainly destroy its rhetoric.

Index

COMPILED BY J. MAX PATRICK

The Index lists names of persons and a selection of leading ideas, technical terms, and the like. An italicized page number indicates that on that page, either in the main text or in the notes or both, either once, twice, or more times, there is bibliographical material relevant to that entry. In other words, the common practice of giving separate references to footnote material has not been followed. Since such information involves the use of italicized titles, the reader will have no trouble in finding it by glancing over the main text and footnotes on that page. The listings under subject-headings such as *brevity* and *courts* could have been multiplied but are intended only to serve as an *entrée* into what Croll has stated concerning them. The task of indexing his works is an exceptionally difficult one, not only because of his wide-ranging erudition and his changing terminology but especially because of his frequent brief but usually significant allusions to authors and ideas; for example, he names Montaigne on at least a hundred pages of the present volume; and on page 98 there are 31 references which had to be recorded in the Index, despite its selectivity.

No attempt has been made to enter subjects such as *rhetoric* which are so continuously treated throughout the volume that almost every page in it would have to be listed.

It is hoped, however, that the Index will provide a key to Croll's most important insights and to the development of his thought and reading. For example, it reveals that although scholars have remarked on his use of *baroque*, they have overlooked his perhaps equally significant use of the terms *positive* and *positivist*.

laconic, 70-71. *See also* brevity, conciseness

Lactantius, Caecilius (or Caelius) Firmianus, 149

Laelius, Gaius, 90

La Fontaine, Jean de, 74

La Moth le Vayer, François de, 66-*67*, 85, 87, *143*, 159, *195*, 222

Landmann, Friedrich, *54*

Latin; influence of Latin: 82-84, *passim*; Latin and the Vernacular Tongues, 181ff.

law; law style; legal studies; jurisprudence: 114, 119, 122, 132-134, 136-138, 146; law French, 123; law Latin, 123. *See also* Barthollism

Le Clerc, J. V., *51*

Leerman, A. D., *46*

L'Estrange, Roger, *173*

letters; letter writing; epistolary genre and style: 28, 29, *60*, 63, 66, 70, 86, 113, 149, 154-*155*, 176, 187, 192, 194

libertine; libertinism; libertins: 47, 68, 75, 105, *111*, 113, 123-124, 139, 142-143, 150, 159-163, 175, 178, 189, 201, 206, 219, 222, 230, 232; =scepticism: 159. *See also* loose style

Linacre, Thomas, 70

linking; linked period; chain of points: 218-219, 221, 224-226, 232

Lipsius, Justus (Joest Lips; Juste Lipse), 1-5, 7ff., *19*; anti-ciceronianism, 16-22; character, 9-10; influence: 31-44; in England, 37-38, 41; in France, 34-40, 43; in Spain, 41-42; modernity, 12, 16, 22, 26-27, 44; opposition to, 34-35, 37; preferred models, 15-20, 24-26; reputation, 7-12; rhetoric, 13-27; stoicism, 12-14; style, 27-31; theory of imitation, 23-26 *et passim*; 47-48, 51, 66, 69, 71, 79-80; 87-89; 95-99; 103, 105, 109, 111-115, 121, 124, 131, 138, 142-143, 149-150, 154-158, 160, 162, 168-181, 186-188, 192-194, 196-197, 200, 202, 215, 231

Livy (Titus Livius), 24-25, 92, 96, 98, 193

Longinus, 47

loose style; loose period: 47, 204, 210; "the informal meditative and 'natural' loose style," 229. *See also* libertine; Seneca

Lyly, John, *5*, 63, 69, 188-189, 204. *See also* euphuism

Lyly, William, *see* Lily

Lysias, 46, 78, 81

Macaulay, Thomas Babington, first Baron Macaulay, 29

Macdonald, Hugh, *49*

Machiavelli, Niccolò; machiavellianism: 64, 113, 126, 142, 151, 153, 160, 196-197

MacIlmaine, Roland, *122*

Maggioni, Sister Julie, *203*

Mâle, Émile, *129*

Malebranche, Nicolas, 67-68, *100*, 199

Malvezzi, Virgilio, 69, 86, 98, 152-153, 186, 201

mannerism, 95, *130*, 183, 216, 218

Manutius, Paulus (Paolo Manuzio), 154

Marino, Giovanni Battista, 109, *203*

Martial (Marcus Valerius Martialis), 96-97, 176

Martin, Louis Aimé, *67*

Marzot, Giulio, 77

mathematics, 88, 100

Mathieu, Pierre, 201

maxims, 87, 135

Mazzeo, Joseph, *77*, *142*

McKeon, Richard P., *56*

medieval; medieval style; Middle Ages: 27, 55-56, 60, 63, 68, 81, 93, 95, 110, 114, 119, 120-121, 147-148, 182, 185, 187-188, 196, 231

Meissner, Paul, *203*

Mejía, Pedro, *188*

melancholy, 10, 36, 162, 178

Melanchthon, Philipp, 10, 14, 16, 21, 116, 145, 167

Mendoza, Diego Hurtado de, 194

Merchant, F. I., *17*

Méré, *see* Gombaud

Mérimée, Ernest, 42-*43*

Mesnard, Pierre, *142*

metaphor, 30, 54, 69, 77, 92, 137, 209, 214, 217-218

metaphysical, 47-49, 163, 201, *203*

Mexia, Pedro, *188*

Michaut, G. L., *188*

Michéa, R., *112*

Middle Ages, *see* medieval

Miller, Perry, *48*

Milton, John, 84

Minozzi, Pierfrancesco, 77

Mirollo, James V., *203*

Mitchell, W. Fraser, 49

modern; modern style; modernism: 93-94, 110, 115, 119; "the 'modern' or positivistic tendency," 130, 138-142, 180-185, 203, 206-207, 213, 229. *See also* positive

Monroe, W. S., 121

Montaigne, Michel Eyquem de, *10*, 12-